Thomas Edward Champion

History of the 10th Royals and of the Royal Grenadiers from the Formation of the Regiment until 1896

Thomas Edward Champion

History of the 10th Royals and of the Royal Grenadiers from the Formation of the Regiment until 1896

ISBN/EAN: 9783337241438

Printed in Europe, USA, Canada, Australia, Japan

Cover: Foto ©ninafisch / pixelio.de

More available books at **www.hansebooks.com**

HISTORY

OF THE

10th ROYALS

AND OF THE

ROYAL GRENADIERS

From the formation of the Regiment until 1896.

BY

THOMAS EDWARD CHAMPION.

Toronto:
THE HUNTER, ROSE COMPANY, LTD.
MDCCCXCVI.

"**Ready, aye Ready.**"

TO

LIEUTENANT-COLONEL JAMES MASON,

AND THE

OFFICERS, NON-COMMISSIONED OFFICERS AND MEN

OF THE

Royal Grenadiers

OF CANADA,

THIS HISTORY

OF THEIR REGIMENT,

FROM ITS FIRST FORMATION TO THE PRESENT YEAR,

IS

RESPECTFULLY DEDICATED

BY

THE AUTHOR,

THOS. E. CHAMPION.

TORONTO, September, 1896.

PREFACE.

"To supply a long felt want." Such is a very common reason given for publishing a new book, or undertaking some new enterprise. In writing this history I have acted from no such motive, on the contrary, I undertook the work thinking that if a readable history of the Royal Grenadiers was written, that it would create a desire for the book, not only from Toronto, but from many places outside the city, where men who formerly served in the 10th Royals or in the Royal Grenadiers have settled, and who would be glad to possess some memento of the corps in which they had passed many pleasant and useful hours. To all those who have assisted in the work by lending me MSS., books, newspapers, or by personally giving me information, I tender my hearty thanks, and I hope that every one who reads the book may take as great an interest in its perusal as I have done in writing it. With these few words I leave the volume to the judgment of the public.

THOS. E. C.

TORONTO, September, 1896.

CHAPTER I.

THE FIRST MILITIA ACT—THE ACT OF 1822—THE TRAINING DAYS—INTERESTING DETAILS.

THE history of the Militia of Upper Canada, or what is now known as the Province of Ontario, in the Dominion of Canada, commences almost with the foundation of the Province. Simcoe's first Parliament met at Niagara, September 17th, 1792, and sat until October 15th following. Eight acts were passed and received the Royal assent, but the question of national defence was not among them, that was deferred until the second session.

The Legislative Assembly met for the second session, May 31st, 1793, and the House in their address in reply to the speech from the throne, thus addressed the Lieutenant-Governor, who had in that speech urged upon the Legislature the necessity of providing for the defence of the country.

" We assure Your Excellency that our utmost diligence shall be used to frame and complete such a Militia Bill as will not only show our own promptness to fulfil Your Excellency's wishes, but our own energy in defending that noble constitution which Great Britain has given us, and which, by enabling us to repel all insults, will secure to us the invaluable blessings that we derive from it."

During the session of 1793 an act was accordingly passed which enabled the Government in case of need to call upon all male adults between the ages of 16 and 60 to bear arms in defence of their country whenever called upon to do so. Commissions from the rank of Colonel to Ensign were granted to prominent settlers in each of the nineteen counties into which the Province was then divided, and on paper the whole thing was as perfect as could be. Each county had its own regiment, with its proper complement of officers; the strength of these "regiments" may be estimated when it is remembered that at that particular period the total population of Upper Canada did not exceed twelve thousand white people, men, women, and children, with about an equal number of Indians.

This Act was repealed *in toto* by the 4th Parliament of Upper Canada, in its 4th session, and a new one passed, which received the Royal assent March 16th, 1808. This act, though being very far from perfect, was framed with care, and was found during the troubles of 1812-14 to work effectively.

The provisions of the Act referred to in the latter part of the preceding paragraph were numerous, almost every possible contingency being provided for, always excepting that of giving the men any payment for their services, on that point nothing whatever was said, or apparently thought of, by the framers.

The preamble set forth as follows:—

"Whereas a well-regulated militia is of the utmost importance to the defence of this province."

The following were its leading provisions: The Lieutenant-Governor, or whoever was acting as administrator had the power to appoint officers, in all ranks, to that of Colonel, who were to rank with officers of H. M. regular forces, only as juniors in their rank. For instance, a captain in the Imperial service would take precedence of an officer of similar rank in the Canadian Militia, though the commission of the latter might bear date anterior to that held by the former officer.

Each militia regiment was to be formed in certain specified districts, and each company of the battalion was to be drawn from certain limits contained within those districts.

Every male from 16 to 60 years of age, was liable to be called upon to serve, but those between 50 and 60 years old, were only to be called out in time of war, or on training-day.

The "training-day" was one of the events of the year, fifty years since, it was on June 4th, George III's. birthday. Anyone who absented himself from muster on that day, without good and sufficient excuse, was liable to a fine of ten shillings currency, or two dollars. It lay with the captains of companies to say what was a good excuse and what was a frivolous one. A good many "summonses" always followed in the wake of training-day.

Within fourteen days after the muster of June 4th, in each year, complete rolls had to be sent to the Lieutenant-Governor of all companies and of all regiments, and if this duty was neglected the captains of each company and the commanding officers of each regiment were liable to penalties, £5, for the former and £10 for the latter.

The militia were liable to serve anywhere in the Province of Upper Canada, or in Lower Canada, if required, for the assistance of that province. They could not, though, be called upon for continuous service of more than six months.

By the 14th clause of this Act it was enacted that each militiaman after enrolment "shall within six months after such enrolment provide himself with a good and sufficient musket, fusil, rifle or gun." If he failed in this duty he was liable to a penalty of five shillings, "unless excused by his commanding officer."

The 31st clause of the same Act authorized the formation of troops of cavalry, and what is now known as the Governor-General's Body Guard, was subsequently enrolled under its provisions.

This Act received the assent of the Lieutenant-Governor on March 16th, 1808, was ratified in due course by the Imperial authorities, and became the law of the land.

During the war of 1812 General Brock and Sir Gordon Drummond, President and Lieutenant-Governor respectively, availed themselves largely of the powers it gave them, and right gallantly at Detroit, Queenston Heights, Stony Creek, Chrysler's Farm, and Lundy's Lane, did the Canadian Militia do their duty.

In the second session of the 8th Parliament of Upper Canada certain amendments were passed in the Act of 1808, or rather incorporated with it, but the amended Act was only to be in operation for four years, unless re-enacted at the expiration of that period, and as the latter was not done, the former one came again into operation

One interesting circumstance though may be mentioned in connection with this Act of 1822; it is among "the things not generally known" in connection with Canadian history, and that is, that "Training day" was changed by it from June 4th to April 23rd. The latter date was chosen as being St. George's Day, the patron saint of England.

In the session of 1823 a short Act was passed, permitting the formation of batteries of artillery, but none appear ever to have existed, except upon paper, for many years after it was passed.

From the close of the war in 1814 until 1837 little was heard of the Militia or of its existence, excepting upon "Training Day," and that was looked upon by many as a big picnic more than as a public duty. The military spirit was only quiescent though, it was not dead. What caused it to blaze forth again will be glanced at in the next chapter.

CHAPTER II.

THE CANADIAN MILITIA IN 1837—THE ROYAL CANADIAN RIFLES—"A DULL TIME"—THE CRIMEAN WAR—THE MILITIA ACT OF 1855.

IN December, 1837, the embers of disaffection, which had been smouldering in many parts of the country, burst into flame, and the inhabitants of the hitherto loyal Province of Upper Canada learned for a certainty that a portion of the population, led by William Lyon Mackenzie and others, had taken up arms against the constituted authorities, and were encamped on Yonge street, at Montgomery's tavern, some few miles north of the city, preparatory to making an attack upon it and its inhabitants.

The whole of the regular troops had been sent by the Lieutenant-Governor, Sir Francis Bond Head, to the Lower Province, as it was his opinion that there was no danger of the malcontents in Upper Canada resorting to arms. Events proved, though, that he was mistaken, and when the outbreak occurred in Toronto there were no soldiers to quell it, excepting such as could be furnished by the unorganized militia. Sir Francis, though, was undaunted, and he at once issued a proclamation calling out the militia, which was promptly and patriotically responded to.

The insurgents were attacked by some 600 hastily-enrolled volunteers about mid-day on December 7th, 1837, and were utterly routed. The loss of life on both sides was happily very small and the list of wounded insignificant. This skirmish was led by Sir Francis Bond Head himself, with Colonel James Fitz-Gibbon as his Adjutant-General.

Among others who served as commissioned officers at this period may be mentioned, Lieutenant-Colonels Fitz-Gibbon, E. W. Thomson, A. McLean, and G. T. Denison, of Bellevue, all veterans of the war of 1812; Sir Alan MacNab, Sheriff Jarvis, Colonel Chisholm, of Oakville, and a very great many more.

Two regiments of militia were subsequently enrolled and kept on duty for several months; they were known as the "Queen's Rangers" and the "Queen's Light Infantry;" they did duty in Toronto and Sarnia, also in other parts of the province, and considering that they were wholly undisciplined troops, officered for the most part by men as inexperienced as themselves, performed their duty remarkably well.

All through the year 1838 the militia were often under arms in different parts of the two provinces and at the battle of the Windmill near Prescott, in the autumn of 1838, did gallant service side by side with the British regulars. The militia troops of cavalry in Toronto also did excellent service on patrol and frontier duty, and with their comrades in the infantry received the hearty thanks of Parliament when the troubles came to an end in 1838.

The Rebellion of 1837-38 paltry as it now appears,

showed the Colonists of Upper Canada in a good light, they were loyal to the crown and they had no sympathy with those who would resort to arms in order to obtain redress for grievances, some of which were real enough, while others were trivial or wholly imaginary. In addition they were willing at the call of duty to hazard their lives in defence of their country and in maintenance of her laws.

The rebellion died out and in 1839 everything was as quiet as possible. There was a regiment of the British regulars stationed in Toronto with their headquarters at Osgoode Hall and some few at the Old Fort, but their duties were of the very lightest character.

In 1840 was formed the Royal Canadian Rifles, and as in the very early days of the history of the 10th Royals some of the non-commissioned officers of the first named corps acted as company drill instructors, a few words respecting the formation of that regiment, now all but forgotten, will not be out of place.

The Royal Canadian Rifles were a corps of veterans drawn from almost every regiment in the British service forming a part of the regular forces of the line, but who could not be called upon for service in any part of the British Dominions excepting those in North America. It is very questionable if they could have been sent to the West Indies had their services ever been required there; happily they never were wanted, so the question was never raised.

They were a magnificent body of men, the very pick of the English army, and possessed medals for war services in every quarter of the globe. When not required for military duty the men were permitted to work at their trades, or to hire themselves out as waiters, messengers, ticket collectors, or in light work of that kind, and most efficient servants they made. They were stationed in detachments all through Upper and Lower Canada and also in Newfoundland, but from the date of their enrolment until their disbandment in 1871, they never saw a shot fired in anger. They were called out in aid of the Civil power in Montreal and Quebec more than once, but that was the extent of their service. They simply did garrison duty, nevertheless the regiment was a most popular one, soldiers who had served in the army for the requisite number of years, which was not less than seven, always being anxious to join it. When it was first enrolled there were several Peninsular and Waterloo veterans among its officers, notably, Colonel Muter, who was for many years a prominent figure in Toronto society.

In the "forties" and early "fifties" the Canadian Militia was less and less prominently before the public, and the military spirit again seemed to be reaching a vanishing point. Every now and then there would be a partial revival of feeling, some more than usually public spirited man venturing to tell the truth, which was that, with the exception of a few scattered troops of cavalry, with here and there a rifle company—both partaking far more of the character of private societies than military organizations—there was no militia force whatever except upon paper.

In 1854 the Crimean war broke out between England and Russia, the former power being aided by France,

Turkey, and subsequently by Sardinia, and in consequence the Imperial troops were withdrawn for the time being from the Upper Province entirely, and also from Lower Canada, excepting in Quebec. During the winter of 1854-5, the only troops in Upper Canada were a very small detachment of the Royal Artillery in Kingston, and the Royal Canadian Rifles.

But some time before this it had been pretty plainly intimated to the inhabitants of both Upper and Lower Canada that they would have to provide for their own defence, that the Home Government had no doubt whatever about their loyalty and devotion to the English monarch, but that actions spoke louder than words, and that Canadians must do more than had hitherto been done. "If you are attacked or in danger of being attacked," said the Colonial Office in effect, "the Mother Country will help you to her last man, but you must do something for yourselves, and do it speedily, for the question of the total withdrawal of British troops from the North American Colonies, with the possible exception of Halifax, is only a question of time."

Fortunately this remonstrance or intimation did not fall on deaf ears, it was listened to with respect, and soon its effects were apparent.

Sir Edmund Walker Head, Bart., was Governor-General of Canada at the time, and his first parliament passed on May 19th, 1855, the famous Militia Act (many times amended and amplified since then), under the provisions of which the 10th Royals, now the Royal Grenadiers, came into existence.

It will be necessary to say a little about this Act.

It was of very great length and drafted with the greatest care, among those who were consulted whilst it was being framed by the ministry of the day, acting on suggestions made by Colonel Baron de Rottenburg, C.B., Adjutant General of Militia, a famous soldier of great experience, were Lieutenant-Colonels Henry Ruttan of Cobourg, E. W. Thomson of Toronto, O'Hara of the same place, George Taylor Denison of Rusholme, also near Toronto, Colonel John Prince of Windsor, Chief Justice Sir John Beverley Robinson, Mr. Justice McLean and some others.

Two classes of militia were created under the Act, namely Active and Sedentary. In the former the number of men per company was strictly limited, as were the number of companies permitted to be formed, but every arm of the service was provided for. The number of officers and non-commissioned officers to each troop battery or company was duly defined and there was no ambiguity in the wording of the act as to how they should be paid disciplined and equipped.

In evidence of this a portion of the xxxii. clause of the Act may be quoted, it read thus : "The Volunteer Militia Companies shall be drilled and exercised * * * * once in each year during ten continuous days, (Sundays not reckoned in either case) and the companies under drill being encamped during the whole or any part of the period if the Commander in Chief shall see fit."

Clause xliv. related to the appointment of Non-commissioned officers, which was to rest with the officers commanding each company of active militia, and not in the hands of the Colonel commanding the battalion or the military district. Of these districts there were eighteen, nine each for Upper and Lower Canada. The lxiv. clause enacted that when the militia were called out for active service the several companies might be embodied into battalions or regiments. We see the working of both these clauses in our country battalions as they now exist.

Immediately after the Act came into operation it was acted upon. Rifle companies were formed all over the country, there being four of them in Toronto, commanded by Captains G. Brooke, D. K. Feehan, and J. Nickinson, and the Highland company under the command of A. M. Smith. Each company for some years had a separate organization and drill shed, and each officer in command was a law unto himself. But about 1860 the " Queen's Own " was formed of several of these independent commands, and in 1861-62 the 10th Royals was organized under Mr. F. W. Cumberland.

Having sketched the history of the militia up till now, the events which led to the formation of the 10th, with the regimental history, will be recounted in our next chapters. Our readers must excuse these few preliminary pages; the object in writing them is that the general public and the militiamen of to-day may, by comparing the past with the present, see how much has been achieved.

CHAPTER III.

THE 100TH REGIMENT—THE TRENT AFFAIR OF 1861—THE MILITARY ENTHUSIASM OF THE PERIOD—THE 10TH GAZETTED.

WE will go back for a very brief period from 1861, the point reached at the conclusion of the last chapter, to the early months of 1858.

At that time the Indian mutiny had not been quelled, and troops were being hurried from all parts of the British Empire to assist in restoring order in the vast Asiatic peninsula.

It was at this time that the Governor-General of Canada, Sir Edmund Walker Head, was authorized by the Imperial authorities to accept an offer made by the Canadian people to raise a regiment of regular troops for service, wherever they might be ordered to proceed. The consequence of this acceptance was that the corps known as the 100th, or Prince of Wales Royal Canadian Regiment was formed, and several of its officers drawn from the Canadian militia. Its first commanding officer was Colonel de Rottenburg, the Adjutant-General of Militia for Upper Canada, he vacating the latter post on assuming command of the 100th. Among the subaltern officers was Ensign John Gibbs Ridout, who afterwards served as a Captain in the 10th Royals. Among the rank and file were several men who served therein for two or three years; then, not caring for the restraints inseparable from regular soldiering, purchased their discharge, and wishing not wholly to sever themselves from army life, served again for the pleasure of doing so in the 10th. In 1867, Mr. Henry James Grasett, of Toronto, was gazetted as an ensign in the 100th. He served therein for several years, and obtained the rank of Lieutenant, and was also, for five years, Adjutant of the regiment. He was a most popular officer, and in his capacity of Adjutant, won the respect and confidence of officers, N. C.O's., and men. The two latter, to use a well-known expression, "swore by him." He knew them all by name, indeed knew many of their regimental numbers, and on his retirement, every man of the 100th whose respect was worth having, regretted his departure.

Returning to Toronto, Mr. Grasett was, upon the reorganization of the 10th as the Royal Grenadiers, appointed Lieutenant-Colonel of the regiment, of which full particulars will be given as this history proceeds. That is all that needs be said respecting the 100th regiment. Its connection with the 10th was not a very close one, nevertheless it existed.

In December, 1861, occurred the difficulty now always spoken of as the "Trent affair" between the United States of America and Great Britain. A British steamer was boarded on the high seas by a United States cruiser, and two men, Messrs Mason and Slidell, who were passengers thereon, were taken by force, and removed in custody to the latter vessel. It was at the beginning of the war of Secession. Messrs. Mason and Slidell were emissaries

LIEUT.-COL. H. J. GRASETT.

from the Confederate States to certain sympathisers in England.

As soon as this act of the United States became known in Great Britain, preparations were made for war, and large numbers of troops and war *materiel* were sent out to Canada. At the same time Canadians were not unmindful of their responsibilities. A proclamation was issued by the Government calling for volunteers from the sedentary militia which would have had the effect of placing more than 30,000 men in the field, irrespective of any troops, batteries or companies that already existed. The proclamation caused an immense sensation, and would, no doubt, have been fully responded to. The gist of it was this "Canada wants some 30,000 men, and she prefers to have volunteers, but if she can't get the latter she must resort to the letter of the law. There is no compulsion, only you must."

Let those who read this book think for a few moments of what a levy of 30,000 men would have meant. At most the entire population of Upper and Lower Canada at that period did not exceed 2,500,000 souls, of those 12 men per thousand would have been required to take up arms. What a sleepy, quiet place is a Canadian village of 1,000 inhabitants. What a blank would it make, were twelve of its unmarried men between the ages of eighteen and forty taken out of it! But wise counsels fortunately were in the ascendency at Washington, an apology was made to Great Britain for the affront offered to her, the difficulty passed away, and so did the necessity for enrolling the sedentary militia.

In the very midst of the turmoil caused by the Trent

affair, and when it was not known whether war would result or not, a meeting at which the late Mr. F. W. Cumberland presided, was held at the Mechanics Institute (the present Central Library), on the evening of December 21st, 1861. At this gathering were men of every trade and of all professions, the lawyer jostled the stonemason, the schoolmaster the carpenter, the banker the butcher, and all were enthusiastic. The object of the meeting was to form a regiment of volunteer militia from the mechanics or working men of the city. It was unanimously decided to try and raise such a corps, and a committee in furtherance of the object was formed. The committee appointed met on December 28th, 1861, and were able to report that somewhat more than $1,500 had been subscribed towards a guarantee fund in aid of the expenses, and that 230 men had been enrolled. On December 30th, the committee met again, and nominated a special committee of forty-eight members to nominate the officers. It had been decided at the meeting of December 28th, that scarlet should be the color of the tunics to be worn by the new regiment. This was a decided novelty in Canadian militia companies, and its adoption was favorably received.

On January 1st, 1862, the following officers were nominated:—

Paymaster, John Stuart; Adjutant, J. G. McGrath Quarter-Master, Thomas Gundry,

Captains, Fred. W. Cumberland, A. J. Brunel, John Worthington, A. DeGrassi, Sandford Fleming, W. G. Storm, James Worthington, John McGee, A. Manning, George Carroll.

Lieutenants, W. Stewart, D. Fleming, E. Coatsworth, Henry Roberts, F. F. Passmore, John Boxall, G. B. Smith, John Albiston, W. Steward, J. Gritz.

Ensigns, J. J. Dickey, W. A. Stollery, George R. Hamilton, R. Dennis, E. Peel, W. W. Colwell, Robert Mitchell, H. F. Bescoby, James Price, David Ramsey.

The first meeting of officers elect was held a week later, when Captain Cumberland was chosen as the Lieutenant-Colonel; Captains John Worthington and Brunel as Majors; Lieutenant Coatsworth, as Captain, to fill the place vacated by Lieutenant-Colonel Cumberland, and Ensign Price was named for the remaining vacant Captaincy. Drs. Buchanan and O'Dea were elected Surgeon and Assistant Surgeon.

It must be understood that all these were merely nominations, they had to be ratified by the Governor-General.

Drill began for the officers on January 7th, 1862. It will be seen that from the date of the first meeting until this one for officers drill, less than three weeks had elapsed, no time had been lost.

On March 14th, 1862, the Canada *Gazette* contained the following notice:—

MILITIA GENERAL ORDERS.

HEADQUARTERS, QUEBEC,
March 14th, 1862.

No. 1. The formation of the following corps is hereby authorized, viz:

CLASS B.

One Volunteer Militia Rifle Co'y. - Jas. Worthington.
" " " - A. J. Brunel.

One Volunteer Militia Rifle Co'y. - S. Fleming.
" " " - John Worthington,
" " " - A. DeGrassi.
" " " - John McGee.
" " " - E. Coatsworth.

This was followed by the following General Order :—

No. 2.—PROMOTIONS, APPOINTMENTS, ETC.

MILITARY DISTRICT, No. 5, U.C.

The 7 Volunteer Militia Rifle Cos. gazetted this day at Toronto, under the command of the following officers, are hereby formed into a battalion under the provisions of Section 26 of the Consolidated Militia Law, and will be styled "The 10th Battalion Volunteer Rifles, Canada,"

To be Major :—
Capt. Fred. Cumberland, from the 3rd Battalion, Toronto.

In the first list of officers of the 10th Battallon it, must be clearly understood that the names given were purely nominations subject to approval or rejection by the Commander-in-Chief.

As a matter of fact some of those whose names have been given as having been chosen by the committee to receive commissions, or rather, to be recommended for commissions, either eventually declined the honor, or from other causes were not gazetted to any rank in the regiment.

The following is the official list of the whole of the captains and subaltern officers on March 14th, 1862, the date upon which the battalion was officially recognized.

Captains, John Worthington, Alfred John Brunel, Sandford Fleming, James Worthington, Alfio DeGrassi, John McGee, Emerson Coatsworth.

Lieutenants, Thomas Gundry, William Steward, Henry

Roberts, David Fleming, Frederick Passmore, John Albiston, John Boxall.

Ensigns, James Isaac Dickey, William Stollery, Edward Moultrie Peele, Robert Mitchell, Richard Dennis, George Hamilton, Henry Bescoby.

In the *Gazette* of March 28th, 1862, appeared the following notification:

MILITIA APPOINTMENTS,

MILITARY DISTRICT No 5, UPPER CANADA.

Tenth Battalion Volunteer Militia Rifles Canada:

To be Lieutenant-Colonel, Major Frederic William Cumberland.

To be Majors, Captain John Worthington, from the 1st Company, and Captain John Brunel, from 2nd Company.

No. 1 Company—To be Captain, George Carroll, Esq., *vice* Worthington, promoted.

No. 2 Company—To be Captain, James G. McGrath, Esq., *vice* Brunel, promoted.

The following is a complete roll of the seven companies which were formed. This was made out and sent to Quebec, March 10th, 1862, and the first G. O. just quoted was issued four days later.

No. 1 COMPANY—A. Brunel, Henry Roberts, Geo. R. Hamilton, James Thompson, Joseph H. Campbell, James Thorn, Charles Parkham, Phillip Kavanagh, Joseph Holman, William Douglas, William H. Simpson, Edward Murn, George Watson, John Degur, Alfred Berry, Alex. Fraser, William Sloggett, John Marsh, P. McCaudahie. W. I. Rolph, I. H. Hickman, Wm. Nicholls, Elias Zeo. P. More, Charles De Francois, Robert Douglas, Thomas

Fennell, James Pim, Richard Lawrence, Thomas Peters, John Harvie, Chas. G. Dunn, Benjamin Dean, Stephen Matthews, Wm. H. Pettigrew, John Henderson, Thomas Flanigan, Joshua Dean, Philip Warren, Reuben Law, George Wilson, Charles Marson, Rich. I. Cole, Henry McCaffrey, Nicholas Holman, David Jack, Lyman Rumour, Thomas Thompson, Taylor Butler, Wm. H. Cheshire, Chris. Verrall, Joseph Benson, Alexander Stewart, Wm. McMullen, M. P. McNulty, Thomas Miller, Michael Burns, Mark Seddan, James Vicars, Michael Larrigan.

No. 2 COMPANY—Wm. Turner, Wilkinson Dean, Chas. Curry, John Knowlton, Fred Warren, James Grant, Geo. Kitson, William Jones, John Keats, John Skidmore, A. Brunel, Jr., Troilus Brunel, Jas. R. Gibson, Joseph Woods, Henry Humphries, Henry Levett, James McIntosh, N. Dickey, Wm. James Hughes, Daniel Livingstone William Armstrong, W. J. McClery, James Cruickshank, Fred. Hood, W. W. Laird, George Hassard, Sandford Fleming, Wm. Hoey, James Yeo, Theophilus Dobie, Jos. Heaslip, Patrick Kelly, Richard Smith, R. McDoryall, J. C. Taylor, Edward Botterill, James J. Hickey, Arthur Carkeek, James Oigan, A. Dickie, Wm. Stewart, E. Moultree Peele, Joseph Green, Edward McGann, Wm. Mara, H. McLaughlin, John Gillett, John Glynn, Michael Curly, John Mullon, James Ross, E. Thornhill, Thomas F. Wilkins, Joseph Waddy, Donald Forsyth, Wm. Mills, John Kelly, A. Taylor, John Taylor.

No. 3 COMPANY—Joseph Taylor, A. DeGrassi, Chas. Simpson, Edward Brookshead, John Huntley, Michael Milton, William Cullen, Thos. Arylesen, A. Wilson, Jas. Murphy, Edward H. Coole, John Kent, Robert McKim.

Richmond Sands, James Fairbanks, Michael Tobin, C. S. Heaps, A. Jackson, Robert Bell, Geo. M. Hall, Christopher Bendon, John Higgins, Austin McNamara, Owen McNally, Wm. M. Middleton, Stewart Burrows, Thos. Hopewood, John Mitchell, John Alliston, William Jones, Elsi Wilson, Jas. McAllister, James McCraw, C. E. Bull, J. G. Gibson, Thos. Snarr, Thos. Scott, George Tate, James Litster, John Ranilson, Andrew Parling, William Fenwick, Andrew Moore, Thos. Gladstone, Henry Moore, John Thompson, John Cull, John Thompson. Geo. P. DeGrassi, John States, Joshua Holdsworth, Alfred T. Shore, John Shanklin, Michael Tobin, Jr., John Wilson, Thos. Jamieson, John Connor, Emerson Coatsworth, John Mossiman.

No. 4 COMPANY—Thos. Hurst, Mitchell Mount, John Ford, John Ellis, Henry Savage, James Murray, James Crother, James 'Dudley, Thos. Dudley, William Dudley, George Peal, John England, John Meddlar, Henry Hurst, Henry Higgins, Edward Durant, Joseph Archer, Thos. O'Connor, David Fleming E. McGann, Edward Higgins, Wm. Thos. Durant, John Dill, Wm. Diamond, Wm. Clowes, Chas. Leight, Wm. Murray, John Taylor, Thos. Hogarth, John Kerr, Alex. McCoy, Wm. T. Crewe, Joseph Archer, Sr., Isaac Johnson, Thos. McMullen, James Bell, Robert Carrace, William Hodson, Robert Mitchell, Joseph Duggan, John Reed, W. C. Manson, Samuel Pettigrew, George Carroll, Thos. Carroll, Thos. W. Crews, John Hillock, John McGuire, S. M. Burney, William Virgo, Geo. Copping, John Gibson, Thos. Skippon, William Harris John Neill, Nathaniel Dickey, William Jaffray, William Boxall, Geo. Boxall.

No. 5 COMPANY.—Wm. Robertson, Wm. Goyen, James Royle, Joseph Marshall, Henry Jackman, Josiah Creys, Jas. Henderson, John Auchifler, Geo. Hutchison, Michael Reardon, John Macintosh, John Boxall, E. Jacobs, Thos. Carfrac, A. Auchincloss, John Burns, Jas. Milligan, John Worthington, William Steward, Richard Dinnis, James Farrall, W. E. Nilson, David Thomas, Jacob Nokes, Simon Strachan, Richard Finlay, Wm. Mulvey, Fenton Burns, Robert Hill, Peter Gall, John Mansall, William Whitcomb, James Campbell, Wm. Ford, Philip Kelly, Michael Keating, James Miller, Jessie Fensome, Edwin Fairchild, Thos. Scott, William Stewart, jr., John W. Reeves, Duncan McWatt, Geo. Guysden, Alex. Beemer, John Greig, John Bomibrick, William Best, Wm. Carter, John Carter, Samuel Stow, William Hill, Augustus Abell, Wm. Black, James Bennett, Wm. John Baxter, Wm. Graham, Walter Grey, Chas. Gould.

No. 6 COMPANY.—Michael McCabe, Robert Tait, John I. Miles, William Wright, William Craig, James I. Pike, Wm. Chas. Snelling, Wm. Davis, Wm. I. Givens, William Wilson, Thomas Gladstone, R. Coulter, Wm. Burns, John Thompson, John Ray, Matthew Peard, James Hawke. William Murphy, Alex. Johnstone, Thos. Barry, J. Hissop, Geo. Husband, James Worthington, J. B. Smith, William A. Stollery, R. W. Coupland, John Worthington, jr., John Greenless, Arthur Coleman, G. L. Parradis, William Cruse, Wm. Crowden, Archibald Campbell, Robert Campbell, John Foster, Thos. Hellem, Samuel Dodd, Wm. H. Edwick, James Hawkes, James Ramsey, James Hobbs, John Stevenson, Thos. Fairbairn, James Thompson, Henry J. Smitt, Edward Hall, John Trevail, James Williams, John

McClain, Wm. D. Rogers, Wm. Gourlay, John Malcolm, Andrew Sander, Thomas Edison, Henry Jackson, Richard Smith, Geo. Rushback, James Edgear, Alex. Wray.

No. 7 COMPANY.—R. E. Gregg, James H. Spring, C. W. Buchanan, jr., John Shannon, William Hughes, John J. Niles, Michael Smith, James Crooks, John Owlger, A. D. Peal, Joseph Rogers, S. Watson, W. J. Stibbs, Henry Jacobs, Thos. Downey, Evan Nicholson, W. R. Adams, Henry Henwood, John Smyth, J. Turner, Wm. Henderson, Robert Mishun, George Tait, Geo. L. Armstrong, R. S. Colley, O. G. McIntie, John Sikath, Alex. Scott, Thos. Coleman, John Rogers, W. D. Rogers, John M. Scott, Geo. Campbell, Peter Jacobs, B. B. Tracy, M. Gardner, W. H. Gough, Francis Tweedie, Samuel McCord, James Waldie, Robert Harrison, John McLoughlin, James Spence, John Bristo, Geo. Steels, Joseph Williams, H. Woodhouse, Wm. Crocker, Wm. Sturgeon.

At a meeting of the officers held in April, 1862, a committee composed of the field officers, together with Captain DeGrassi, Lieutenant Gundry, Ensign Bescoby and Captain Worthington, were appointed to draft by-laws, for the general government of the battalion. It was arranged that the field officers post officers to each company as follows:—

No. 1 Company—Captain ———, Lieutenant Stewart, Ensign Dennis.

No. 2 Company—Captain McGrath, Lieutenant Roberts, Ensign Hamilton.

No. 3 Company—Captain Fleming, Lieutenant Passmore, Ensign Peéle.

No. 4 Company—Captain James Worthington, Lieutenant Gundry, Ensign Stollery.

No. 5 Company—Captain DeGrassi, Lieutenant Albiston, Ensign Bescoby.
No. 6 Company—Captain Coatsworth, Lieutenant Fleming, Ensign Mitchell.
No. 7 Company—Captain George Carroll, Lieutenant Boxall, Ensign Dickey.
Captain McGee, unattached.

Another meeting of officers was held in May, 1862, when it was decided to procure 350 stand of new arms, those which had been purchased having proved unsatisfactory. At this meeting the recently issued Militia-General orders that the active militia should put in twenty-eight days consecutive drill were discussed. This was considered to be an obstacle in the way of getting suitable recruits. The officers in meeting assembled, passed a motion stating that, in their opinion, the period of drill should be left to the discretion of the Commander-in-Chief. It was also suggested that six day's drill would be more easily executed.

At a meeting of officers held on November 20th, 1862, at which Lieutenant-Colonel Cumberland presided, the following resolution, proposed by Captain Fleming, and seconded by Ensign Dickey, was carried unanimously :

"That the filling up of vacancies among the officers, and the posting of officers to companies, be left in the hands of field officers."

At the same meeting a committee was appointed to make arrangements about officer's uniform. A Building Committee was also appointed, which consisted of the following members: Major John Worthington, Captain James Worthington, and Lieutenant William Steward.

The officer commanding the 10th received an official notice from Quebec in the end of November, reading as follows :

MILITIA GENERAL ORDERS.
ACTIVE FORCE.
HEADQUARTERS, QUEBEC,
21st November, 1862.

No. 1. His Excellency the Commander-in-Chief approves of the 10th Battalion, Volunteer Militia Rifles, Canada, at Toronto, being organized as an Infantry Battalion, instead of Rifles under the designation of "The 10th Battalion Volunteer Militia (Infantry), Canada." Captain Latham's company of Volunteer Rifles, at Toronto, is hereby incorporated with the said Battalion, and will be known as the 8th Company.

On November 28th another fully attended meeting of the officers was held, when a band committee was appointed, and the question of supplying clothing to the regiment was discussed.

There were several changes among the commissioned ranks of the regiment early in the new year, the following promotions and appointments appearing in the *Gazette* of January 30th, 1863 :

10TH BATTALION VOLUNTEER MILITIA (INFANTRY).

No. 1 COMPANY.

To be Captain—Lieutenant William Steward from No. 2 Company, *vice* Carroll resigned.

To be Lieutenant—Ensign Dennis from No. 1 Company, *vice* Gundry, whose commission has been cancelled.

To be Ensign—George McMurrich, gentleman, No. 2 Company.

No. 2 COMPANY.

To be Lieutenant—Lieutenant Henry Roberts from No. 3 Company, *vice* Steward promoted.

To be Ensign—Ensign Hamilton from No. 6 Company, *vice* Stollery, promoted.

zation, but from some reason not stated the officer commanding the proposed 8th Company failed in his endeavors, and on May 15th the following notification appeared in the *Canada Gazette:*

10TH ROYAL REGIMENT OF TORONTO VOLUNTEERS.

The 8th Company of this Battalion, under the command of Captain Latham, having failed in its organization, the formation of another Company is hereby authorized in its room and stead, viz. :

No. 8 COMPANY.

To be Captain—Samuel Sherwood.
To be Lieutenant—John Edwards.
To be Ensign—Levius Peters Sherwood.

At the Queen's Birthday parade, May 24th, 1863, several of the officers of the 10th Royals were present in undress uniform on the invitation of Lieutenant-Colonel Durie, commanding Q.O.R. The regiment was unable to be present on parade owing to the fact that their uniforms, which had been ordered in England, had not reached Canada.

On May 25th, 1863, a Drum Major's Mace was presented to the Battalion. The Mace is the one still in use, and it bears a small silver escutcheon, upon which is engraved the date when it became the property of the regiment.

CHAPTER IV.

PRESENTATION OF COLOURS TO THE REGIMENT BY MRS. CUM-
BERLAND.—LIEUTENANT-COLONEL CUMBERLAND RETIRES.—
THE FENIAN RAID.

THE History of the 10th Royals has now reached the point where they had become properly organized as an eight-company battalion, had learned their drill and were ready to respond to any call for duty that might be made upon them.

July 6th, 1863, was a red-letter day in the regiment's history, for upon that date was given to the corps those colours which, in the thirty-two years that have since elapsed, neither the 10th Royals or the Royal Grenadiers have ever disgraced, but have, on the other hand, fought bravely in maintaining their honor, the credit of their regiment and shewing their devotion to their Sovereign and their country.

The scene was thus described by one of Toronto's daily papers at the time of its occurrence :—

" It is always a pleasing duty to chronicle the fact that any portion of the community are giving 'aid and comfort' to the volunteer movement, but it is doubly gratifying when that aid and comfort comes from the fairer sections of the community. The officers and men of the 10th Royals may well feel proud of marching under the colours presented by the ladies of this city. Great preparations had been made for the important ceremony, both on the part of the officers and men. The scarlet uniforms, lately supplied by the Government, looked bright and gay, and it was the first time that the entire regiment had turned out in full-dress uniform. That they made a fine appearance, all who saw them admit. That each officer and man looked every inch a soldier nobody can deny.

"At half past two in the afternoon the regiment left headquarters, King street west, headed by the Pioneer Company and their band, in a neat white uniform like the regulars, and playing in capital style on the new instruments presented with their colours. They marched to the Queen's Park, where they executed a number of battalion movements, under command of Lieut.-Col. Cumberland, and then marched to the cricket ground where refreshments were served. The citizens were assembling at this time in great numbers on the common to witness the presentation. The spectators were estimated at five thousand persons. About four o'clock, the sound of martial music was heard in the distance, and in a few moments the companies, comprising the Queen's Own Battalion, under command of Lieut.-Col. Durie, marched on to the common with a firm tread, headed by their band playing a lively quickstep, and took up their position on the south side of the field. They had hardly got the word 'Stand at ease' when the tune of the 'British Grenadiers' was heard, and on came the gallant 10th and wheeled quickly in line on the right of their companions-in-arms.

"Both battalions were eagerly scanned by their friends and fellow-citizens. To those who judged by color only the scarlet tunics gave the men of the 'Royals' a decided advantage over the rifle green of the Queen's Own. Much regret was expressed when it was announced that owing to sickness, Major-Gen. Napier would be unable to be present to review the troops, and take part in the ceremony. He had, however, delegated Col. Robertson Royal Engineers, Commandant of the garrison, to take his place. Col. Robertson and staff took up their position in front of the brigade now in line, and Col. G. T Denison, of Rusholme, having assumed the command the troops presented arms.

"An altar covered with a white cloth was placed a short distance from the line, Lieut.-Col. Cumberland, Ensign Worthington, and Ensign Sherwood, these two last being the junior officers of the regiment, advanced and took up their position in front and the Colours were brought out from the tent under charge of Sergeant-Major Helm, and four colour sergeants with fixed bayonets, and placed on the altar. On a signal from Lieut.-Col. Cumberland, the committee of ladies, headed by Mrs. Cumberland, Col. Robertson and staff, and Rev. Dr. McCaul, in full academic costume, left the tent and approached the altar facing the brigade. On coming to the front, Mrs. Cumberland in a clear tone of voice read the following address:—

'*To Lieut.-Col. Cumberland, the officers, non-commissioned officers and men of the* 10th *Royal Regiment of Volunteer Militia:—*

'The ladies of Toronto request that you will do them

the favor to accept the accompanying stand of Colours for the regiment, together with a set of instruments for its band, as an evidence of the warm interest they take in the welfare of your corps, and their high appreciation of the spirit by which it is animated.

'In confiding these Colours to your charge, the donors are persuaded that they entrust them to those who will ever keep them in safety and in honor, nor do they doubt that if unhappily a necessity should arise for unfurling them in defence of the province, you will promptly rally around them at the call of duty, and, emulating the historic gallantry of your comrades of the regular service you will bear them with a valor which will evince affectionate attachment to your homes, patriotic love of your country, and loyal devotion to your Queen. (Applause.)

"The Rev. Dr. McCaul, President and Professor of the University of Toronto, consecrated the Colours by offering up prayer."

Colonel Robertson then handed first the Queen's then the Regimental Color to Mrs. Cumberland, who in turn handed the former to Ensign Worthington, the latter to Ensign Sherwood, who received them with bended knee. Mrs. Cumberland then said how pleased she was on her own behalf and on that of the Ladies' Committee to have had the pleasure and the privilege of giving these colours to the regiment that the people of Toronto would ever be jealous for the honour of that regiment, and that they trusted and believed the 10th would ever maintain their own honour and retain their standards unsullied.

Lieut.-Colonel Cumberland, in a few brief words becoming to him both as "a soldier and a man," thanked

the ladies for their gift. He then called upon th Reverend John McCaul, D.D., to address them.

Dr. McCaul then said it was with no ordinary pleasure he addressed them, the occasion was gratifying and honourable to all concerned, to the givers and receivers, to the ladies who had presented the colours, and to those who had received them, and he could with perfect propriety term the act a noble one. It was a most noble act on the part of the ladies, as they testified by it to the interest they felt in the corps, and at the same time gave a proof of their liberality. By this public recognition they had shown that they felt the practical utility of the force to the Province, and in explicit terms said, that if war should come, they were ready to do their parts to send forth their husbands, brothers and sons in defence of their country, trusting that God in His infinite mercy would bring them back to them unharmed. The act was also honourable to the corps, as the donors in their address said they felt they were confiding the colours to worthy men, who, in the event of war, would stand side by side with the regiments of the regular service that might be sent out from the Mother Country. When they looked at the Queen's colour they would remember their duty to the Empire of which they formed a part and to the happiness they enjoyed under the benign rule of its Most Gracious Sovereign, and when they looked at the regimental colour they would remember that they might be called on to defend their happy homes in this fair and fertile country, the birth-place or the land of adoption of them all, and in defending their homes they were also protecting their wives, daughters, mothers and sisters. Dr. McCaul brought his remarks to a close by saying that he was sure the men who formed the Royals would sustain the honour of the colours and that they would be handed down to their successors, without a blemish upon the regiment, as emblems of the love they bore their country and their devotion to their Queen.

On the close of Dr. McCaul's speech, Colonel Robertson and staff took up their positions at the saluting point on the western side of the grounds. The troops were drawn up in brigade order, "right in front," opposite.

Then commenced the time-honoured and picturesque ceremony of "trooping the colours." To the vast majority of those present the scene was an absolutely new one, but to some on the ground, veterans who had served their country in various parts of the globe, it brought back memories of the Alameda in Gibraltar, of Edinburgh and Holyrood, of Dublin and the Phœnix Park, of Parkhurst, Isle of Wight, and its famous drill field, or of Malta and the parade ground near Fort Ricasoli.

Cheer after cheer was given as, in response to the word of command "officers and non-commissioned officers, to your guards, slow march!" officers and sergeants who were drawn up in line at attention about one hundred yards in front of and facing the battalion, at once brought their swords and rifles to the "recover" and moved slowly towards the line, the band playing a slow march. Arrived at the line the captains took up position on the right flank of the company, their covering sergeants in the rear, while the remaining officers and sergeants passed to their proper places in the supernumerary rank.

PRESENTATION OF COLORS. 41

Then the "troop" took place and afterwards the brigade marched past in open column in slow and quick time, and in quarter distance column in quick time. The march past in slow time was splendidly done, and as company after company marched past the saluting point, the officers giving the old-fashioned stately double salute, first with the sword and then with the left hand, the applause from the onlookers was unstinted.

Colonel Robertson made some very complimentary remarks and the troops marched off the field.

On July 10th, 1863, The *Gazette* contained the following notification "10th or Royal Regiment of Toronto Volunteers."

To be adjutant with the rank of Lieutenant:

James Benson, Gentleman, late 2nd Volunteer Rifle Company, St. Catharines.

Though it is scarcely necessary in writing a military history, to refer to the social life of the officers and men of any particular regiment, yet there are certain social events which have an historic interest. Such was the celebrated ball given by the Duchess of Richmond, on the eve of Waterloo, and such also, was the first ball ever given by the officers of the 10th Royals on December 20th, 1863. It marked the commencement of the Regiment's role as entertainers of the pleasantest order, a distinction which in the long years that have since elapsed has not grown less, even in the slightest degree.

The Canada *Gazette* of April 29th, 1864, giving a list of those Militia Corps who had become entitled by proficiency in drill and discipline, to the money prizes which had been awarded by Government in the several Military Districts of Upper Canada, remarked:

"His Excellency, the Commander-in-Chief, has observed, with much satisfaction, that in addition to the Corps named, the 10th or Royal Regiment of Infantry, Toronto, Lieutenant-Colonel Cumberland, with others, although not entitled to prizes, have been favourably reported upon for general proficiency."

Queen's Birthday passed off with the usual parade and with the firing of a *feu de joie*. The birthday parade of 1864 was the first of that kind that the 10th had been able to hold.

On July 14th, 1864, it was announced, under the heading "General Order" that Ensign George A. Shaw, who afterwards commanded the 10th, and who was then a candidate for a Commission in the 10th Royals, had received a second-class certificate for efficiency from the Commandant of the School of Military Instruction at Toronto.

There was a change in the officers of No. 8 Company on September 23rd, 1864. Ensign L. P. Sherwood being promoted to the Lieutenancy caused by the resignation of Lieutenant Edward Stewart.

Owing to the disturbed state of political affairs in the United States towards the end of the year, 1864, much trouble was caused to the Canadian Government by certain persons committing acts which tended to infringe the conditions of neutrality assumed by Great Britain, regarding the great internecine contest that was then waging. On December 19th, 1864, were issued the following "General Orders."

No 1. His Excellency, the Commander-in-Chief, is pleased to state he has given orders to call out for actual service, under the provisions of "The Volunteer Militia Act," a part of the Volunteer Militia of this Province and that the same will consist of thirty companies of Rifles of Infantry to be hereafter named.

No. 2. His Excellency desires that all officers commanding Battalions, and officers commanding Companies (not in Battalion), will forthwith increase the strength of their several Companies of Rifles or Infantry to 65 non-commissioned officers and men, and will hold themselves in readiness for immediate actual service when His Excellency may see fit to call out the same or any part thereof.

On December 19th, 1864, a General Order was issued to the following effect:—

"His Excellency the Commander-in-Chief is pleased to state that he has given orders to call out for active service, under the provisions of the Volunteer Militia Act, a part of the Volnnteer Militia of this Province, and that the same will consist of thirty companies of rifles, or infantry, to be hereafter named."

Four days later this was followed by the following order, dated—

HEAD-QUARTERS, QUEBEC, 23RD DEC., 1864, VOLUNTEER MILITIA GENERAL ORDER.

No. 1. Referring to the General Order of December 19th, is pleased to call out for active service the following companies of the volunteer force.

Then followed the names of the companies called out, and directions that they should be formed into three administrative battalions, and the names of the staff officers for each battalion were duly gazetted.

The Commander-in-Chief, in a General Order addressed to the force, impressed upon them " that they were embodied, not for the purpose of warfare, but with the object of aiding the civil power in its efforts to prevent aggression on the territories of a friendly state, on the part of persons enjoying the right of asylum in Her Majesty's dominions; and to maintain, as regards Canada, complete neutrality with respect to the war existing in the United States, which Her Majesty has enjoined on all her subjects."

None of the companies of the 10th were included in these first battalions, which on April 21st were relieved, and three new battalions formed in their stead, in the third of which No. 1 and 2 companies were composed by men of the 10th Royals, under the command of Captains G. W. Musson and John Gibbs Ridout; the subaltern officers being Lieutenant G. McMurrich, Ensigns C. Connon and H. J. Browne.

On Queen's birthday, 1865, the 10th were brigaded with the Queen's Own and other troops in garrison, and fired a *feu de joie*. The detachment at Laprairie indulged in a series of athletic contests in which the men of Captain Musson's company carried off most of the prizes.

The Laprairie camp broke up October 13th, 1865, the two companies of the 10th had returned to Toronto a short time previously.

Under date January 13th, 1865, the *Gazette* announced the retirement from the 10th of Captains McGrath, Sandford Fleming and DeGrassi, also of Lieutenant Bescoby and Ensign Edward Murphy.

The following appointment was gazetted :

To be Captain, Ensign George W. Musson *vice* De-Grassi.

The next appointment in connection with the 10th was gazetted April 20th, 1865, it was as follows :

To be Adjutant with the rank of Captain, Lieutenant John Gibbs Ridout *vice* Benson, resigned.

Lieutenant Ridout had just retired from the 100th, P. W.R.C.R., in which he had served since its formation in 1858. Lieutenant Ridout, when at the Staff College, took the highest place in the examinations of his final year; distancing by far every other officer of every branch of the service then at the Staff College.

Lieutenant-Colonel Cumberland, who had commanded the 10th since its first formation, retired from the service on July 21st, 1865, when the *Gazette* contained the following notice :

10th Battalion Royal Regiment, Toronto Volunteers.

To be Lieutenant-Colonel, Major Alfred Brunel *vice* Cumberland, resigned.

To mark the high appreciation of the services rendered not only to the 10th but to the militia force of Canada generally, by Lieutenant-Colonel Cumberland, it was officially notified in the *Gazette* as follows :

The Governor-General and Commander-in-Chief has been pleased to appoint Lieutenant-Colonel Frederic W. Cumberland to be an extra Aide-de-Camp to His Excellency.

When Lieutenant-Colonel Cumberland severed his connection with the 10th Royals he issued as a regimental order, on August 8th, 1865, this valedictory address:

"Lieutenant-Colonel Cumberland, having been permitted by His Excellency the Commander-in-Chief to resign the command of the 10th Royal Regiment, cannot retire without expressing to the officers, non-commissioned officers and men his warm appreciation of the soldierly spirit evinced by all ranks throughout the period (nearly four years) during which he has had the honor of commanding the regiment, of their willing obedience to his orders and of the good-feeling which has so happily united them as a military organization.

"The Lieutenant-Colonel deeply regrets the necessity for his severance from the Regiment, arising, as it solely does, from engagements no longer admitting of a divided duty.

"He will always remember his associations with it as a very high honor and as a most acceptable and happy service; and he leaves it with the fullest confidence that under the zealous and devoted energy of the able officer succeeding to the command, the Regiment will uphold and extend its reputation.

"By the favor of His Excellency the Commander-in-Chief, Lieutenant-Colonel Cumberland continues attached to the Volunteers, and has been appointed to the personal staff of the Governor-General. He cannot doubt that for this honor he is largely indebted to the high standing of the Regiment it has been his priviluge to command, and he hopes that such a special mark of favor to it, in his person, will stimulate the pride of all ranks to maintain the Royals in a condition of permanent and honorable efficiency.

"In bidding the Regiment heartily farewell, Lieutenant-

Colonel Cumberland desires to express his best and most friendly wishes for the future well-being of every member in it."

In the Regimental Orders of August 8th, 1865, appeared the following:

The Lieutenant-Colonel commanding directs that the farewell order of Lieutenant-Colonel Cumberland be posted in the orders of the day, and in doing so he refers with great pleasure and satisfaction to the honors conferred on Lieutenant-Colonel Cumberland by His Excellency the Commander-in-Chief, a satisfaction which he is convinced will be felt by the Regiment, both on account of the gratification it must afford to Lieutenant-Colonel Cumberland and of the incentive which this precedent must give to increased efficiency in the Regiment.

By order,
(Signed,) J. GIBBS RIDOUT,
Captain and Adjutant

Lieutenant-Colonel A. Brunel succeeded to the vacant command and at once issued the subjoined orders:

HEADQUARTERS 10TH ROYAL REGIMENT, TORONTO VOLUNTEERS.

TORONTO, Aug. 8th, 1865.

Regimental Order:

1. The Lieutenant-Colonel, in assuming command of the Regiment, earnestly invites the active co-operation of all ranks in maintaining the corps in a state of efficiency worthy of the spirit in which it was organized, and such as while sustaining the reputation of the Regiment will satisfy the just expectations of the Commander-in-Chief.

2. The Lieutenant-Colonel commanding is convinced that every officer will zealously devote himself to the maintenance of efficiency and the support of discipline, and that while doing so they will take such a generous interest in the welfare of their men as will in some measure compensate them for any sacrifices they may be called upon to make in discharging their duty as volunteers.

3. And he is equally confident that the non-commissioned officers and men will evince a soldierly appreciation of the value of discipline and of the importance of the implicit obedience to orders while on duty, which is essential to the efficiency of the Regiment, and will best demonstrate the manly self-respect characteristic of men who know the value of the privileges they are armed to defend.

4. In urging on every member of the corps the zealous discharge of their respective duties, the Lieutenant Colonel desires not to be forgetful of his own responsibilities. While on duty with the regiment, he will require such obedience to orders as is due to the Queen's commission, which he has the honor to hold, and he will insist on the maintenance of that discipline, without which a regiment degenerates into an armed mob, dangerous only to its friends. But he will also recognize in every well-conducted member of the corps a comrade and a friend, whose welfare it will be his pleasure and his duty to promote on all fitting occasions.

By Order,

(Signed,) J. GIBBS RIDOUT,
Capt. and Adjt.

There was a good soldierly ring in this order, and every one who wished well to the 10th, was pleased that Lieutenant-Colonel Brunel had the courage to say plainly what he meant, what he wanted, and what, so far as he was able, he intended to exact.

Towards the close of the year 1865, much anxiety was caused throughout the Province by the possibility, if not the extreme probability of troubles arising on the Canadian frontier, by raids from what were known as the Fenians, an alien body inimical to Great Britain, located in the United States, and who pursued their nefarious modes of procedure in defiance of the American Republic and of everyone else but themselves. In consequence of this state of feeling, the following "General Order" was issued.

HEAD-QUARTERS,
OTTAWA, 15th Nov., 1865.

MILITIA GENERAL ORDERS,—

His Excellency, the Administrator of the Government, and Commander-in-chief, having had under consideration the possibility of raids or predatory incursons on the frontier of Canada, may be attempted during the winter, by persons ill-disposed to Her Majesty's Government, to the prejudice of the Province, and the annoyance and injury of Her Majesty's subjects therein.

And being impressed with the importance of aiding Her Majesty's troops in repelling such attempts, and with that purpose of placing a portion of the Volunteer Force on active service. His Excellency directs

That one Volunteer company be called out for service, for as long a period as may be thought necessary by

D

His Excellency, from each of the undermentioned places, viz. :

Quebec, Montreal, Ottawa, Morrisburg, Toronto, Port Hope, Hamilton, Woodstock, London—the companies so called out to be stationed at such places as His Excellency, the Lieutenant-General commanding shall direct.

And that the said Volunteer Force shall, during the time it remains on active service, be placed under the command of His Excellency, Lieutenant-General Sir John Michel, commanding Her Majesty's forces in North America ; that it shall be subject to the Queen's regulations and orders for the Army, to the Rules and Articles of War, to the Act for punishing mutiny and desertion, and to all other laws applicable to Her Majesty's troops in this Province, not inconsistent with the Acts respecting the Volunteer Militia.

Consequent upon the resignation of Lieutenant-Colonel Cumberland, Captain James Worthington succeeded to the Majority rendered vacant by Major Brunel's promotion to the command of the regiment, Lieutenant William Stollery obtaining the Captaincy thus vacated.

In Nov. 1865, Major John Worthington retired from the regiment retaining his rank, his resignation being published in the *Gazette* issued on Nov. 10th.

Captain Ridout also resigned the Adjutancy, but did not sever his connection with the regiment.

Lieutenant George McMurrich was appointed Adjutant in place of Captain Ridout, and the following promotions and appointments were also gazetted on the same day.

10th Royals, No. 4 Company—

To be Lieutenant, Ensign Arthur Coleman *vice* Stollery, promoted.

To be Surgeon, Dr. James H. Richardson, M.D.M.R.C.S.
To be Assistant Surgeon, Dr. James Newcombe, M.D M.R.C.S.

A little later there were yet more appointments and promotions notified thus:—

HEAD-QUARTERS.
OTTAWA, Dec. 1st, 1865.

General Orders.

10th Battalion Royal Regiment Toronto Volunteers.

To be Lieutenants, Ensign John M. Lawrence, *vice* McMurrich, appointed Adjutant; Ensign Charles Connon, *vice* James Isaac Dickey, removed.

To be Ensigns (temporary), Charles James Henry Winstanley, Gentleman, Military School, *vice* Lawrence, promoted; Lewellyn H. Robertson, Gentleman, Military School, *vice* Connon, promoted; Walter H. Barrett, Gentleman, Military School, *vice* Coleman, promoted.

Lieutenant L. P. Sherwood severed his connection with the 10th. Dec. 16th, 1865, he on that day being promoted to a Captaincy in the Q O. R Ensign Harry J. Browne was promoted to the Lieutenancy made vacant by the promotion of Captain Sherwood.

There are various contradictions in the *Gazette* respecting the ranks of officers, for instance, Ensign Hetherington is mentioned January 10th, 1866, as having obtained a Certificate, whereas Mr. Hetherington's appointment to an Ensigncy does not appear in the *Gazette* until Feb. 2nd, just one fortnight later.

On Feb. 2nd, the *Gazette* contained the following notifications:

10th Battalion Royal Regiment Toronto Volunteers.

52   HISTORY OF THE ROYAL GRENADIERS.

To be Major, Captain John Boxall, *vice* Worthington, resigned.

To be Captain, Lieutenant and Adjutant McMurrich, *vice* Steward, whose resignation is hereby accepted.

To be Ensign, John W. H. Hetherington, Gentleman.

Lieutenant C. H. Connon assumed the duties of Adjutant in succession to Lieutenant McMurrich, promoted on the same date.

March, 1866, was a stirring time for the Militia. On the 8th day of that month was issued the following " General Order."

" His Excellency the Governor-General and Commander-in-Chief directs that the 10th Royal Regiment Toronto Volunteers be called out for service ; that the said corps be immediately assembled and billeted at their respective headquarters, there to await such orders as may be directed by the Commander-in-Chief."

Of course the 10th Royals was only one among a great many others who received a similar order.

A long list of promotions and appointments appeared in the *Gazette* of March 23rd, 1866. They were as follows :

10th Battalion Royal Regiment Toronto Volunteers.

To be Captain, Lieutenant J.W. Lawrence, *vice* Richey, appointed Pay Master.

To be Lieutenants—

Ensign James H. Winstanley, temporary, Military College, *vice* Lawrence, promoted.

Ensign Frederick Richardson, *vice* Connon, appointed Adjutant.

To be Acting Ensigns (temporary)—

Captain J.W. Rolph, from 5th Battalion Service Militia, York.

Lieutenant G. A. Shaw, from 3rd Battalion Service Militia, York.

To be Pay Master—

Captain John Richey, from No. 7 Company.

10TH BATTALION ROYAL VOLUNTEERS OF TORONTO.

To be Captain—

Lieutenant T. Brunel, *vice* Boxall, promoted, to date from the 22nd.

To be Lieutenants—

Ensign John W. Hetherington, *vice* Brunel, promoted.

Lieutenant Mitchell is allowed to retire, retaining his rank.

To be Ensigns (temporary)—

George Brunel, Gentleman, Military School.

Alexander James Robertson, Gentleman, Military School.

The following letters appeared in the *Gazette* on the date given, they were as follows:

HEAD QUARTERS.

OTTAWA, 20th April, 1866.

GENERAL ORDERS.

VOLUNTEER MILITIA.

No. 1.

His Excellency the Governor-General and Commander-in-Chief has pleasure in publishing the following letter for the information of the Volunteer Force in Canada:

" DOWNING STREET, 31st March, 1866.

" MY LORD,—

" I have the honor to acknowledge the receipt of your Lordship's despatch of the 9th March, transmitting a copy of an Approved Minute of the Executive Council of Canada, in which your Ministers signify their concurrence in the recommendation of the Minister of Militia for calling out a force of ten thousand volunteers in consequence of the threatened raid of the Fenian conspirators upon Canada.

"Your Lordship also reports, in the same despatch the alacrity with which the summons has been answered.

"I have to signify to your Lordship the unqualified gratification felt by Her Majesty's Government, at the prompt and loyal spirit which the volunteers of Canada have so signally manifested on this occasion.

"I have, etc.,

"(Signed,) EDWARD CARDWELL."

On May 24th, 1866, the 10th paraded, six companies strong, under command of Lieut. Col. Brunel, the other troops with whom they were brigaded, being H. M. 47th Foot, the Q. O. R. of Canada, Garrison Militia Artillery and the Governor-General's Body guard. After parade, Sergeant Rogers, No. 5 Company, was presented by the officers and men of the company with a sword, he being appointed armorer sergeant to the battalion.

On May 25th, 1866, the following regimental order was published :

" The Lieutenant-Colonel desires to express his high appreciation of the good conduct of the officers, N. C. O's., and men of the regiment since they have been called out for active duty, and to thank them for the readiness with which they have yielded to discipline."

The regiment had been under arms in anticipation of trouble from Fenian sources, but it was thought that the

Fenians had given up their foolhardy projects, and that it was not necessary to keep the 10th embodied; a very few days though sufficed to dispel this illusion. So completely was the fear of trouble at rest, that even the guard over the drill shed, which had been furnished by the various regiments, was discontinued by Garrison order, dated May 28th, 1866.

The Fenian Raid of 1866, is now a matter of somewhat ancient history, and excepting for the part played in assisting to restore order by the 10th Royals and other Canadian militia regiments, would possess little interest to any one. On the morning of June 1st, the 10th Royals assembled and received peremptory orders to proceed to St. Catharines by train, at 4.30 the same day, Major Boxall commanded, with the following officers in command of companies 1 to 8 respectively. Captains McMurrich, Hamilton, Moberley, Stollery, Musson, Lawrence, Hetherington and Brunel, Lieut.-Colonel Brunel was in Montreal at the time, and as the troops were ordered off at only a few hours notice he was unable to get back so as to march with his men, though he assumed the command on the frontier a few days later. The 10th saw no actual warfare on this occasion, but were greatly praised for their excellent behaviour and discipline.

While in camp at Fort Erie no passes were allowed on any pretence, sickness, of course, excepted, and officers were required to report themselves to the commanding officer before leaving and on returning to camp.

The 10th while at Fort Erie furnished each day a patrol, consisting of one sergeant, one corporal and six men, also an outlying picquet, to "guard the rear of the camp;" the orders do not say how many men were on the picquet.

In the camp orders issued June 5, 1866, Lieutenant Dawson, 47th Regiment, was appointed Brigade Major. This same officer subsequently served as Major with the Royal Grenadiers in the North-West campaign, and eventually commanded the regiment.

A general order was issued after the Fenian Raid; it was as follows:

HEAD QUARTERS,

OTTAWA, 22nd June, 1866.

GENERAL ORDERS

VOLUNTEER MILITIA.

No. .

In releasing the volunteers for the present from active duty, the Commander-in-Chief desires to make known to the officers, non-commissioned officers and men of the force, the pride and satisfaction with which he has witnessed the patriotism and energy displayed by them in their instantaneous response to the call to arms.

The Commander-in-Chief wishes to express his admiration of the promptitude with which, on the only occasion when an opportunity was afforded them of meeting the enemy, the volunteers went under fire, and his deep sympathy with the friends and relatives of those who there met a soldier's death.

The discipline and good conduct of the force while on service has secured the approbation of their military commanders, and has been most favorably reported on to the Commander-in-Chief.

LIEUT.-COL. G. D. DAWSON.

The Commander-in-Chief wishes to impress on the minds of the volunteers that though the late attack on the Province has proved a failure, the organization by means of which it was attempted still exists, and that its leaders do not hesitate to declare publicly that they meditate a renewal of the invasion. Under these circumstancees the Commander-in-Chief trusts the Volunteer Force generally will continue at all convenient times to perfect themselves in drill and discipline, so that they may be able successfully to repel any future aggresion that may be attempted.

At a complimentary dinner given by Mr. Carlible of the Terrapin restaurant on July 12th, to the officers of the Queen's Own, Major Robert B. Denison, replying to the toast of the "Volunteers of Canada," said "he regretted very much that the 10th Royals had not been with the Queens Own at Lime Ridge. Had they been there he was sure the retreat to Port Colborne would never have taken place." At the same dinner, Major Gilmor, Q.O.R., proposed the health of the 10th Royals coupled with the name of Captain Moberly, who in his reply said, "If the Queens Own had had the honor of shooting the Fenians, the 10th Royals had enjoyed the pleasure of burying them."

The services rendered by the Canadian Militia though were destined to receive yet further recognition, as is thus evidenced :

HORSE GUARDS,
July 21st, 1866.

SIR,—With reference to the several reports which have been received from the General Officer commanding in

Canada, relative to the Fenian movement in that province and to the measures taken by the Colonists for repelling any Fenian attack, I am directed by the F. M. Commanding-in-Chief, to request that you will acquaint the Secretary of State for War that H.R.H. having observed the alacrity, loyalty and zeal shown by the Volunteers and Militia forces of Canada, in having come forward for the defence of the colony on the late trying occasion in support of the troops, is very desirous of expressing to the Force his full appreciation of their gallant and energetic behaviour, and the very great gratification and satisfaction he has thereby experienced. * * *

I am Sir,
Your obedient servant,
(Signed) W. F. FOSTER,
Military Secretary.

The Under Secretary of State for War.

On August 13th, 1866, the 10th were by Brigade order ordered to be ready to move into camp on August 17, they were "to take no personal effects beyond knapsacks." Accordingly on Friday, August 17, the 10th took their departure from Toronto on board the steamer Osprey for St. Catharines, en route to Thorold. They were served out each man with fifty rounds of ball cartridge, though only going "into camp" for eight days, military authorities evidently thought it best to be ready for the worst.

The camp passed off though without any incident occurring outside the daily routine of military duty, drills and parades followed each other with regularity, and there was nothing to disturb anyone.

There were yet more changes in the Regiment towards the end of the year, they were as contained in the following extract:

OTTAWA, December 28th, 1866.

10th Battalion Royal Regiment Toronto Volunteers.

To be Captains, Lieutenant John Patterson, *vice* Sherwood whose resignation is hereby accepted; Lieutenant Arthur Coleman, *vice* Lawrence whose resignation is hereby accepted.

To be Lieutenants, Ensign George Brunel, M.S., *vice* Patterson promoted; Ensign George Alexander Shaw, M.S., *vice* Coleman promoted.

To be Ensigns, Frederick Barlow Cumberland, gentleman, temporary, M. S., *vice* Hetherington promoted; Francis E. Boswell, gentleman, temporary, M.S., *vice* Richardson promoted; F. H. Noverre, gentleman, *vice* Barrett promoted; Robert L. Killaly, gentleman, temporary, M.S., *vice* Brunel promoted; Lewis H. Moffat, gentleman, temporary, M.S., *vice* Shaw promoted.

It is worthy of note that up to 1867 the rank and file of the battalion were obliged to pay for their own forage caps, an order appearing in the Regimental Orders on March 20th, that the men "should procure them through their captains, by the payment of their cost, fifty cents."

In January, 1867, Quarter Master Rufus Skinner was appointed Paymaster of the regiment *vice* Richie deceased. In the next month and in the one succeeding it the *Gazette* contained the following G.O. and appointments:

HEAD QUARTERS,
OTTAWA, 15th February, 1867.
GENERAL ORDERS.

No. 3. The following officers of the Volunteer Militia and candidates for appointments therein, having appeared before Boards of officers at Kingston and Toronto, for the purpose of having their qualification tested have received certificates as follows, viz.:

Captain Harry John Browne, 10th Royals, Toronto.

Captain John Watson Hetherington, 10th Royals, Toronto.

10th Battalion Royal Regiment Toronto Volunteers.

April 5th, 1867.

To be Ensign, William D. Rogers, gentleman, *vice* Shaw promoted.

A very important change in the armament of the corps took place in June, 1867, when the Spencer rifles in possession of the regiment were called into store, and "Snider Enfields" issued in their place. What a change from the armament of the active militia as it had been only a few years earlier. Then, anything was good enough to arm them with, but in 1867 nothing was too good.

Queen's Birthday parade in 1867 passed off as usual, and on July 1st, 1867, the first Dominion Day was celebrated by a parade of the 10th and other militia regiments.

Under the new Constitution of the country it is interesting to note who were the first Dominion officers in the 10th Royals. Their names are contained in the following extract from the *Gazette*:

HEAD QUARTERS,
OTTAWA, 9th August, 1867.
GENERAL ORDERS.
VOLUNTEER MILITIA.

No. 1. Tenth Battalion Royal Regiment Toronto Volunteers.

To be Lieutenants, Ensign W. D. Rogers, *vice* Musson resigned.

Ensign Fred. B. Cumberland, M.S., (temporary), *vice* Patterson promoted.

George A. Boomer, M.S., (temporary).

To be Ensigns, (temporary), Philip Vankoughnet, M.S., *vice* Rogers promoted.

James L. Capreole, M.S., *vice* Cumberland promoted.

To be Adjutant, Captain H. J. Browne, *vice* Connon, who resigns the adjutancy only.

To be Quarter Master, with rank of Ensign, David McLellan, *vice* Skinner promoted.

The resignation of Ensign R. L. Killaly is hereby accepted.

There were yet more and more changes as the year wore on, many well-known names appearing and also disappearing. The following *Gazette* was issued at the end of October:

HEAD QUARTERS,
OTTAWA, 31st October, 1867.
GENERAL ORDERS.
VOLUNTEER MILITIA.

No. 2. Tenth Battalion Royal Regiment of Toronto Volunteers.

To be Captains, Lieut. Geo. A. Shaw, M.S., *vice* Brunel, resigned.

Thomas Thompson, Esquire, *vice* Musson, resigned.

To be Lieutenant, William Adamson, *vice* Connon, resigned.

To be Ensigns (temporary), James Wiley and William John Ramsey, M. S.

There was little to note in the next few months, but in the late spring of the next year there were again many changes notified officially thus:

HEAD QUARTERS,
OTTAWA, 8th May, 1868.

GENERAL ORDERS.

VOLUNTEER MILITIA.

No. 2. Tenth Battalion Royal Regiment of Toronto Volunteers.

To be Captains, Lieut. Walter H. Barrett, *vice* J. Paterson, resigned.

Lieut. Fred B. Cumberland (temporary), M. S., *vice* G. R. Hamilton, resigned.

Lieut. Wm. D. Rogers, *vice* Browne, appointed adjutant.

Lieut. George A. Boomer (temporary), M.S.

To be Lieutenants, Ensign Alex. J. Robertson (temporary), M.S., *vice* Barrett, promoted.

Ensign W. H. Noverre, *vice* Cumberland, promoted.

Ensign Lewis H. Moffatt (temporary), M. S., *vice* Rogers, promoted.

Ensign Philip Vankonghnet (temporary), M. S., *vice* Boomer, promoted.

Ensign William John Ramsey (temporary), M.S., *vice* C. J. H. Winstanley, resigned.

Joseph Marshall, *vice* Frederick Richardson, resigned.

To be Ensigns, Andrew Fleming, acting till further orders, *vice* Robertson, promoted.

Wm. H. Dudley, *vice* Noverre, promoted.

Ebenezer Bryant, *vice* Moffatt, promoted.

The resignation of Ensign J. W. Rolph is hereby accepted.

HEAD QUARTERS,
OTTAWA, 15th May, 1868.

GENERAL ORDERS.

VOLUNTEER MILITIA.

No. 2. Tenth, or Royal Regiment of Toronto Volunteers.

Ensign Andrew Fleming, having obtained the necessary certificate of qualification, is now confirmed in his rank from the date of his appointment.

There was the usual Queen's Birthday parade on May 24th, 1868, at which the regiment made a good showing, and on Monday, June 22nd, formed a portion of the Brigade which assembled on the Spadina-avenue common for inspection by the Major-General commanding the troops in Canada.

Only one change took place in the commissioned ranks of the 10th during the rest of year, it was this:

To be Ensign (temporary), Edwin G. Curtiss, M.S., *vice* Rolph, resigned. Dated, July 12th, 1868.

Promotions and appointments, resignations and retirements, followed thick and fast in those days among the officers of the 10th. In the seven and a half years the corps had been embodied, it had had nearly one hundred officers, and yet they came and yet they went.

A long list of changes appeared in the *Gazette* of July 16th, 1869, and to understand them better, G. O.'s issued on September 10th and November 12th, 1869, are also given. They were as follows:

HEAD QUARTERS,
OTTAWA, 10th July, 1869.
GENERAL ORDERS.
VOLUNTEER MILITIA.

No. 2. Tenth Royal Regiment of Toronto Volunteers.

To be Major, Captain William Stollery, *vice* James Worthington, who is allowed to retire, retaining his rank.

To be Captain, Lieutenant Lewis H. Moffatt, M.S., *vice* Stollery, promoted.

To be Lieutenants, Ensign Wm. H. Dudley, *vice* Moffatt, promoted.

Ensign Edwin G. Curtiss, *vice* Robertson, resigned.

The resignations of the following officers are hereby accepted, viz.:

Captain G. A. Boomer.

Captain and Adjutant, H. J. Browne.

Ensign F. E. Boswell.

HEAD QUARTERS,
OTTAWA, 23rd July, 1869.
GENERAL ORDERS.
VOLUNTEER MILITIA.

No. 3. Tenth Royal Regiment of Toronto Volunteers.

To be Captain, Ensign Andrew Fleming, *vice* Boomer, resigned.

HEAD QUARTERS,
OTTAWA, 10th Sept., 1869.
GENERAL ORDERS.
VOLUNTEER MILITIA.

No. 2. Tenth Battallion or Royal Regiment of Toronto Volunteers.

With reference to the General Order No. 2, of the 16th July last, Captain and Adjutant H. J. Browne, is now permitted to retire, retaining his rank.

THE FENIAN RAID. 65

HEAD QUARTERS,
OTTAWA, 12th Nov., 1869.
GENERAL ORDERS.
UNATTACHED LIST.
No. 1.

To be Captain, Lieutenant Edwin G. Curtiss, from 10th Battalion Volunteer Militia, Toronto.

The regiment was inspected by the Adjutant-General, on September 23rd, 1869, and the result was that they received unstinted praise from that official, he complimenting them "on the excellent condition of their arms, clothing and accoutrements, and of their manly and soldierlike appearance on parade."

On October 2nd, 1869, the regiment paraded for inspection by H.R.H., Prince Arthur, who distributed the prizes gained by the men in the rifle matches. On October 4th, appeared the following Regimental Order, which speaks for itself:

REGIMENTAL ORDER.

" The Lieut.-Colonel has been commanded by H.R.H., Prince Arthur, to express to the regiment the gratification he felt in presenting the prizes on the 2nd inst., and the more especially as never before having been called upon to act in a similar capacity, it was peculiarly agreeable to H.R.H. that the first occasion of such a nature should be in connection with a regiment of Canadian volunteers."

The regiment received a General Order from Head Quarters, dated 2nd June, 1870, to the effect that: " Referring to paragraph 54 of the " Regulations and Orders for the Active Militia, etc.," 1870, it is hereby notified

E

66 HISTORY OF THE ROYAL GRENADIERS.

that promotions are, and shall so continue to be, made 'according to seniority.'"

The year 1870 saw just as many changes among the commissioned ranks of the 10th, as had any of those which had preceded it, there being no less than twelve new appointments in June alone. In that month the *Gazette* contained the following notice:

HEAD QUARTERS,
OTTAWA, 30th June, 1870.
GENERAL ORDERS.
VOLUNTEER MILITIA.

No. 2. Tenth Battalion or Royal Regiment of Toronto Volunteers.

To be Captains, Lieutenant William Adamson, V.B., *vice* G. McMurrich, retired retaining rank.

Lieutenant William John Ramsey, V.B., *vice* W. H. Barrett, retired retaining rank.

Lieutenant Joseph Marshall, V.B., M.S., *vice* W. D. Rogers, retired retaining rank.

To be Lieutenant, Ensign Ebenezer Brant, V.B., *vice* Marshall, promoted.

Benjamin Coleman, V.B., *vice* Adamson, promoted.

To be Ensigns, Andrew Anderson, M.S., *vice* Bryant, promoted.

John B. Allison, M.S., *vice* J. S. Capreole, resigned.

Powell Martin, M.S., *vice* J. Wiley, left limits.

N. Gordon Bigelow, (provisionally.)

Malcolm Morrison, (provisionally.)

Charles Price, (provisionally.)

Daniel Spry, (provisionally.)

The resignation of Lieut. A. J. Robertson is hereby accepted.

In October, 1870, a General Order was issued ordering that "The drill of the regiment will hereafter be in accordance with the Field Exercise published by authority for 1870."

Two more appointments were gazetted just at the end of the year, they were these:

HEAD QUARTERS.
OTTAWA, 7th December, 1870.

GENERAL ORDERS.

VOLUNTEER MILITIA.

No. 2. Tenth Battalion or Royal Regiment of Toronto Volunteers.

To be Lieutenants, Ensign P. Martin, M.S., *vice* E. Bryant, left limits.

John Patterson, M.S., *vice* P. Van Koughnet, left limits.

Lieutenant-Colonel Brunel retired from the command of the 10th Royals in January, 1871, though it was not officially announced until the following month, when on February 24th the *Gazette* contained this notice:—

GENERAL ORDERS (6)

ACTIVE MILITIA.

No. 2. Tenth Battalion or Royal Regiment, Toronto.

To be Lieutenant-Colonel, Major John Boxall, V.B., vice A. Brunel, retired, retaining rank.

On April 6th following, Captain John Watson Hetherington was promoted to the majority rendered vacant by Major Boxall's promotion.

In June, 1871, the regiment went into camp at Niagara and when it was broken up was favorably reported on by the inspecting officers. In the following year they were also encamped at the same place, from June 13th to 26th, and again received commendation for their appearance and drill.

On June 2nd, 1871, the following appointments and resignations appeared in the *Gazette* :—

No. 4. Tenth Battalion or Royal Regiment of Toronto.

To be Lieutenant, Ensign Andrew Anderson, M.S., *vice* B. Coleman, left limits.

The resignations of Ensign Malcolm Morrison and Daniel Spry are hereby accepted.

This was succeeded on June 6th by the order following :—

GENERAL ORDERS.

No. 8. Tenth Battalion or Royal Regiment of Toronto.

To be Captain, Lieutenant George Brunel, M.S., *vice* Hetherington, promoted.

From May, until September in 1872, almost every officer in the 10th Royals who had held a commission on the preceding New Year's Day, left the corps, as is witnessed by the following extracts from the *Gazette* :—

HEAD QUARTERS,
OTTAWA, 10th May, 1872.

GENERAL ORDER (12).,

ACTIVE MILITIA.

No. 3. Tenth Battalion, or Royal Regiment, Toronto.

To be Lieutenant, Robert F. Joseph, M.S.

To be Ensigns, Edward A. Millard, M.S., *vice* Anderson, promoted.

Thomas T. Rolph, M.S., *vice* Martin, promoted.

R. G. Hirschfelder, M.S., *vice* Morrison, resigned.

John T. Thompson, M.S., *vice* Spry, resigned.

William Henry Weston, M.S., *vice* J. B. Allison, left limits.

John Bailey, M.S., *vice* C. Price, retired on account of ill-health.

W. A. Phipps (provisionally).

Captain and Paymaster Rufus Skinner is hereby permitted to retire with the honorary rank of Captain.

HEAD QUARTERS,
OTTAWA, 7th June, 1872.

GENERAL ORDERS (16)

ACTIVE MILITIA.

No. 1. Tenth Battalion or Royal Regiment of Toronto.

To be Captains, Lieutenant Frank H. Noverre, V.B., *vice* William Adamson, who is hereby permitted to retire retaining rank, as a special case.

Lieutenant John Patterson, M.S., *vice* Lewis H. Moffat, retired retaining rank.

Lieutenant Andrew Anderson, M S., *vice* F. B. Cumberland, left limits.

To be Lieutenants, Ensign Edward A. Millard, M.S., *vice* Noverre, promoted.

Ensign T. Rolph, M.S., *vice* Patterson, promoted.

Ensign R. G. Hirschfelder, M.S., *vice* Anderson, promoted.

Ensign John T. Thompson, M.S.

Ensign William Henry Weston, M.S., *vice* W. H. Dudley, resigned.

Ensign John Bailey, M.S.

Ensign W. A. Phipps, M.S.

To be Ensigns, Samuel Lawrence, M.S., *vice* Bigelow, appointed Paymaster.

W. B. Canavan, M.S., *vice* Millard, promoted.

Robert T. Martin, M.S., *vice* Rolph, promoted.

Albert Bradley, provisionally, *vice* Hirschfelder, promoted.

James Ramsay, provisionally, *vice* Thompson, promoted.

Gilbert Brown, provisionally, *vice* Bailey, promoted.

E. F. Green, provisionally, *vice* Phipps, promoted.

Arthur Chapman, provisionally, *vice* Weston, promoted.

Robert S. Martin, provisionally.

To be Paymaster, Ensign Nelson Gordon Bigelow, *vice* Skinner, retired.

To be Quartermaster, John Metcalfe, *vice* D. McLellan, left limits.

To be Assistant-Surgeon, James Elliott Graham, Esquire, M.D., *vice* James Newcombe, left limits.

HEAD QUARTERS,
OTTAWA, 12th July, 1872.

GENERAL ORDERS (19),

ACTIVE MILITIA.

No. 1. Tenth Battalion, or Royal Regiment, Toronto.

To be Ensign from 13th June, 1872, William Henry Cooper, M.S.

HEAD QUARTERS,
OTTAWA, 6th September, 1892.

GENERAL ORDERS.

ACTIVE MILITIA.

No. 1. Tenth Battalion or Royal Regiment, Toronto.

To be Lieutenant, Ensign Samuel Lawrence, M.S.

From many causes, during the command of Lieutenant-Colonel Boxall, the 10th Royals did not progress or even maintain its standing; for one thing, the excitement caused by the Fenian Raid had entirely subsided, and for another, there was not much interest at that time taken by the general public either in the corps or in its affairs.

The following promotions and appointments occurred early in 1873. They were thus gazetted:

HEAD QUARTERS,
OTTAWA, 14th Feb., 1873.

GENERAL ORDERS.

ACTIVE MILITIA.

No. 1, Tenth Battalion of Infantry, or Royals, Toronto.

To be Captain: Lieutenant Powell Martin, M. S., *vice* J. Marshall, left limits.

To be Lieutenant: Ensign William B. Canavan, M. S., *vice* Martin promoted.

To be Ensigns: H. J. Hill, M. S., *vice* Canavan promoted.

J. T. Jones, provisionally, *vice* R. T. Martin, left limits.

The foregoing were shortly afterwards followed by these:

72   HISTORY OF THE ROYAL GRENADIERS.

HEAD QUARTERS,
OTTAWA, 25th April, 1873.
GENERAL ORDERS.

ACTIVE MILITIA.

No. 1. Tenth Battalion of Infantry, or Royals, Toronto.

To be Captains: Lieutenant Thomas T. Rolph, M.S., *vice* P. Martin, appointed Adjutant.

Lieutenant Rudolph G. Hirschfelder, M.S., *vice* George Browne, left limits.

To be Ensigns: Alfred E. Hirschfelder, M.S., *vice* G. Browne, deceased.

Frederick W. Unitt, M.S., *vice* R. S. Martin, deceased.

To be Adjutant: Captain Powell Martin, M.S., *vice* H. J. Browne, retired.

The resignation of Lieutenant Robert F. Joseph is hereby accepted,

Memo.—Adverting to G. O., 14th February, 1873, Captain Powell Martin takes rank as Captain from 7th June, 1872, next after Captain Frank H. Noverre.

On November 21st, 1873, Lieutenant-Colonel Boxall retired from the command of the 10th, accompanied by Major J. W. Hetherington, and Major Stollery assumed command. For two years the 10th had no Lieutenant-Colonel, Major Stollery, though in command, not being gazetted to the Lieutenant- Colonelcy until November 5th, 1875.

On December 26th, 1873, the following General Order appeared:

No. 1. Tenth Battalion of Infantry, or Royals, Toronto.

To be Major, Captain and Brevet Major, Arthur Coleman, V.B., *vice* J. W. Hetherington.

On February 27th, 1874, Captain and Adjutant Powell retired from the regiment, the fact of his doing so being duly published from Head Quarters.

There were several more changes in the 10th during April and May in the same year, they were published thus:

HEAD QUARTERS,
OTTAWA, 10th April, 1874.

GENERAL ORDERS.

ACTIVE MILITIA.

No. 1. Tenth Battalion, or Royal Regiment, Toronto.

To be Captains: Lieutenant John T. Thompson, M.S., *vice* A. Coleman promoted.

Lieutenant William Birch Canavan, M. S., *vice* G. A. Shaw appointed Adjutant.

To be Lieutenant: Ensign Arthur Chapman, M.S., *vice* E. A. Millard, deceased.

Ensign Henry J. Hill, M.S., *vice* T. T. Rolph, promoted.

Ensign Alfred E. Hirschfelder, M.S., *vice* R. G. Hirchfelder promoted.

Ensign F. W. Unitt, M.S., *vice* J. T. Thompson promoted.

To be Ensign: Frederick A. Caston, M.S., *vice* Albert Bradley left limits.

Samuel Platt, M.S., *vice* James Ramsay resigned.

Edwin D. A. De la Hooke, M.S, *vice* J. T. Jones resigned.

Allan Stuart Scott, provisionally, *vice* W. H. Cooper resigned.

To be Adjutant: Captain and Brevet Major George Alexander Shaw, M.S., *vice* P. Martin.

HEAD QUARTERS,
OTTAWA, 8th May, 1874.
GENERAL ORDERS.
ACTIVE MILITIA.

No. 2. Tenth Battalion, or Royal Regiment, Toronto.

Adverting to No. 1 of General Orders, 25th April, 1873, the acceptance of the resignation of Lieutenant Robert F. Joseph is hereby cancelled, Lieutenant Joseph reverting to his former position in the Battalion.

The usual drills and inspections took place in 1874 and 1875, but unfortunately matters in the 10th were at a very low ebb, and it was felt by everyone that changes must, sooner or later, be effected or the regiment would cease to exist except upon paper.

Ensign Caston, now the senior Captain of the Royal Grenadiers had joined the 10th in April, as did several others whose names have already been given. In the course of the summer yet more changes were made and thus notified:

HEAD QUARTERS,
OTTAWA, 13th August, 1875.
GENERAL ORDERS.
ACTIVE MILITIA.

No. 1. Tenth Battalion, or Royal Regiment, Toronto.

To be Captain: Lieutenant William Henry Weston, M.S., *vice* R. G. Hirschfelder, left limits.

To be Lieutenant: Ensign F. A. Caston, M.S., *vice* Robert F. Joseph, resigned.

To be Ensign provisionally: Charles Reid, *vice* Caston, promoted.

Edwin Alf. Mumford, *vice* Allan Stuart Scott, resigned.

HEAD QUARTERS,
OTTAWA, 1st October, 1875.
GENERAL ORDERS.
ACTIVE MILITIA.

No. 2. Tenth Battalion, or Royal Regiment, Toronto.
To be Captain: Lieutenant John Bailey, M.S., *vice* William John Ramsay, retired retaining rank.

HEAD QUARTERS,
OTTAWA, 5th Nov., 1875.
GENERAL ORDERS.
ACTIVE MILITIA.

No. 3. Tenth Battalion, or Royal Regiment, Toronto.
To be Lieutenant-Colonel: Major and Brevet Lieutenant-Colonel, William Stollery, V.B., *vice* Boxall, retired.

HEAD QUARTERS,
OTTAWA, 19th Nov., 1875.
GENERAL ORDERS.
ACTIVE MILITIA.

No. 1. Tenth Battalion, or Royal Regiment, Toronto.
To be Ensign, Joseph H. Mead, M.S., *vice* Hill, promoted.

HEAD QUARTERS,
OTTAWA, 3rd Dec., 1875.
GENERAL ORDERS (32).
ACTIVE MILITIA.

No. 2. Tenth Battalion, or Royal Regiment, Toronto.
To be Major: Brevet Major and Adjutant, George Alex. Shaw, M.S., *vice* Hetherington.

To be Adjutant: Lieutenant Frederick W. Unitt, M.S., *vice* Shaw.

For a time in 1876 it looked as if the 10th were going to pull themselves together, there being very few resignations among the officers, and the companies maintaining their strength. On June 2nd, Ensign Scott retired, and G. B. Gordon was appointed to the vacant Ensigncy. In December the *Gazette* contained this notification :—

HEAD QUARTERS,
OTTAWA, 15th December, 1876
GENERAL ORDERS.

ACTIVE MILITIA.

No. 3. Tenth Battalion, or Royal Regiment, Toronto.

To be Lieutenants : Ensign Edwin D. A. De la Hooke, M.S., *vice* Samuel Lawrence, retired.

Ensign Joseph H. Mead, M.S.

To be Ensigns, provisionally : L. A. Lovekin, *vice* Samuel Platt, resigned.

W. G. Andrews, *vice* Edwin Alfred Mumford, resigned.

Alexander A. Leith, *vice* De la Hooke, promoted.

Frederick Deane Griffith, *vice* Mead, promoted.

Among the winners of gold medals by the Wimbledon detachment of 1875, were three members of the 10th Battalion, *viz.* :—Privates James R. Mills, Wm. Crint, and A. Bell. Their names were recorded and published in the General Orders issued from Ottawa on March 9th, 1877, more than eighteen months after the event.

The changes in the Regiment during 1877 were not very numerous. They are thus recorded :—

HEAD QUARTERS,
OTTAWA, 9th March, 1877.
MILITIA GENERAL ORDERS.
ACTIVE MILITIA.

No. 4. Tenth Battalion, or Royal Regiment, Toronto.
To be Ensign, provisionally, William Alexander Bell.

HEAD QUARTERS,
OTTAWA, 22nd June, 1877.
GENERAL ORDERS.
ACTIVE MILITIA.

No. 1. Tenth Battalion, or Royal Regiment, of Toronto.

To be Ensign, provisionally : Quarter-Master Sergeant-George Maurice Furnival, *vice* G. B. Gordon, resigned.

The resignation of Ensign W. G. Andrews is hereby accepted.

HEAD QUARTERS,
OTTAWA, 24th August, 1877.
MILITIA GENERAL ORDERS.
ACTIVE MILITIA.

No. 1. Tenth Battalion, or Royal Regiment, Toronto.

To be Ensign, provisionally : Henry McCulloch, *vice* Andrews, resigned.

HEAD QUARTERS,
OTTAWA, 21st December, 1877
GENERAL ORDERS.
ACTIVE MILITIA.

No. 6. Tenth Battalion, or Royal Regiment, Toronto.

Captain Frank A. Noverre and Lieutenant Arthur Wellesley Chapman are hereby permitted to retire, retaining their respective ranks.

On March 18th, 1878, a detachment of the 10th were ordered out for active service, "in aid of civil power," consisting of Captains Anderson, Thompson, a subaltern and 80 men. They were under arms for two days.

Unhappily in 1878 the changes in the 10th were very numerous. They were the following:—

HEAD QUARTERS,
OTTAWA, 15th March, 1878.
GENERAL ORDERS.
ACTIVE MILITIA.

No. 4. Tenth Battalion of Infantry, or Royal Regiment Toronto.

To be Ensigns: Sergeant Thomas Flynn, M.S., *vice* Hirschfelder, promoted.

Sergeant William M. Cooper, provisionally, *vice* Unitt, promoted.

HEAD QUARTERS,
OTTAWA, 18th April, 1878.
GENERAL ORDERS.
ACTIVE MILITIA.

No. 7. Tenth Battalion of Infantry, or Royal Regiment, Toronto.

To be Captain: Lieutenant William Arthur Phipps, M. S., *vice* Noverre, retired.

HEAD QUARTERS,
OTTAWA, 19th July, 1878.
GENERAL ORDERS.
ACTIVE MILITIA.

No. 2. Tenth Battalion of Infantry, Royal Regiment, Toronto.

To be Captain: Lieutenant Henry J. Hill, M.S., *vice* William Birch Canavan, retired, retainiug rank.

To be Lieutenants: Ensign Charles Reid, V.B., *vice* Chapman, retired.

Ensign Thomas Flynn, M.S., *vice* Hill, promoted.

Lieutenant and Adjutant Frederick W. Unitt, M.S., to have the rank of Captain.

HEAD QUARTERS,
OTTAWA, 2nd August, 1878.

GENERAL ORDERS.

ACTIVE MILITIA.

No. 5. Tenth Battalion of Infantry, Royal Regiment, Toronto.

To be Assistant-Surgeon: John Henry McCollum, Esquire, *vice* James Elliott Graham, whose resignation is hereby accepted.

HEAD QUARTERS,
OTTAWA, 6th September, 1878.

GENERAL ORDERS.

ACTIVE MILITIA.

No. 2. Tenth Battalion of Infantry, Royal Regiment, Toronto.

To be Captain: Lieutenant Edwin D. A. De la Hooke, M.S., *vice* Thomas Thompson retired retaining rank.

To be 2nd Lieutenants: John Cleghorn, V.B., *vice* Henry McCulloch, left limits.

Sergeant Neil McEachren (provisionally) *vice* Flynn, promoted.

HEAD QUARTERS,
OTTAWA, 4th October, 1878.
GENERAL ORDERS.

ACTIVE MILITIA.

No. 4. Tenth Battalion of Infantry, Royal Regiment, Toronto.

Memo.—No. 2 of General Orders (20), 6th September, 1878, is hereby amended in the appointments " To be Lieutenant" by substituting the words " John Cleghorn, V.B., from Retired List of Captains," for John Cleghorn, Gentleman, V.B.

HEAD QUARTERS,
OTTAWA, 27th December, 1878.
GENERAL ORDERS.

ACTIVE MILITIA.

No. 3. Tenth Battalion of Infantry, Royal Regiment, Toronto.

Major Arthur Coleman is hereby permitted to retire, retaining rank.

The resignation of Captain Andrew Fleming is hereby accepted.

In 1879 Captain Anderson and 2nd Lieutenant Mills of the 10th Royals formed a portion of the team sent from Canada to Wimbledon to the great annual rifle shooting contest.

The year 1879 was an eventful one for the 10th Royals if the changes among its officers is any criterion, they were very numerous, a long list appeared early in the year, it was as follows :

HEAD QUARTERS,
OTTAWA, 7th February, 1879.

GENERAL ORDERS.

ACTIVE MILITIA.

No. 1. Tenth Battalion of Infantry, Royal Regiment, Toronto.

To be Captain: Lieutenant F. A. Caston, M.S., *vice* Fleming, resigned.

To be Lieutenants: 2nd Lieutenant and Hon. Captain, John Cleghorn, V.B., *vice* Caston, promoted.

2nd Lieutenant George Maurice Furnival, V.B., *vice* Hill, promoted.

2nd Lieutenant William M. Cooper, V.B., *vice* De la Hooke, promoted.

To be 2nd Lieutenant: William M. McSpadden, M.S., *vice* Cleghorn, promoted.

Sergeant C. H. Smith (provisionally), *vice* Furnival, promoted.

William Manly German (provisionally), late Lieutenant No 1. Company, 15th Battalion, *vice* Cooper, promoted.

The foregoing was followed by this:—

HEAD QUARTERS,
OTTAWA, 16th May, 1879.

GENERAL ORDERS.

ACTIVE MILITIA.

No. 2. Tenth Battalion of Infantry, Royal Regiment, Toronto.

To be Lieutenant: 2nd Lieutenant W. M. McSpadden, M.S., *vice* Hirschfelder, transferred.

To be 2nd Lieutenants: Edwin A. Smith, M.S., *vice* Flynn, promoted.

Private James Robert Mills (provisionally) *vice* McSpadden, promoted.

The following interesting G. O. was issued towards the end of the summer of 1879 :—

HEAD QUARTERS,
OTTAWA, 1st August, 1879.

GENERAL ORDERS.

ACTIVE MILITIA.

No. 2. Tenth Battalion of Infantry, Royal Regiment, Toronto.

This Battalion is hereby permitted to adopt and use on the helmet plate, the following description of badge : In centre on shield, figure 10 with crown on top; behind both, and showing above crown and 10, a sheaf of spears ; on dexter side, Thistle and Shamrock ; on sinister side, Roses, and in base, Maple Leaves. The shield surrounded with garter, bearing the motto, "Ready, aye Ready," which is surrounded by a wreath of laurel leaves, behind which and extending outside wreath, a military star. The whole surmounted by a Royal Crown.

The resignation of 2nd Lieutenant Charles H. Smith was notified on the same date.

On December 5th, 1879, Lieutenant-Colonel Stollery retired from the regiment, retaining his rank.

Captains Thomas T. Rolph, W. H. Weston, and Henry J. Hill, retired on the same date, and the *Gazette* contained in addition the following notifications :—

2nd Lieutenant L. A. Lovekin having left limits, his name is hereby removed from the list of officers of the active Militia.

The resignation of 2nd Lieutenant Frederick Deane Griffith is hereby accepted.

No. 3 of General Orders (27), 27th December, 1878, is hereby amended by substituting the words, " The resignation of Major Arthur Coleman is hereby accepted," for the words, " Major Arthur Coleman is hereby permitted to retire, retaining rank."

Just a week later appeared the following in the *Gazette* :—

HEAD QUARTERS,
OTTAWA, 12th December, 1879.

GENERAL ORDERS.

ACTIVE MILITIA.

No. 1. Tenth Battalion, Royal Regiment, Toronto.

Captains Andrew Anderson and John Bailey are hereby permitted to retire, retaining rank.

Memo.—That portion of No. 4 of General Orders of 5th December, 1879, in which the services of Captain Henry J. Hill are dispensed with, is hereby amended by permitting that officer to resign his commission from 7th October last. Captain Hill's letter of resignation, being attached to the correspondence relating to another case, was overlooked when the General Order above referred to was issued.

The two following General Orders require no comment. They speak for themselves.

HEAD QUARTERS,
OTTAWA, 23rd January, 1880.

GENERAL ORDERS.

ACTIVE MILITIA.

No. 3. Tenth Battalion Royal Regiment, Toronto.

Captain and Adjutant Frederick W. Unitt, M.S., is hereby permitted to resign the Adjutancy only.

The resignation of 2nd Lieutenant William A. Bell and Quartermaster John Metcalfe is hereby accepted.

HEAD QUARTERS,
OTTAWA, 12th March, 1880.

GENERAL ORDERS.

ACTIVE MILITIA.

No. 3. Tenth Battalion, Royal Regiment, Toronto.

Surgeon-Major James H. Richardson is hereby permitted to retire, retaining rank.

Memo.—That portion of No. 4 of General Orders (29), 5th December, 1879, dispensing with the services of Captains Thomas T. Rolph and William Henry Weston is hereby cancelled. Those officers are therefore restored to the rank and positions previously held by them in the Battalion. That portion of the same General Order which substitutes the resignation of Major Arthur Coleman for his retirement, " retaining rank," is also hereby cancelled, which restores Major Coleman to the list of " retired " officers, retaining rank.

After a period of four months, the vacancy in the command of the 10th was filled up by this Order :—

HEAD QUARTERS.
OTTAWA, 9th April, 1880.

GENERAL ORDERS.

ACTIVE MILITIA.

No. 4. Tenth Battalion, Royal Regiment, Toronto.

To be Lieutenant-Colonel : Major George Alexander Shaw, M.S., *vice* Stollery, retired.

To be Major : Captain Thomas Taylor Rolph, M.S., *vice* Shaw, promoted.

To be Surgeon : Assistant-Surgeon John Henry McCollum, M.D., *vice* Richardson, retired.

To be Assistant-Surgeon : Robert Allan Pyne, Esquire, M.D., *vice* McCollum, promoted.

Lieutenant-Colonel Shaw had served in the Active Militia for about ten years, and was the grandson and great grandson of two famous soldiers. His father had also served in the Militia of Canada during the rebellion of 1837. His grandfather was at Waterloo, and his great grandfather, Major-General Æneas Shaw, was a veteran of the Revolutionary War, 1776-1783, and had served in Canada during the war of 1812.

The fortunes of the 10th Royals at this particular date were at a very low ebb, the corps had, from many causes, ceased to be popular in the city, and the question " what was to be done ? " exercised the minds of both officers, ex-officers and men. What was done will be told in the next chapter.

CHAPTER V.

THE REORGANIZATION OF THE REGIMENT UNDER LIEUTENANT-COLONEL
GRASETT.—FIVE EVENTFUL YEARS.

THROUGHOUT the summer of 1880 many rumors were current in the city as to the future of the 10th Royals. It was painfully evident to the general public, and fast becoming equally evident to the whole of the members of the corps, no matter of what rank, that radical changes must be effected. Either the regiment had to be completely reorganized or it had to be disbanded, the question was, which of these two was the better course?

The Government of the day had decided, in consequence of the disorganized state of the corps, to disband it, but, owing to the persistent efforts of Lieutenant-Colonels Cumberland and Brunel, the first two commanding officers, the former practically the founder of the regiment, this determination was reconsidered and a milder course was adopted, it was decided to entirely reorganize the battalion under new officers.

Lieutenant-Colonel Shaw was willing to retire, being greatly chagrined at the course events had taken in the 10th Royals. He was also willing if any aid was required from him in reconstructing the regiment to give it.

THE REORGANIZATION OF THE REGIMENT.

After serious and careful deliberation the Government decided to accept Lieutenant-Colonel Shaw's proffered resignation, and to allow him—despite the fact of his having held the command for only a very brief period—to retain his rank. They also decided that the rest of the officers should also be retired, while in many cases they too were allowed to retain their rank. In some instances where officers were retired, they did not retain their rank through the fact that they omitted to apply for the privilege. Assistant-Surgeon R. A. Pyne is a case in point, he was simply retired, yet afterwards was one of the Medical Officers chosen by the Dominion Government in 1885, to report on the claims for pension made by the wounded men who served in the North-West campaign, this appointment showing that he was an officer in whom confidence was placed.

The Government decided to appoint a new commanding officer, who, with an entirely different set of officers under him, would at least have the opportunity of refilling the ranks of the 10th, and of regaining for the corps the prestige they had enjoyed under the spirited *regime* of Lieutenant-Colonels Cumberland and Brunel.

In accordance with this plan, simultaneously with the retirement of Lieutenant-Colonel Shaw, a new but not untried man was gazetted in his place. *Le Roi est mort. Vive le Roi.*

The following was the order for reconstruction ;

HEAD QUARTERS,
OTTAWA, 5th Nov., 1880,
GENERAL ORDERS.
ACTIVE MILITIA.

No. 4, Tenth Battalion of Infantry, Royal Regiment, Toronto.

To be Lieutenant-Colonel: Henry James Grasett, Esq., late of Her Majesty's 100th or Royal Canadian Regiment, *vice* George Alexander Shaw, who is hereby permitted to retire, retaining rank, as a special case.

Captains John T. Thompson, W. H. Weston, and Edwin D. A. de la Hooke, are hereby respectively permitted to retire, retaining rank; and the resignation of 2nd Lieutenant William M. German is hereby accepted.

In order to facilitate the re-organization of this Battalion, the following officers are placed on the Retired List, as stated opposite their respective names:

Major Thomas Taylor Rolph, with rank of Captain.
Captain John Patterson, retaining rank.
Captain William Arthur Phipps, retaining rank.
Captain Frederick W. Unitt, retaining rank.
Captain Frederick A. Caston, with the rank of Lieutenant.

And the following officers are removed from the list of officers of the Active Militia:—

Lieutenants Charles Reid, Thomas Flynn, John Cleghorn, George M. Furnival, William M. Cooper, and W. M. McSpadden; 2nd Lieutenants Edwin A. Smith, James R. Mills, Neil McEachren and Alexander A. Leith (prov.); Paymaster, Nelson Gordon Bigelow; Surgeon, John Henry McCollum, M.D., and Assistant Surgeon, Robert Allen Pyne, M.D.

THE REORGANIZATION OF THE REGIMENT. 89

As will be seen a little later on this order was somewhat altered by subsequent notices, readers must, so as to get a clear idea of the proceedings, read the foregoing with the notifications that appeared in the *Gazette* at later dates.

The General Orders issued during December, 1880, and the first three months of 1881 are given without note or comment, they were these:—

HEAD QUARTERS,
OTTAWA, 17th December, 1880.
GENERAL ORDERS.
ACTIVE MILITIA.

No. 1, Tenth Battalion of Infantry, Royal Regiment, Toronto.

To be Majors: George Dudley Dawson, Esquire, (late Lieutenant H. M's. 47th Foot); appointment to date from 16th December, 1880.

Thomas Taylor Rolph, M.S., from the retired list of Captains.

To be Lieutenant: Lieutenant Frederick Fitzpayne Manley, V.B., from the 2nd Battalion.

To be Paymaster: Robert Mearse Wells, Esquire.

To be Surgeon: John Henry McCollum, Esquire, M.D.

To be Quarter-Master: George Strachan Cartwright Bethune, Esquire.

MEMO.—Adverting to No. 4 of General Orders (21), 5th November, 1880, in which Lieutenant John Cleghorn is removed from the list of officers of the Active Militia, that portion of the General Order is hereby amended by permitting Lieutenant Cleghorn to revert to the Retired List of Captains.

HEAD QUARTERS,
OTTAWA, 13th January, 1881.

GENERAL ORDERS.

ACTIVE MILITIA.

No. 3. Tenth Battalion of Infantry, Royal Regiment, Toronto.

To be Captains : George Anthony Boomer, Esq., M.S.
Lewellyn Henry Robertson, Esquire, M.S.
To be Lieutenants: Charles Reid, Esquire, V.B.
Edwin Arthur Smith, Esq., M.S.
John Bruce, Esquire, provisionally.
To be 2nd Lieutenants provisionally : Lionel Vernon Percival, Esquire.
George William Allan, Esquire.
To be Assistant-Surgeon : George Sterling Ryerson, Esquire, M.D.

HEAD QUARTERS,
OTTAWA, 28th, January, 1881.

GENERAL ORDERS.

ACTIVE MILITIA.

No. 1. Tenth Battalion of Infantry, Royal Regiment, Toronto.

To be Captains : Frederick Albert Caston, M.S., from retired list of Lieutenants.
Arthur Bagshaw Harrison, Esquire, C.C.
Nicholas Weatherston, Esquire, provisionally.
Frank Darling, Esquire, provisionally.

HEAD QUARTERS,
OTTAWA. 25th February, 1881.
GENERAL ORDERS.
ACTIVE MILITIA.

No. 2. Tenth Battalion, Royal Regiment, Toronto.

MEMO-Adverting to No. 4 of General Orders (21) 5th November, 1880, in which certain officers are removed from the list of officers of the Active Militia for the purpose of completely re-organizing the Tenth Battalion, it is now considered advisable to amend that General Order by placing Paymaster N. G. Bigelow, having relative rank of Captain, on the Retired List, with the honorary rank of Captain, and by permitting, as a special case, the following officers who held substantive rank, to retire retaining their respective ranks, viz:—Lieutenants Charles Reid, Thomas Glynn, George M. Furnival, W. M. Cooper, and William M. McSpadden; and 2nd Lieutenants Edwin A. Smith, James Robert Mills, and Neil McEachren.

The next General Order which appeared in the *Gazette* is interesting from the fact that it is the last one issued respecting appointments in the old "10th Royals." The officers named therein were the final appointments. The order read thus:

HEAD QUARTERS,
OTTAWA, 8th April, 1881.
GENERAL ORDERS.
ACTIVE MILITIA.

No. 6. Tenth Battalion of Infantry, Royal Regiment, Toronto.

To be Lieutenants: Lieutenant William Twiname MacFarlane, M.S., from 6th Battalion.

John Henry Paterson, Esquire, (provisionally).

If anybody imagined that Lieut.-Colonel Grasett meant to " play at soldiers " when he assumed command of the regiment, they were soon undeceived. The N. C. O's. and men at once learned that he said what he meant, and the officers also were not left in ignorance of what was required of them. Witness the following extract from Regimental Orders, dated May 17th, 1881:

" The Lieut.-Colonel commanding having observed that some officers are in the habit of absenting themselves from parade without leave, he desired it to be distinctly understood that any officer wishing to obtain leave must make the usual application through the Adjutant."

By a General Order issued from Ottawa on August 5th, 1881, the title of the Regiment was changed from the 10th Royals to that of 10th Royal Grenadiers. The former title had been borne by the corps since its formation in 1861-62, under Lieutenant-Colonel Cumberland, the additional title of Grenadiers was greatly appreciated by all concerned.

But before dealing with the remainder of the Battalion's History as the Grenadiers, let us glance briefly at some salient points in the twenty year's life of the " Old 10th."

When they were first organized in 1861-62-63, they provided themselves in great measure at their own expense with uniforms and shakos, the latter were of peculiar shape, being blue with a broad red band, very similar to those now worn by the Toronto postmen in summer. In 1862-3 the 2nd Regiment, Queen's Own Rifles, had their Armoury in St. Lawrence Hall and

THE REORGANIZATION OF THE REGIMENT.

drilled in the large main Hall. There not being room enough for the 10th Royals also, the officers of this Regiment purchased a large factory building, removed and re-erected it on the Baldwin leasehold property on King-street, almost opposite the present Romaine building. In this building, which was of very considerable size, the first examinations of officers as to the qualifications for their rank were held, and the Regiment drilled there until the Government erected the new drill-shed on the south side of Wellington-street, in 1864.

In succeeding years the efficiency of the regiment was fully maintained, and in 1866, when the Fenian Raid occurred, the 10th Royals, although not notified until late in the morning of Friday, June 1st, that they would have to leave for the front, were mustered and ready at noon on that date, leaving by special train at 4:40 p.m., from the Old Queen's Wharf Station, to which they were accompanied by a very large number of the citizens. After a stay at Suspension Bridge, of two hours for supplies, they went on to Chippewa, where they arrived at 5 a.m. They were here brigaded with H.M. 16th Regiment and a Battery of Artillery under Col. Peacocke, 16th Regiment. The brigade marched in the early morning to form junction at Stevensville, near Ridgeway, with the Queen's Own and 13th Battalion from whence the two columns thus combined were to advance together to meet the invading forces who were advancing from Fort Erie, this junction unfortunately was not effected by reason of the Queen's Own leaving Port Colborne some hours too soon.

A portion, two companies, of H.M. 47th Regiment were included in Col. Peacocke's brigade.

The 2nd of June was exceedingly hot and owing to reports being received that an engagement was already in progress the march was made at an excessive rate of speed. At noon a halt took place near New Germany. The 16th Regiment who were in heavy marching order with knapsacks, had suffered greatly from the heat, many of their men having fallen out by the way, some of the companies reaching the halting place not half their strength. The 10th Royals fortunately less encumbered, showed the stamina of the workingmen who then and ever since have filled its ranks, by coming in almost full strength.

It is true that some men helped comrades by, at intervals, carrying two rifles but the earnest spirit of the companies carried them through the day. Reports reaching camp that the engagement at Ridgeway was over and that the Fenians were in retreat. immediate pursuit was made in the direction of Fort Erie. The rear of the Fenians was caught up to just as night fell and together with the 16th the Royals camped out during the night in line of extended pickets in the ploughed fields, in front of the bush into which the Fenians had disappeared.

The tug *Robb*, detailed to patrol the river and cut off any attempted return of the Fenians, had been sent to Port Colborne, and thus, as will presently be shown, the marauders escaped.

Next morning the forces advanced at daylight and encircling the town of Fort Erie closed in upon the remainder of the Fenian column. During the night the bulk of the force under General O'Neil was taken on board some scows and removed to United States waters on the south side of the river, had it not been for this an action would have taken place and it was with the full expectation of such a meeting that the column made its advance. The 16th Regiment and the 10th Royals were in the first line having their companies thrownout in advance engaged in searching houses etc., which were on the line of march. In this way the Regiment captured a number of Fenian prisoners who were forwarded next day to the jail at Toronto. It is true that there were no shots fired in anger but the only reason was that the prisoners gave themselves up without much resistance. Some of the Queen's Own who had been taken prisoners were also released. During the time the Regiment was in camp at Fort Erie it performed a large amount of technical and mechanical work for the Brigade, being composed as it was of mechanics and artisans, there were men in its ranks available for every trade, and the Commander of the Brigade made full use of them. The 10th Royals buried the Fenian dead, repaired road-bridges, relaid the railway tracks which had been torn up, repaired the damaged rolling stock, drained the whole camp and generally did all such services as are usually done in the Regular Service by the Corps of Royal Engineers.

When the Queen's Own marched in from Port Colborne to join the Brigade at Fort Erie they received a royal welcome from the 10th. The Regiment in connection with the others of the Brigade did its usual share in supplying pickets down the river and at the American Ferry of the Grand Trunk where the trains were for some time thoroughly inspected. On the occasion of a night alarm when the whole Brigade was suddenly called to arms the Regiment received special commendation from Col. Lowry, Commander of the Brigade for its ready preparation for duty and the steadiness of the men. The larger portion of the Volunteer Regiments, composing the Brigade, returned to their headquarters on the days following their arrival, but the Royals remained in camp at Fort Erie, together with H.M.'s 16th and 47th Regiments doing frontier duty for three weeks longer when all expectations of a further invasion being dispelled, they also returned to Toronto. Throughout its service the Regiment proved its capacity for actual work and received the warm approval of the Staff Officers.

While at Fort Erie, the regiment had the pleasure of meeting their former and first commanding officer, Lieutenant-Colonel Cumberland, who had volunteered for service on the staff of Colonel Lowry, 47th Regiment, and received special mention in General Orders for his valuable services in controlling the railway operations.

Some of these matters may be considered trivial, but the reason they are referred to, is not to seek any special credit for them, but to show that the 10th, both officers and men, were prepared to and did act up to the spirit as well as the letter of their motto, "Ready, aye ready."

The official order creating the "Royal Grenadiers," was worded in a somewhat peculiar manner, first the corps is described as "Royal Grenadiers," and then a note signifying the change of title is added.

THE REORGANIZATION OF THE REGIMENT.

It reads thus,—

HEAD QUARTERS,
OTTAWA, 5th August, 1881.

GENERAL ORDERS.

ACTIVE MILITIA.

No. 5. Tenth Battalion Royal Grenadiers.

The title of this Battalion will in future be Tenth Battalion, Royal Grenadiers.

To be Lieutenant: 2nd Lieutenant, George W. Allan, M.S., *vice* Edwin A. Smith, who reverts to the retired list of 2nd Lieutenants.

To be 2nd Lieutenant, provisionally : Oliph Leigh Leigh-Spencer, Esquire, *vice* Allan, promoted.

Throughout 1881 the regiment steadily increased in numbers and efficiency, all ranks worked harmoniously together, and an excellent spirit of *esprit de corps* was developed, which has happily pervaded the regiment ever since.

The remaining appointments to commissions in 1881 were these :—

HEAD QUARTERS,
OTTAWA, September 30th, 1881.

GENERAL ORDERS.

ACTIVE MILITIA.

No. 5. Tenth Battalion, Royal Grenadiers.

To be Captain, provisionally : Hon. Captain and Quarter-Master Robert Swanton Appelbe, from 20th Battalion, *vice* Nicholas Weatherstone, resigned.

HEAD QUARTERS,
OTTAWA, 11th November, 1881.

GENERAL ORDERS.

ACTIVE MILITIA.

No. 4. Tenth Battalion, Royal Grenadiers.

To be Adjutant, with rank of Captain, from 28th October, 1881 : Lieutenant Frederick Fitzpayne Manley, V. B.

To be Lieutenants, from 28th October, 1881, taking rank in the Militia from 13th January, 1881 : George S. Ryerson, M.S. (late Assistant-Surgeon), *vice* Manley, promoted.

To be 2nd Lieutenant, provisionally : Robert Goodall Trotter, Esquire.

It will simplify matters considerably, and make this volume of greater usefulness as a work of reference if in the remainder of its pages the promotions and retirements are given together for each year. In 1882 they were as follows :

HEAD QUARTERS.
OTTAWA, 28th April, 1882.

GENERAL ORDERS.

ACTIVE MILITIA.

No. 2. Tenth Battalion, Royal Grenadiers.

To be Lieutenant : 2nd Lieutenant, L. V. Percival, V. B., *vice* William Turnance MacFarlane, resigned.

To be Paymaster : Nicol Kingsmill, Esquire, M. S., *vice* Rupert Mearse Wells, resigned.

THE REORGANIZATION OF THE REGIMENT. 99

HEAD QUARTERS,
OTTAWA, 12th May, 1882.
GENERAL ORDERS.
ACTIVE MILITIA.

No. 2. Tenth Battalion Royal Grenadiers.

To be 2nd Lieutenants, provisionally : Francis J. Gosling, vice Percival, promoted.

Duncan Arthur Duntroon MacIntyre, Esq.

HEAD QUARTERS,
OTTAWA, 18th September, 1882.
GENERAL ORDERS.
ACTIVE MILITIA.

No. 2. Tenth Battalion, Royal Grenadiers.

To be Captain : Lieutenant John Bruce, M.S., vice Frank Darling, resigned.

To be Lieutenants : 2nd Lieutenant Peter Brown Ball, V.B., vice Charles Reid, who reverts to retired list of Lieutenants.

2nd Lieutenant Donald MacDonald Howard, V.B., vice George William Allan, resigned.

HEAD QUARTERS,
OTTAWA, 29th September, 1882.
GENERAL ORDERS.
ACTIVE MILITIA.

No. 1. Tenth Battalion, Royal Grenadiers.

The formation is hereby authorized of two additional Companies of this Battalion.

To be Captains : James Mason, Esquire, M.S.
John Weir Anderson, G.S.

HEAD QUARTERS,
OTTAWA, 27th October, 1882.
GENERAL ORDERS.
ACTIVE MILITIA.

No. 3. Tenth Battalion, Royal Grenadiers.

To be Lieutenant: 2nd Lieutenant Oliph Leigh Leigh-Spencer, M.S., *vice* Bruce, promoted.

To be 2nd Lieutenants, provisionally : L. E. Leigh, Esquire, *vice* Ball, promoted.

Andrew Maxwell Irving, Esquire, *vice* D. A. Duntroon McIntyre, resigned.

HEAD QUARTERS,
OTTAWA, 24th November, 1882.
GENERAL ORDERS.
ACTIVE MILITIA.

No. 3. Tenth Battalion, Royal Grenadiers.

To be Lieutenant : 2nd Lieutenant, Robert Goodall Trotter, V.B.

HEAD QUARTERS,
OTTAWA, 1st December, 1882.
GENERAL ORDERS.
ACTIVE MILITIA.

No. 4. Tenth Battalion, Royal Grenadiers.

To be 2nd Lieutenant, provisionally : Charles Hector Symons, Esq., V.B.

The first Regimental order of any note issued in 1882 was dated February 16th, and it showed that the Commanding officer was determined to know exactly how the regiment was equipped and the condition of every-

THE REORGANIZATION OF THE REGIMENT. 101

thing belonging to it. The order has the true military ring in it, it was as follows:

"With a view of ascertaining the disposition of the clothing, etc., that has been issued to the regiment, the Lieutenant-Colonel commanding will make a minute inspection of every article in possession of each company prior to the commencement of the annual drill. Officers commanding companies will therefore take such steps as are necessary to have everything ready for the inspection, the exact date of which will be notified hereafter."

The inspection was duly made and Lieutenant-Colonel Grasett had the satisfaction of knowing from personal observation exactly how his command was equipped.

The annual drill for 1882 commenced on Tuesday, March 21st, and was continued each week until May 24th. The C.O.'s parade was held on Thursday evenings, Tuesday evenings being reserved for company and recruits' drill.

A church parade was held on Sunday, April 30th, the battalion attending divine service at the Church of the Ascension in the morning.

The regiment made steady progress in 1882, though there was nothing to vary the ordinary routine of weekly drills. The whole battalion had confidence in their commanding officer and as a natural consequence progress followed.

On May 24th, the spring drills terminated by the regiment "trooping" the Queen's Colour in Queen's Park. This always pleasing ceremonial was attended by an immense crowd of spectators.

Autumn parades commenced on September 12th, and

continued until Thursday, November 9th, when the Grenadiers were inspected by Major-General Luard, commanding the Canadian Militia. A complimentary order expressing his approval of the regiment was issued by the General after it was concluded. The regimental church parade was on Sunday morning, October 8th, to St. James' Cathedral, the battalion mustering at "The Guns" in the Queen's Park.

It may also be noted that Lieutenant Egerton Denison of the 3rd battalion Staffordshire Regiment was attached to the Grenadiers in September, 1882, and continued to do duty with them for that year. Lieutenant Denison subsequently served in the Soudan campaign of 1885 under Lord Wolseley, and died at sea as he was returning home from South Africa in 1886.

A General Order was issued on October 3rd, 1882 authorizing the increase of the Grenadiers from a six to an eight company battalion. This order caused the greatest satisfaction to the regiment. James Mason and John Weir Anderson, Esquires, were the two officers selected to command the new companies.

The various companies after augmentation were commanded as follows:

A. Company, Captain Boomer.
B. " " Robertson.
C. " " Caston.
D. " " Mason.
E. " " Anderson.
F. " " Appelbe.
G. " " Bruce.
H. " " Harrison.

LIEUT.-COL. J. MASON.

THE REORGANIZATION OF THE REGIMENT.

There was no change of moment in the regiment during the remainder of the year. The appointments and promotions in the following year were as follows:

HEAD QUARTERS,
OTTAWA, 27th April, 1883.

GENERAL ORDERS.

ACTIVE MILITIA.

No. 1. Tenth Battalion, Royal Grenadiers.

Captain Robert Swanton Appelbe is hereby permitted to retire retaining rank, as a special case.

The resignation is hereby accepted of Lieutenant George Sterling Ryerson, who reverts to the position of Assistant-Surgeon in the Battalion, with his previous seniority.

HEAD QUARTERS,
OTTAWA, 11th May, 1883.

GENERAL ORDERS.

ACTIVE MILITIA.

No. 3. Tenth Battalion, Royal Grenadiers

To be Captain, Lieutenant John Henry Paterson, V.B. *vice* Appelbe, retired.

HEAD QUARTERS,
OTTAWA, 6th July, 1883.

GENERAL ORDERS.

ACTIVE MILITIA.

No. 1. Tenth Battalion, Royal Grenadiers.

The resignation of Captain George Anthony Boomer is hereby accepted.

HEAD QUARTERS,
OTTAWA, 10th August, 1883.

GENERAL ORDERS.

ACTIVE MILITIA.

No 3. Tenth Battalion, Royal Grenadiers.

The resignation of Captain Llewellyn H. Robertson is hereby accepted.

No. 1, of General Orders, 6th July, 1883, is hereby amended by permitting Captain George Anthony Boomer to retire retaining rank.

HEAD QUARTERS,
OTTAWA, 9th November, 1883.

GENERAL ORDERS.

ACTIVE MILITIA.

No. 3. Tenth Battalion, Royal Grenadiers.

To be Major: Captain Arthur Bagshaw Harrison, C.C., *vice* T. T. Rolph, retired retaining rank.

To be Captains: Lieutenant Peter Brown Ball, V.B., *vice* Boomer, retired.

Lieutenant Oliph Leigh Leigh-Spencer, V.B., *vice* Robertson, resigned.

To be 2nd Lieutenant, provisionally:

John Irvine Davidson, Esquire.

The resignation of Lieutenant Lionel V. Percival is hereby accepted.

HEAD QUARTERS,
OTTAWA, 30th November, 1883.

GENERAL ORDERS.

ACTIVE MILITIA.

No. 2. Tenth Battalion, Royal Grenadiers.

THE REORGANIZATION OF THE REGIMENT.

To be Lieutenants: 2nd Lieutenant Francis J. Gosling, V.B., *vice* Percival, resigned.

2nd Lieutenant A. M. Irving, V.B., *vice* Ball, promoted.

2nd Lieutenant C. H. Symons, V.B., *vice* Percival, resigned.

To be 2nd Lieutenants, provisionally: John Morrow, Esquire, *vice* Spencer, promoted.

Granville Percival Eliot, Esquire, *vice* Trotter, promoted.

HEAD QUARTERS,
OTTAWA, 14th December, 1883.

GENERAL ORDERS.

ACTIVE MILITIA.

No. 3. Tenth Battalion, Royal Grenadiers.

To be Lieutenant: Charles Greville Harston, formerly Lieutenant in the Royal Marine Light Infantry, *vice* Ryerson.

Spring drill began for the Grenadiers in 1883, a little later than in the preceding year, the first parade being held on April 9th; drill continued until May 24th, when the regiment under command of Lieut.-Colonel Grasett went to London, Ont., being brigaded there on the date just named with the 7th Fusiliers. It may be mentioned that this, the first excursion made by the Grenadiers was most successful. The regiment returned to Toronto early in the morning of May 25th.

In September of the same year His Excellency the Governor-General, Marquis Lansdowne, paid a state visit to Toronto. A guard of honor composed of one captain, two subalterns, four sergeants, and one hundred rank and file, was furnished by the Royal Grenadiers.

This guard was on duty during the whole of H. E. visit, under the command of Captain James Mason.

In Regimental Orders of September 20th, 1883, the following letter was published for the information of the officers commanding corps which formed escorts and guards of honor to His Excellency the Governor-General during his visit to Toronto:

"His Excellency (the Governor-General) desires to express his approbation of their soldier-like appearance and the manner in which they performed their several duties, and he trusts that the Militia of Toronto will maintain that high character for discipline and smartness which they have held in the past, the Governor-General will always take an interest in their future career."

By a District Order dated October 29th, 1883, the Royal Grenadiers were ordered to hold themselves in readiness for inspection by the Major-General commanding the Canadian militia. On October 31st, the following Regimental Order was issued:

"In accordance with District Order No. 1, of 29th October, 1883, the regiment will parade in marching order with leggings at the drill shed, on Thursday, November 8th, at 1.30 p.m., and proceed to the Exhibition Grounds, where the annual inspection by Major-General Luard, commanding the Canadian Militia, will take place."

It is satisfactory to record that the inspection proved satisfactory to all concerned, to those commanding and to those commanded.

With the inspection, drill ceased for the year 1883, and in the following year these were the changes in the commissioned ranks of the regiment, notified by successive General Orders as follows :

THE REORGANIZATION OF THE REGIMENT.

HEAD QUARTERS,
OTTAWA, 4th January, 1884.
GENERAL ORDERS.
ACTIVE MILITIA.

No. 2. Tenth Battalion, Royal Grenadiers.

To be 2nd Lieutenant, provisionally: 2nd Lieutenant John Dunlop Hay, from Toronto Field Battery, *vice* Gosling, promoted.

HEAD QUARTERS,
OTTAWA, 25th January, 1884.
GENERAL ORDERS.
ACTIVE MILITIA.

No. 4. Tenth Battalion, Royal Grenadiers.

To be 2nd Lieutenant, provisionally: Charles Egerton McDonald, Esquire, *vice* Irving, promoted.

HEAD QUARTERS,
OTTAWA, 14th March, 1884.
GENERAL ORDERS,
ACTIVE MILITIA.

No. 2. Tenth Battalion, Royal Grenadiers.

No. 1 of General Orders, 7th June, 1872, is hereby amended, with reference to Captain Frederick Barlow Cumberland, by substituting "is hereby permitted to retire, retaining rank," for "left limits."

HEAD QUARTERS,
OTTAWA, 18th April, 1884.
GENERAL ORDERS.
ACTIVE MILITIA..

No. 2. Tenth Battalion Royal Grenadiers.

To be Lieutenant: 2nd Lieutenant John Irvine Davidson, V. B.. *vice* Ball, promoted,

To be 2nd Lieutenants, provisionally: Forbes Michie, Esquire, *vice* Symons, promoted.

William Charles Fitch, Esquire, *vice* Davidson, promoted.

The resignation of Quarter-Master George Strachan Cartwright Bethune is hereby accepted.

HEAD QUARTERS,
OTTAWA, 16th May, 1884.
GENERAL ORDERS.
ACTIVE MILITIA.

No. 2. Tenth Battalion, Royal Grenadiers.

To be 2nd Lieutenant, provisionally: Alexander Cecil Gibson, Esquire, *vice* Davidson, promoted.

HEAD QUARTERS,
OTTAWA, 3rd October, 1884.
GENERAL ORDERS.
ACTIVE MILITIA.

No. 3. Tenth Battalion, Royal Grenadiers.

The resignation of 2nd Lieutenant, Charles Egerton McDonald, is hereby accepted.

The regiment pursued a useful, but not especially exciting course throughout 1884. As will be seen on reference to the promotions and appointments, there were not many changes in the commissioned ranks and among the rank and file there was a small, though gratifying increase in numbers.

Drill commenced as usual in March, continuing until the Queen's Birthday. The regiment paraded on Saturday, 24th May, 1884, in Review Order with leggings and cross belts, at 9.15 a.m., and proceeded by special train

THE REORGANIZATION OF THE REGIMENT. 109

to Hamilton, where, in conjunction with the 13th Battalion, under Lieut.-Col. Gibson, a short review was held.

After the review, the officers of the Grenadiers were hospitably entertained by the officers of the 13th, and the men's comfort was not neglected by their comrades of the "Ambitious City." The regiment returned to Toronto the same night.

In accordance with instructions received, the regiment paraded in marching order with leggings, at the drill shed, on Thursday, 6th November, 1884, at 2.30 o'clock. and marched to the Queen's Park, where they were inspected by Major-General Middleton, commanding the Militia.

The inspecting officer, after a minute inspection of the Battalion, expressed himself as being well satisfied, and notified his satisfaction in General Orders.

The year 1885 was destined to be a most eventful one for the Royal Grenadiers particularly, and for the militia forces of the Dominion generally, though when the new year arrived, there was nothing to foretell the arduous and eventful work that the Grenadiers were to accomplish before its close.

Towards the end of March, 1885, rumours were prevalent all over the Dominion of impending troubles with the Indians and half-breeds in the Northwest, but no one took these reports very seriously to heart while warfare was never even contemplated. "At the worst," people said, "it is only a case for the mounted police," and calmly. turned to the discussion of other subjects.

The term "North-West," just used is slightly ambiguous and may mean a great deal or else a very little. In the particular instance mentioned it includes the whole of the territories, comprised in the Canadian Dominion north of the Province of Ontario. This part of Canada then, as now, contained a scattered population of Indians and half-breeds. Besides these there were the settlers who had taken up land throughout the various Northwest Provinces, they for the most part living at wide distances from one another, though of course a city had sprung into existence at Winnipeg, while there were some few moderately sized towns and villages in addition, although at great distances apart.

The fancied state of security just referred to was rudely disturbed on March 27th by the news received at Ottawa on that date from Colonel Irvine commanding officer of the North-West Mounted Police of the insurrection and fight at Duck Lake on March 26th, and of the death in action with Gabriel Dumont and his halfbreeds of several loyalist residents in that locality.

A few words must be said about the Duck Lake fight. Louis Riel who had given the Dominion Government a great deal of trouble in 1870 when he was the head and front of the Red River rebellion, for which acts he had subsequently been pardoned, again in 1885 incited the Indians and half-breeds to rebellion and armed resistance to constituted authority. That the classes whose cause Riel espoused had real grievances cannot be denied, but the mode resorted to by Riel and his followers to obtain redress of these grievances cannot for a moment be defended or even palliated.

In March, 1885, the stores belonging to Messrs. Walters, Baker & Kerr Bros., residing at St. Laurent were

THE REORGANIZATION OF THE REGIMENT. 111

raided; and Indian agent Lash, Astley, a surveyor, Tompkins, the telegraph repairer, and other Government employees were taken prisoners. Major Crozier, who was stationed at Fort Carlton, received this news on the 19th, and at once sent over to Prince Albert to Captain Moore asking for reinforcements. A meeting was held and it was determined to send a force of forty men, who on the 20th marched to Fort Carlton, forty miles distant, arriving there about ten o'clock the same night.

Major Crozier was already the recipient from Riel through Mr. Mitchell a store-keeper at Duck Lake, of a demand that he should surrender Fort Carlton. In reply to this the Major sent a half-breed named McKay with Mitchell to try and persuade the half-breeds to disperse. This occurred March 21st. Riel received Mitchell and McKay with little else than abuse and told them that unless Major Crozier surrendered Fort Carlton it would be attacked at twelve o'clock. Mitchell and McKay then returned to Fort Carlton. It had been arranged with Mr. Mitchell by a committee acting under Riel's instructions says Major Boulton in his book on the rebellion "that Riel should send two delegates to meet Major Crozier half way; and an hour after the arrival of McKay at Fort Carlton, he turned round and accompanied Captain Moore to meet the delegates. At the appointed place they were met by Charles Molin and Maxime Lepiere, who had been sent as delegates to demand the surrender of Fort Carlton, with all its stores and property, undertaking if it were quietly given up that the police should be allowed to go unharmed. As Major Crozier's instructions to the delegates were that the people should disband, and give up the leaders at once, or suffer the penalty of their criminal acts, the meeting resulted in nothing; and Lepiere did not present the document intended for Major Crozier. It was afterwrrds found among Riel's papers in Batoche subsequent to its capture.

Things rapidly grew from bad to worse until on the morning of March 26th when Major Crozier sent a small detachment with a dozen sleighs to remove the stores and food that were in Mitchell's store at Duck Lake to place of greater safety. It is not necessary to say more on this subject excepting that they were attacked by the rebels and in the fight that ensued which lasted for nearly three-quarters of an hour, nine Prince Albert volunteers and three policemen were killed and about twenty-five wounded. The rebels were in large numbers under the command of Gabriel Dumont; Crozier's force consisted of about one hundred men.

The news reached Toronto late in the evening of March 27th and an hour or so later Lieutenant-Colonel R. B. Denison, D.A.G. received the following peremptory telegram from Ottawa:

"Call out the Queen's Own and 10th Battalion for immediate service.

POWELL, ADJUTANT GENERAL."

Lieut.-Col. Denison at once communicated with Lieutenant-Colonels Miller, Q.O.R. and Grasett, R.G., giving them the order and they with equal promptitude transmitted the order to their officers, summoning a parade for 8 a.m. on Saturday, March 28th, and ordering the officers to warn their men.

THE REORGANIZATION OF THE REGIMENT. 113

It was 11 p.m. on Friday, March 27th when Colonel Grasett received his orders and in a short time all officers whom he could communicate with by telephone were duly warned and messengers were on their way carrying the order to such as could be reached in no other way.

In most houses the officers who had telephones had retired for the night when the bells rang.

"Is not that the telephone bell," queried the husband to his wife?

"Telephone bell, no; who would be telephoning at this time of night?"

A few moments silence and there was no mistaking the fact that the telephone bell was ringing, and ringing furiously. Up jumped the officer and going to the "phone," shouted "Hello?"

"Is that you Captain A?"

"Yes, what is wanted, who is speaking?"

"Colonel Grasett." You are warned with your company and your subordinate officers for immediate service in the Northwest, you will parade at 8 a.m. tomorrow. Good night." There was no more sleep in such houses that night and there were many aching hearts and tearful faces when the family met for their early breakfast on the Saturday morning. The wife and mother was quiet and subdued, the children scarcely knew what it all meant, only this, "that Father was going away and they might never see him again." The head of the house said little but gulped down his coffee and when he kissed his wife and children "good-bye for the present," adding for their comfort "we shan't go before evening at anyrate." There was a suspicious tremor in his voice and moistness in his eye that told what a trial and sacrifice he was making, though doing so cheerfully and loyally at the call of duty. In other houses, perhaps it was an only son or an elder brother who was warned, they too obeyed the summons with alacrity assuring their parents it would be "only a picnic" and laughing at and turning into ridicule the fears of their agitated sisters.

All that night the officers and sergeants were busy warning the men and in every case was the warning received with the utmost cheerfulness.

"Does Thomas Brown live here?" queried the officer or N.C.O. after he had knocked up the sleepers in the house where T.B. resided.

"Yes, he does," shouts out T. B. from his bedroom," what do you want?"

"I am captain A. of the Grenadiers and I want to speak to you."

"Yes, sir," says T. B., "be with you in a moment," on his appearance he was duly told what was required of him.

T. B.'s mother had opened the door and coming up to the officer asked "what it all meant?" "Nothing, mother, nothing, all right Sir, I'll be there" and the officer departed, to go through a similar experience at other houses. This is no fancy sketch, it is but the reproduction of scenes that transpired in hundreds of Toronto homes in the early morning of Saturday, March 28th, 1885.

The following are the various brigade orders issued touching the despatch of the expedition, they are all duly dated and read as follows:

THE REORGANIZATION OF THE REGIMENT. 115

TORONTO, 28th March, 1885.

Northwest Expeditionary Force.

BRIGADE ORDERS.

No. 1. The Queen's Own Rifles and 10th Royal Grenadiers having been ordered to furnish 250 N.C.O. and men each ; to proceed with 85 non-commissioned officers and men of "C" Company, Infantry School Corps, to the Northwest under the command of Lieut.-Col. Otter, the two former Corps parade in marching order at the drill-shed Saturday evening at 7.30 p.m. for inspection.

The inspecting officer was Lieutenant-Colonel Otter.

Officers baggage was restricted by Brigade order No. 2 of same date to a small trunk, capable of carrying a change of uniform or underclothing; each non-commissioned officer and man was required to take with him the following kit to be carried in their knapsacks:—

1 Pair marching boots.	Knife, fork and spoon.
1 Flannel shirt.	Soap, towel and comb.
1 Under shirt.	Needle and thread.
1 Pair drawers.	Tin of dubbing.
1 Pair socks.	

No. 3.

The Corps to parade in drill order with great coats on Sunday 28th inst. The Queen's Own at 2.30 and Grenadiers at 3.30 to receive orders.

There was a full muster of the various companies of the Regiment at 8 a.m. on Saturday, March 28th, and the eight companies "doubled" so as to form four companies as follows:

No. 1 by C. and H. Companies.
" 2 " D. " F. "
" 3 " B. " E. "
" 4 " A. " G. "

The only difficulty that presented itself was what men to leave behind, every man was anxious to go. In one case at any rate—perhaps in more than one—a young fellow who was ordered to remain at home, managed to escape observation and was found with his comrades in the train some hours after leaving Toronto.

At last though the selection was made and the following regimental orders issued.

HEAD QUARTERS, ROYAL GRENADIERS,
28th March, 1885.

REGIMENTAL ORDERS.

No. 1. In accordance with Brigade Order No. 1 of this date the 250 non-commissioned officers and men selected to proceed to Northwest will parade at 7.30 p.m. this evening in marching order for inspection.

No. 2. The men chosen will be divided in four companies with the following officers, and to each company will be attached one pioneer, four fifers and drummers and buglers, and two Ambulance Corps, four Sergeants will be with each company in addition to the Staff Sergeant viz., 1 Quarter Master Sergeant, 1 Hospital Sergeant, 1 Pioneer Sergeant, 1 Sergeant Drummer and 1 orderly room clerk.

The regimental orders of the same date as just quoted further stated:

Referring to Brigade Order No. 2 of this date each non-commissioned officer and man will have with him in his knapsack, one pair of boots, one flannel shirt, and under shirt, one pair drawers, one pair socks, knife, fork, spoon soap, towel and comb, needle and thread, tin of dubbing.

In accordance with Brigade Order No. 3 of this date the regiment will parade to-morrow, Sunday 29th inst., at 3.30 p.m. in drill order with great coats.

Further brigade orders were these, they tell their own tale so plainly that any comment would not add to but would detract from their interest.

NORTHWEST EXPEDITIONARY FORCE.
TORONTO, 29th March, 1885.
BRIGADE ORDERS.

No. 1. The officers and men of the Queen's Own and Royal Grenadiers detailed for service in the Northwest will parade at the drill shed in marching order at 10 a.m. to-morrow (Monday) with twenty-four hours cooked rations.

Officers baggage and regimental stores must be ready packed in waggons at the above hour.

29th March, 1885.

No. 4. The hour for the departure of the corps has not yet been fixed, but will probably be on Monday. Cooked rations for 24 hours subsistence must be provided by each officer, non-commissioned officer, and man.

No. 5. Lieut. J. W. Sears, I.S.C., will until further orders act as Staff Officer, and Sergeant Major Spackman, I.S.C., will act as Brigade Sergeant Major to the force.

By order,
J. W. SEARS,
Staff Officer.

30th March, 1885.

No. 1. The force will leave the shed at 11 a.m. for the Union Station, and embark as under :—

No. 1. Train, Staff "C" Company, Infantry School Corps, and Queen's Own Rifles, with baggage and horses belonging thereto.

No. 2. Train—Royal Grenadiers with baggage and stores.

No 2. Corps will entrain as speedily as possible, officers remaining with their men, arms and accoutrements to be left on until train moves.

No. 3. Orderly Officers to be detailed daily throughout the journey, whose duty it will be to see that order is maintained—that no men are allowed to get out at the stations without leave, or to stand on the platform, and that after 10 p.m. perfect quietness is maintained throughout the train.

No. 4. Upon all ranks must be imposed the necessity of absolute discipline throughout the whole of the service.

Though the following Regimental Order is simply a repetition of a Brigade Order already given it will make the story complete if it also is added.

HEAD QUARTERS, ROYAL GRENADIERS,
MARCH 29th, 1885.

REGIMENTAL ORDERS.

No. 1. In accordance with Brigade Orders, No. 1 of this date the Regiment will parade in Marching Order with leggings, at 10 a.m. to-morrow. Each Non-Commissioned Officer and man will have 24 hours cooked rations in his haversack.

Officers' baggage and regimental stores will be packed in a waggon in East Market Square under the directions of the Quarter Master. The Ambulance men will act as a baggage guard.

The story of the departure of the Northwest contingent from Toronto, on the morning of Monday, March 30th, 1885, has often been told, but it will bear being again referred to. At 10 a.m. on that date the Queen's Own and Royal Grenadiers paraded in the Old Drill Shed; for some of them it was "their last parade" in that building, for they fell as gallant soldiers ought to fall with their faces to the foe, "their last thought for their country, their last cheer for their Queen."

To return to the departure of the troops, Lieutenant-Colonel Otter briefly addressed the brigade in the Drill Shed when they were ready to march, then the Jarvis-street doors were opened, and the contingent, headed by their bands, marched out turning from Jarvis into King-street and thence by York-street to the Union Station. It was a wonderful sight, thousands and tens of thousands of people were assembled to cheer the departing soldiers, to wish them "God speed" and a safe return.

Fathers and mothers parting from their sons were there, old soldiers who had experienced the rigors of the Crimean winter and had seen the carnage at Alma, Balaclava and Inkerman came to wish "the boys" farewell. Veterans of the Cape War, of the Indian Mutiny, and of the March to Kandahar were present, not to condole, but to urge the citizen soldiers to do their duty, to submit to discipline, and if needs be to die like men.

At last all were on board the train and as the

bands played "Auld Lang Syne," they moved slowly out of the station and the journey to the Northwest was begun.

Since the preceding Saturday the citizens of Toronto had moved in a whirl of military excitement, and it is scarcely an exaggeration to say that every household was more or less interested in the departure of the troops.

The city fathers had not been unmindful of the comforts necessary for the men and they presented them for their service kits with complete sets of underclothing.

So far as the officers and men of the expeditionary force were concerned, they could have left Toronto on the Saturday but it was necessary to delay their departure until Monday so that the requisite transport and commissariat arrangements might be made.

MAJOR JOHN BRUCE

MAJOR J. D. HAY.

CHAPTER VI.

ON THE WAY TO THE NORTHWEST.—INCIDENTS OF THE JOURNEY.—THE BATTLES AT FISH CREEK AND BATOCHE—THE KILLED AND WOUNDED.

READERS of this volume must kindly bear in mind that it is not intended to be a history of the whole of the operations in the Northwest and that the fact of the services rendered by Strange's and Otter's columns and by the various cavalry corps as well as those of other troops not being fully related, is not because the part they took in the campaign is underrated but because it is only sought to tell the story of the Grenadiers share in the expedition and of those troops who being brigaded with them shared their work and the credit that was gained by it.

The Grenadiers had only reached Peterboro' on March 30th, when the following order was issued.

PETERBORO', 30th March, 1895.
BRIGADE ORDERS.

Officers commanding corps will at once caution their men to be sparing of their rations in order to meet any emergency that may arise.

Carleton Place was reached late in the evening of March, 30th, the troops getting their supper there·

There was lots of jollity and every one was in good spirits, despite the fact that they had then been travelling for many hours and had the prospect of very arduous work before them.

A pleasing incident occurred at Carleton Place, Mrs. Blake wife of the Honorable Edward Blake, presenting to the expeditionary force through Lieutenant-Colonel Otter, a flag, the Union Jack, from members of the House of Commons. Mrs. Blake was accompanied by Mr. W. Mulock, M.P., who addressed the commandant in brief but felicitous sentences.

Mrs. Blake then presenting the flag said:

"A number of my friends in the House of Commons, desirous of expressing their sympathy and good wishes for the men under your command and on the expedition on which they have now started, have desired me to present you with this flag. I do so with great pleasure and at the same time would like to add my own heartfelt prayer for your speedy success and safe keeping."

Lieutenant-Colonel Otter in thanking Mrs. Blake and the donors said. " * * * On an occasion like this, nothing more fitting could be presented than the British flag, the emblem of law, justice and freedom. It will be ours to preserve it and guard it carefully, as a reminder that the people of Canada are with us in our undertaking. I acknowledge the kindness which has prompted the representatives of the people to make this presentation to us, and I thank you as the bearer of the gift."

The Grenadiers reached Biscotasing on April 1st, having passed the previous day on the train where they had breakfast and on the night of the same day the end of the C.P.R. track was reached, and the gallant soldiers found themselves at Dog Lake.

A long gap now had to be crossed, this was done in open sleighs with the thermometer varying from a few degrees below freezing point to twenty degrees below zero, the men at the same time having but little protection against the winter's blast beyond the clothing that they wore.

This first gap began at Dog Lake and extended for forty-two miles north of the river Michipicoten to a point near Jack Fish Bay on Lake Superior.

The following letter written at Dog Lake by one of the Grenadiers will prove interesting.

DOG LAKE, C.P.R.,
Thursday, 2nd April, 1 o'clock A.M.

"This is actually Thursday morning and we started on Monday. The time has gone very fast. We have come to the gap in the rail and are waiting till sleighs come back which have transported the Queen's Own over the 40 odd miles to the re-continuance of the railroad. As the train is at last not jolting along, as it has been incessantly almost since we started, I can write a connected letter.

"Things are carried on in proper military fashion—guards at the door of every carriage, and no man allowed to go from one to another except the medical staff."

* * * * * * * * *

"There is generally one large building at these places where we go in by companies to have meals, bread and tough something or other, with hot water flavored with green tea but altogether considered a good square meal. Lots of chaff and high spirits enliven the work which is down-right hard, being turned out at night without overcoats to tramp through the snow to get wood, and pails of water—no water to drink half the time.   *   *   *

Our number with those ahead of us makes about 800 or 900 and there are 1,200 close behind I believe, but we know very little news from want of telegraph communication and papers.

"A" Battery from Kingston I hear have been sent out."

The same writer under date Good Friday of 1885, remarks: "It is no playing at soldiers. We are at present in the open snow about four feet deep, waiting for the train to come, as we have got through our 50 mile drive, going 30 miles in an open sleigh for 12 hours without grub and then having to stand for one hour and a half in line waiting for our turn at tea, chilled through to the bone, while we saw those who had finished their tea crowding into huts with roaring fires."

There had been a break-down in the transport arrangements, one of the locomotives having been injured, consequently there was but one engine available for the transport of the troops, and it was engaged taking on the Queen's Own, this caused very great delay but at 11 p.m. on Good Friday, April 3rd, the Grenadiers embarked for a run of 150 miles, this time they had nothing but flat open cars with the roughest of seats and no other comforts of any kind.

An unlucky accident happened at Camp Desolation to Lieutenant Morrow of the Grenadiers who was shot by the accidental discharge of a revolver in the hands of a newspaper correspondent. One of the Grenadiers also had a fall, breaking his arm, but he showed true grit and instead of being "sent home sick" as he could have been, he insisted upon going on, serving throughout the whole of the campaign.

The weather during the stay at Camp Desolation was warm and pleasant and the men were in excellent spirits.

Captain Spencer was attacked with rheumatic fever at the same time and place and was obliged to be invalided home greatly to his own regret and that of his brother officers. Saturday, April 4th, saw the arrival of the Grenadiers at Port Munro late in the afternoon, where the regiment found barracks in a schooner named the *M. L. Breck*, On Easter Sunday at 9 a.m. the Grenadiers proceeded on a march of 20 miles across the ice to an inlet of Lake Superior, reaching McKellars Bay late in the day, where cars were again taken for about 12 miles till Jack Fish Bay was reached, where the night was passed.

On Monday, April 6th, a march of 22 miles was made to Winston and from there the Grenadiers took train to Nepigon which was reached at 10 p.m. the same day.

Leaving Nepigon the Grenadiers made a further march of 14 miles which brought them to Red Rock which they reached at a tolerably early hour on the morning of April 7th.

Not long after this Port Arthur was reached where the whole of the troops received a hearty welcome from the residents.

Leaving Port Arthur the regiment proceeded on its journey to Winnipeg where it arrived early on Wednesday, April 8th. After arriving at Winnipeg such of the force as could be spared and who applied for leave to do so, were allowed to make calls, either of pleasure or business, throughout the city. Many pleasing re-unions took place between the officers and men of the Queen's Own, the Grenadiers, and inhabitants of Winnipeg who had formerly resided in Toronto.

The people of Winnipeg had a lively interest in the struggle which was then impending with the Indians, half-breeds and nondescripts generally in the Northwest. They were also furnishing a large contingent of troops and it was only natural that they, who like the people of Toronto were sending their fathers, husbands and brothers to the field, should be intensely interested in all troops who were going on the same errand.

A great many of the men during their forced marches had been very badly frost-bitten, and it is no disparagement to them to say that when they once more reached civilization in Winnipeg, they were intensely weary.

The arrival of the Grenadiers at Winnipeg was thus notified by telegram to Toronto from that city:

"Grenadiers arrived here this morning, April 8th, at 6 o'clock, and notwithstanding Monday night's terrible march all were in capital condition except a few slight colds and frost-bites. The men breakfasted in the hotel and are now viewing the city till 2 p m. when they leave for Qu'Appelle where they will overtake the Queen's Own who went west yesterday. From Qu'Appelle the whole force will proceed to Middleton's present position a few miles north.

The distance from Toronto to Carleton Place Junction was 234 miles. From the latter place to Sudbury an additional 265 miles to Dog Lake, where occurred the first gap, was 261 miles. After crossing the gap to Nepigon was yet 255 miles more. From the latter station to Port Arthur covered 68, and from Port Arthur to Winnipeg 435 miles, where at present we find the Grenadiers on their way to Qu'Appelle. The total number of miles thus far travelled had been 1,518, with 532 still to accomplish before reaching their destination.

The Grenadiers left Winnipeg at 4 p.m. on Wednesday April 8th, and reached Troy or Qu'Appelle station about 7 o'clock a.m. next day. From there, after a brief rest, they started for Fort Qu'Appelle, 20 miles farther on, which they reached the same evening having received orders from General Middleton at Qu'Appelle station to join him at Humboldt.

When the train stopped at Brandon great hospitality was shown to the troops by the residents of that locality. Ladies boarded the train, bringing with them baskets of preserved fruit, hard boiled eggs, cakes, pies, and other delicacies for the benefit of the men. These kind attentions were greatly appreciated by all concerned, and just before the train resumed its journey, Major Manley returned thanks to the fair donors on behalf of the battalion.

A corps of mounted infantry which were known throughout the campaign as "Boulton's Scouts," under Major Boulton, were encamped at Qu'Appelle station when the Grenadiers arrived there, the orders the Major received being similar to those given to Lieutenant-Colonel Grasett.

The march of 250 miles across the prairie began on

April 9th, and on the 18th General Middleton was caught up to at Clarke's Crossing.

This campaign was not the first that the valley of the Qu'Appelle had looked upon. The feuds of the Black Feet and the Crees, Indian tribes, had been both remorseless and undying. These internecine contests had to a certain extent subsided, the blessings resulting from western civilization having extended themselves even to this remote region of the north.

The troops after leaving Qu'Appelle passed on towards the Saskatchewan by the Touchwood Hills and Humboldt, arriving at Clarke's Crossing in the afternoon on April 18th.

General Middleton speaking of the arrival of the Grenadiers in an official despatch dated April 18th, says: "Lieut.-Colonel Grasett and 10th Regiment Royal Grenadiers joined my force this day. This regiment had come through the gaps and made remarkably good marching to catch up to my column."

On April 20th, General Middleton made up his mind to divide his force, which now consisted of about 800 of all ranks, and to move forward on both the east and the west sides of the river. The force he commanded on the right or east bank of the river, comprised the 90th Winnipeg Battalion, 304 of all ranks; " A " Battery R.C.A., 120 men; half " C " Company I.S.C., 40 men; armed teamsters, 66 men; Boulton's Scouts, 60 men, a total of 590.

The force under Lieut.-Colonel Montizambert and Lord Melgund on the left or west bank of the river was as follows:—Royal Grenadiers, 270; Winnipeg Field Bat-

CAPT. F. A. CASTON.

CAPT. R. G. TROTTER.

tery, 52; French's Scouts, 40; armed teamsters, 80, a total of 422. Communications were kept up between both sides. The idea that evidently actuated General Middleton was, that by advancing on both sides of the river it would be impossible for the insurgents to escape from him.

The General had been informed, as he believed, credibly, that Riel's force only consisted of about 400 men, and doubtless considered that he had sufficient force on either side of the river to overcome the rebels should he meet with them. The difficulties presented were great, for on both banks of the Saskatchewan, and for some miles in the interior, were groves of high timber and deep ravines quite sufficient to afford complete cover for a large body of troops.

On April 22nd, the Division was halted by the order of the General to complete arrangements for the advance and also to formulate a scheme both for night and day signalling. On April 23rd, a distance of 18 miles was reached from where the troops had been encamped the day previously. On April 24th, the march was resumed, the enemy met with and engaged at Fish Creek.

We will let the account of how this battle began be told in the words of General Middleton himself, contained in a despatch dated from Fish Creek, May 1st, 1885, he says :

"Though I had not been led to believe that the rebels would come so far to the front to attack us, still I was aware of the existence of a rather deep ravine or creek about five or six miles ahead, consequently I was on this occasion, with the supports under Major Boulton, accompanied by Captain Haig, R. E., A. Q. M. G. and my two aides-de-camp Captain Wise and Lieutenant Doucet, and Mr. MacDowell attached to my staff. On approaching some bluffs, just as the left advanced scouts were circling round, we suddenly received a heavy fire from a bluff and some ground sloping back on our left, which fire was luckily too high to do mischief, having been evidently fired in a hurry, owing to the approach of the left scouts. Major Boulton instantly ordered his men to dismount, let loose their horses (two of which were immediately shot) and hold the enemy in check. This was done by them most gallantly—the flankers and files in front falling back on the main body. I sent Captain Wise back with orders to bring forward the advance guard and main body which was soon done. The advance guard on arrival extended and took cover in the bluff nearest us, and, as the main body came up, two more companies of the 90th were extended, the Rebels advancing up out of the ravine into which, however, they again speedily retired and a heavy fire was exchanged; but having sent a party round to the house on the enemy's right, the enemy gradually retired along the ravine, while our men advanced slowly to the crest of a deeply-wooded part running out of the main ravine. In this former ravine a small part of the Rebels made a stand in what we found afterwards to be some carefully constructed rifle pits. These men were evidently their best shots—Gabriel Dumont being amongst them, but were, so to speak caught in a trap. A great number of their horses and ponies being in this ravine, and, what is said to be very unusual, were tied up—thus showing, I am informed, that the Rebels were pretty confident of success—55 of these horses were killed. These men were gradually reduced in number until, from the position of our men, it was almost impossible for them to retire, and they continued to fire at intervals, doing a great deal of mischief. Captain Peters with great pluck and dash, led the dismounted men of "A" Battery, supported by a party of the 90th under Captain Ruttan, and gallantly attempted to dislodge them, but they were so well covered and were able to bring such a heavy fire on the party advancing without being seen, killing three men, two artillerymen and one of the 90th, (the body of one artilleryman was afterwards found within eight or ten yards of their pits) that I resolved to leave them, contenting myself with extending more of the 90th in front to watch them, and sending some shells into the bluff now and then. * * *

During the action a messenger from the left column arrived, asking if they should bring troops across, and I directed the 10th Grenadiers to be brought over, which was done by means of the scow, most expeditiously, one company with Lord Melgund arriving about 1 o'clock p. m., and two other companies under Lieutenant-Colonel Grasett later on, with two guns of the Winnipeg Field Battery, under Major Jarvis. As the affair was nearly over then, I contented myself with extending a company of the 10th on the right centre to assist in watching the ravine where the enemy's rifle pits were, the other companies being on the extreme right in support and ultimately remaining there until the wounded were removed to the camp-ground, which had been selected in the meantime. I would here beg leave to draw particular attention to the crossing of these troops, who, though luckily not required might well have been. To fully appreciate the rapidity with which this was done, in spite of the difficulties that existed, the river must be seen; wooded heights on each side 100 feet high—at bottom, large boulders encrusted in thick sticky mud—a fringe of huge blocks of ice on each side, a wretched scow carrying about sixty men at most, pulled with oars made with an axe and a rapid current of about 3 or 4 miles an hour, were the obstacles that were surmounted by dint of determination and anxiety to join with and aid their comrades.

An amusing story is told by General Middleton, in connection with the battle of Fish Creek, of a little bugler of the 90th Regiment named William Buchanan who "made himself particularly useful in carrying ammunition to the right front when the fire was very hot, this he did with peculiar nonchalance walking calmly about crying, ' now boys whose for cartridges?'" It is sad to have to add that at Fish Creek there were 2 gunners of " A " Battery and 4 privates of the 90th killed, and no less than 15 others dangerously wounded, 4 of whom subsequently died and 30 wounded in addition but not so dangerously.

On April 25th, were buried the dead who had fallen the day previously and in the next few days the remainder of the western column crossed to the eastern side. Their crossing was effected by means of the scow which the General had floated down the river between the two columns It was a difficult as well as a most hazardous operation.

From the 26th until the 30th of April the column remained in Camp at Fish Creek waiting for the arrival of the steamer *Northcote* which was expected with supplies and reinforcements. It was the General's intention upon the arrival of this steamer to remove his wounded to the hospital at Saskatoon, the settlers of which had kindly offered to do all that was in their power for those who had been injured.

A few details may be given respecting the fight at Fish Creek which have not been mentioned or even glanced at in the General's despatch. When the order was given to cross the river, No. 2. Company Grenadiers under the command of Captain Mason who had volunteered for the privilege, was the first to do so. Once across the Grenadiers soon showed the metal that they were made of by setting resolutely to advance. As they were moving forward they were met by Captain Haig, R.E., who was A.Q.M.G. to the expedition. This officer was asked by Captain Mason "how is the fight going?" "Badly" replied Captain Haig, "the rebels are in that ravine and cannot be dislodged." Captain Mason hearing this asked Captain Haig to get him permission to see the General, which permission was given and Captain Mason preferred his request that he and his company might be allowed to clear out the enemy's rifle pits at the point of the bayonet. Captain Mason knew that his subalterns, Lieuts. Irving and Hay, with the men of the company were to be relied on to the last.

General Middleton considered the request and then said "No, too many valuable lives have been lost already."

A little later Captain Mason's company was ordered to relieve a company of the 90th, who had been engaged for some time and were very greatly fatigued. As the company took up position, which they did under the dropping fire from the concealed Indians they were met with a hearty cheer from the Winnipeg men. The other two companies of the Royal Grenadiers relieved those of the 90th who were yet engaged.

The good feeling displayed by the 90th to the Grenadiers was of the very warmest; the accommodation they themselves possessed in the way of tents, bedding and eating and drinking utensils were barely sufficient for their own needs and yet they "shared and shared alike" with their comrades of the Grenadiers. Imagine a small tent built to contain four, with seven sleeping in it and not more than blankets enough for half of them. Tea had to be drunk out of wash bowls, empty meat tins, dippers, which had "once been new" and other miscellaneous articles. Of these very primitive utensils too there were only about half enough to go round.

Shortly after the fight at Fish Creek, there was a night alarm, which was groundless. It was marked though by a most pathetic incident, D'Arcy Baker of Boulton's Horse was lying wounded in his tent, life's moments fast passing away from him. Hearing the shots fired, in half delirium, he rose to his feet got to the door of the tent and shouting "bring me my horse" fell to the ground—dead.

The following lines describe this tragic occurrence:

* * * * * * *
With shattered heart, the stricken soldier lies,
　The fatal wound has almost ceased to bleed;
The dying warrior vainly seeks to rise,
　And begs once more, his rifle and his steed.

* * * * * * *

ON THE WAY TO THE NORTHWEST.

> Forever more the youthful limbs are still,
> The young, the gallant, and impulsive brave
> Now rests beside the far-off western hill,
> And wild flowers blossom by his lonely grave.
> —MURDOCH.

When the Grenadiers crossed the river for Fish Creek they had breakfasted at 6 a.m., and it was 12 o'clock midnight and later before food again passed their lips. Since the Northwest Expedition, remarks have been occasionally made by those whose ignorance of the real facts of the case is only equalled by their own insolence in making the assertion that the whole affair in the Northwest was "only a picnic." If it was, it was a picnic under extremely disagreeable circumstances and one in which the niceties of life and the comfort of the guests were very badly considered and provided for by those who were responsible for the enjoyment of the company.

One more word before passing on to the further story of the campaign. The picquet duty, night and day, at Fish Creek, was incessant and neither Grenadiers or 90th ever had more than a few hours off duty.

On May 1st, General Middleton ascertained that the *Northcote* was not likely to arrive for perhaps a week, and acting on the advice of Dr. Orton, of the 90th Battalion, he ordered waggons to be made ready to take the wounded men back to Saskatoon. They left upon May 1st under escort, reaching there *via* Clarke's Crossing in perfect safety. From May 2nd to 4th nothing of any particular moment occurred, although the General made a reconnaissance through that territory by Boulton's and French's scouts to within four miles of Batoche, when some of the enemies' scouts were sighted but speedily disappeared.

On May 5th, the long looked for steamer *Northcote* arrived, bringing besides the necessary welcome supplies and requirements, Lieut.-Col. Van Straubenzie, formerly of the 100th Regiment, whom the General immediately appointed second in command.

On May 6th, the General writes, " Prepared for marching and the *Northcote* was made defensible against musketry fire under the direction of Captain Haig, R.E., A. Q.M.G., as I intended that it should take part in my intended attack on Batoche, and perhaps draw off some of its defenders from my front. I placed on board Major Smith and 35 men of C. School ; Capt. Wise, my A.D.C., who was wounded in the foot, and Mr. Bedson. Lieuts. Eliot and Gibson, Royal Grenadiers, and Lieut. Hugh J. Macdonald, 90th Battalion, also were on board, being all on the sick list."

On May 7th, the General, whose force then consisted of 850 men, made up of the " A " Battery, the Winnipeg Field Battery and half of " C " company of Canadian Infantry, the Royal Grenadiers, the 90th, two companies of the Midland Battalion with Boulton's and French's Scouts, moved forward and reaching Gabriel Dumont's Ferry, there halted.

On the 8th May, it had become well-known that it would be a fight to the bitter end between the Canadian forces and the rebels, and that in the event of the latter being victorious, few belonging to the former would be allowed to live to tell the tale.

Colonel Grasett was fully aware of the position of affairs, and on the evening of May 8th, assembled the officers of the Grenadiers together in one of the tents and put the probabilities and possibilities of what might happen fairly before them.

Maxwell Drew, in his "Sergeant's Story" quaintly refers to this incident thus:

"Kurnel Grasett, he calls all the officers into the Quarter Master's tent, and sez, 'Gintlemen,' says he. 'things has come to a head at last,' he sez, 'In a short time we will have met the inimy in foorce, an' there's no knowin' what the ind ov it all will be; we must bate thim,' he sez, 'because we have no place fer to fall on, an' no place fer to retreat to—an' we will lick thim I know, but gintlemen,' sez he 'we must'ent lose soight ov the fact that some ov us who are here to-night, won't be here at the finish, when the 'Cease Fire' sounds an' the day is won; I merely wish to remind yez ov this, gintlemen, so that if any ov yez have any matters to arrange or any letters yez want fer to wroite—well, gintlemen—yez understand, o'im sure; that will do, gintlemen,' sez he, 'an' out ov the tint they came.'"

"'Now wus'nt that jist like him, sor, an' you know him, too, ivery inch a soldier, an' not only a soldier, but a man as well.'"

It may be mentioned that General Middleton's orders to the Grenadiers were that they were to have the post of honor and lead the attack.

On May 8th, the General writes:

"As I had received information that there were several bad and difficult spots on the river trail, I marched the force to the East, and then struck across the prairie, striking the main trail from Humbolt to Batoche, at about nine or ten miles from Batoche, and camped. I then rode forward with a small party of scouts to within two miles of Batoche, seeing nothing but one scout of the enemy, who disappeared at once."

On the morning of May 9th, General Middleton's force advanced on Batoche, no hindrances occurred to impede them until they arrived about half a mile from a Roman Catholic Church that had recently been erected at a point where the trails struck the river bank, before it turned down to Batoche. There were some houses near the church, and some men were seen in their neighborhood, they speedily decamped after two or three shells and some rounds from the Gatling gun, under the command of Captain Howard, late U.S.A., had been fired at them. The General advanced cautiously with his infantry, Nos. 1 and 2 Companies of the Grenadiers in front, the other two companies in support, and the 90th in reserve, in extended or skirmishing order, driving the enemy back until the crest of the hill was reached. There he was enabled to bring his guns into action, and shell the houses of Batoche, which could be seen, and where it was known the rebels were entrenched. The General himself describes this part of the action in the following words: "As the houses were of a light construction and not very large, not much damage was done, and just then as some shots came from across the river, from a bluff along the bank, and as the spot the guns were in was completely exposposed to this fire, I directed the guns to retire, and as they were doing so, suddenly a very heavy fire was opened from what we afterwards found were some rifle pits in a bluff, just below where the guns had been, but which was stopped by a rattling fire from the Gatling, which was splendidly handled by Captain Howard, ably supported by Lieut. Rivers, 'A' Battery."

I then went off to the right of my extended line behind the church and found the men (of the Grenadiers) holding their ground, but exposed to a fire from a bluff with a newly-made grave in front of it railed in with wood. I then ordered the gatling round to try and silence their fire, which it did at first, owing probably to the novelty of this weapon, as regards the enemy, but shortly afterwards the enemy's fire was renewed, and we afterwards found that they were firing from carefully-constructed rifle-pits which completely covered them from any fire. During this time Captain Peters "A" Battery had endeavored to drive the enemy out of the pits from whence had come the fire which caused me to retire the guns, with a portion of the Garrison Artillery of "A" Battery School, but the fire was too hot, and they had to retire, leaving a wounded man behind.

On my returning to that part of the attack, and hearing of this, I advanced a part of the Midland Battalion down a coulee or bluff on the left, between the cemetery and the church, with orders to keep up a hot fire, so as to distract the attention of the enemy from the spot where the wounded man was lying, and also directed a part of the 90th and 10th (Grenadiers) who were lying down in advance across the trail, to do the same, and sent down a party of the Artillery with a stretcher to bring the man back, which they did without hesitation; and to my great satisfaction they succeeded in bringing him back, without losing another man, which was what I feared, but unfortunately the man himself was dead."

Very heavy fatigue duty fell upon the Grenadiers at this time. It was work in camp making trenches, or work in the open under fire from the rebels day in and day out. The state of affairs was very much like which it is said used to exist on the old East India sailing vessels among the sailors described pithily thus :

> " Seven days shalt thou work
> And do all thou art able
> On the seventh
> Holystone the deck and scrape the cable "

The casualities after the fighting on May 9th consisted of two men killed, one officer and nine men wounded. One of the men killed was Private Thomas Moore of the Grenadiers. Captain Mason also of the regiment and Privates Stead and Cantwell were among the latter.

On May 10th little more was done than to keep an eye upon the enemy though the Grenadiers were out all day. There was some slight skirmishing on both sides, one man being killed and five wounded among the General's command.

On May 11th General Middieton started to reconnoitre the prairie ground about Batoche taking with him Boulton's scouts or Mounted Infantry and the Gatling gun. Speaking of the day's work the General says, " I found it was a good large plain of an irregular shape about two miles long and one thousand yards in the broadest part with a sort of slight ridge running down the centre and some undulations. We saw a good many men moving about on our left front, and fired two or three rounds from the Gatling, at the same time lining the crest of the ridge with some of Boulton's men which soon drew a pretty smart fire from the edge of the bluffs running parallel to the ridge, which we soon saw was defended by a series of rifle-pits. * * * After firing for some time at the pits, I retired the force in good order and regained the camp. Here we found that we had regained all our lost ground owing to my feint on the enemy's left, which had drawn a good many of the enemy from their right to repel what they feared was a general attack, as, owing to the lay of the ground, the enemy could not see what my force was. Some of the Midland Battalion led by Lieut.-Col. Williams, gallantly rushed to some rifle-pits beyond the cemetary, and drove the Indians, who had been left on their right out of them, capturing some blankets and a dummy which had been used to draw our fire. In the morning one gun of "A" Battery shelled the cemetery and pits near the church. In the afternoon I brought up two guns from the Winnipeg half battery to a spot held by the Midland advance party, near the cemetery, from whence they were able to see to shell a house on the opposite side of the river, which was flying Riel's white flag, with some design on it, and about which a great many people were moving. The range was a large one and the material of the house so light that not much harm was done, but the people all dispersed at once and seemed to take to the woods. During the afternoon some few shots were fired from the opposite bank, but the fire was kept under and silenced by a party of men posted on the ground overlooking the river on the left of the camp. In the evening my advanced parties were withdrawn to the camp as usual but the enemy hardly pursued at all ; there was no firing into our camp, and our casualties of the day, consisted of four wounded all very slightly. This showed that my men were becoming more at home in this mode of warfare, and though as yet we had not made much progress I resolved, to use a historical expression, "to peg away" until I succeded in my object of taking Batoche which I was sure I should do. During the day the men left behind to protect the camp and the teamsters added to the slight parapet and trenches already made, and made a traverse across the south side of the Zareba, which would have effectually prevented any shots from doing mischief in the camp." ·

About midday on May 12th the events were as is further told by the General, thus:

* * * * * * * *

May 12th, 1885.

"Two companies of the Midland, 60 men in all, under Lieut.-Col. Williams, were extended on the left and moved up to the cemetery, and the Grenadiers, 200 strong, under Lieut.-Col. Grasett prolonged the line to the right beyond the church, the 90th being in support. The Midland and Grenadiers, led by Lieut.-Cols. Williams and Grasett, the whole led by Lieut.-Col. Straubenzie, in command of the brigade, they dashed forward with a cheer and drove the enemy out of the pits in front of the cemetery and the ravine to the right of it, thus clearing the angle at the turn of the river. During all this time a heavy fire was kept up from the other side of the river, which annoyed our advance. This was kept down as best we could by a few of the Midland Regiment in pits on the bank of the river, and one company of the 90th Regiment was sent to support Lieut.-Col. Williams on the extreme left. The Midland Regiment and Grenadiers kept pushing on gallantly, led by Cols. Straubenzie, Williams and Grasett, until they held the edge of the bluffs surrounding the left part of the plain, where the houses were. Just before this a most promising young officer, Lieutenant Fitch of the Grenadiers was killed."

"It was at this period that the late lamented Captain French was killed by a shot from the ravine while looking out of the window at Batoche's house. This officer's loss was keenly felt and mourned by the whole force. He had been with the force from the commencement and he was always ready for the front and his cheerfulness and good humour was proverbial and had a cheerful effect on the whole camp.

A company of the Grenadiers was sent along the river on our left up to the house of the rebel Champagne and a company of the 90th was sent well forward on the right, as a few desultory shots were fired from a ravine there. By evening all firing ceased and I went up to the camp for the men's blankets and food and we bivouacked for the night round the buildings."

E. J. C. in the Montreal *Star* writing on Batoche said: * * " The rebels stuck to their rifle-pits with great tenacity and several of them were run through with the bayonet while taking aim. One Indian whose face presented a horrible picture from the hideous war-paint, discharged his rifle without success against a captain, and although the bayonets were close upon him, opened the breech block to insert another cartridge when he received his quietus at the hands of a stalwart Grenadier who ran his bayonet through the Indian with such force that the savage was lifted from his feet and carried over the edge of his pit at the point of his rifle. But very few shots were fired by our men during the dash down the slope, but every one told and rebels were seen tumbling over like nine-pins among the brushwood. In the bluffs, a short distance across the open from the bottom of the slope a large number of the rebels gathered and for some minutes held in check the troops. * * * * * *

"The men were as steady as rocks. The rebels were scattered in all directions, the puffs of smoke from the bush and the whizz of bullets overhead, showed that they had retired, not retreated and were bound on contesting every bluff."

Another account of the fight at Batoche is given by "Maxwell Drew," the late (alas that I should have to write 'the late') Captain A. M. Irving in his sketch entitled "The Sergeant's Story," published in 1895 in the Toronto *Evening Telegram.*

"Now all this toime the Gineril had'nt bin sayin' a word, but the old man had bin sawin' wood just the same oi'm thinkin', and the next day the 12th of May, he gave us all the excitemint we were wantin' an' Riel an' Dumont an' the rest ov thim a blame sight more than they bargained for oi'm thinkin', Ye see, sor, it wuz jist this way. The Gineril thought fer to attack wid all the mounted min from the plain to the north, draw the inemy from the cinter an' let the infantry push on beyond the roifle pits. Then ye see, would attack wid the whole foorce an' capture the position wid a ringin British cheer as laid down in the Field exercise of 1882: thin the rest wud be a walk-over. He gives orders to Kurnel Straubenzie fer to push on wid the infantry as far out as we wuz the day before an' lay down an' wait, jist as soon as he heard the scouts firing over on the right. Ye see, there wuz a strong 9 o'clock wind blowin' acrost the camp an' divil a bit of firin' did any ov us hear at all at all, so uv coorse divil a step did we stir. Bime by up rides the Gineril as mad as the divil thinkin' that 'some one had blundered.' He kicks up the very ould Harry because we had'nt advanced whin the firin' began. Kurnel Straubenzie he ups an' tells him the whyfore an' the Gineril he sez, 'very well, we'll try over again,' sez he. Now sor, oi ain't no military expert, but to my way ov thinkin' it's a lucky thing we did'nt hear the firin' fer ye see the Rebels not hearin', nor seein' anythin' ov us in the cinter an' on the left very naturally supposes that we wuz all goin' fer to let go at thim from the right an' let it go at that. Well sor, thin we gets a bit uv somethin' to eat an' were soon out to the front agin. There was'nt goin' to be no mistake nor nothin' this toime. We wuz drawn up in extended order two companies ov the Midland on the left, the Grenadiers 200 strong right plum in the cintre an' the 90th in support. We had a koind ov a feelin' that things so fur was a koind of a 'saw-off' loike, but by the Lord Harry we got roight down to work in rale earnest now, an' what's more, we done overtoime in the bargain. We pushed on steadily into the bush. The guns tuk up an advanced position an' kept on peggin' away fer all they wuz worth. The mounted men prolonged the line to the right. We kept goin' on an' on

J

an' thin the long looked for command to 'double' came at last an' off we wint. We got a terrific volley from a batch ov roifle pits, that koind ov staggered some ov us fer a minit.

"'God save us!' sez Mac.

"Thin koind ov half turnin' towards me he sez.

"'Good bye, old man,' sez he, 'there aien't no knowin' what may——God bless ye, Oirish, stick close to me, an'——.'

"Tut, tut, sez I, luck to yerself Mac, its always thinkin' ov me ye are, an' whatever else he moight have bin goin' to say wuz drowned in the ringin' shout that broke from ivery mothers son ov us, as we fixed our bayonets an' cleared over the first bluff. That was the first 'bluff' the Grenadiers ever tuk sor, an' it did'nt take thim long aither.

"'Come on Grenadiers' sez Kurnal Straubenzie 'keep steady an' we'll clear thim out' he sez, an' on we wint wid a cheer that moight have bin many a poor soul's death cry, yellin' an' runnin' loike the very mischief. What's that yer sayin' sor? wuz oi froightened? God save ye sor there was'nt no toime fer to be froightened, no toime fer to be thinkin' about it, wid the guns crackin', the 'hurdy-gurdy' grindin' away, the shells burstin', the Injin's ki-yi-in' an' ivery mother's son ov us cheerin', there wuz no toime fer to git scared loike. On we wint helter-skelter ivery wan ov us wuz that excited loike, that the showers ov bullets from the roifle pits wuz fergotten loike. On we wint likity-split ivery man fer himself an' the divil take the hindermost, leavin' the church an' the school-house far behoind, chargin' pit after pit, past the grave yard into the ravine, past the bluffs an' acrost the open through a shower of bullets. Hard work wuz it? well I should say so, the Rebels fought loike the very mischief, they stuck to their pits an' kept up a steady foire, till they seen it wuz no use. We had bin joined by the 90th who prolonged the line to the roight, an' the scouts wuz on the roight of thim agin. The first house we struck, off scampered some half-breeds an' we knew the end wuz near. There was'nt much ov the line left by this toime, men ov the left flank wuz mixed up wid men ov the roight, an' ivery wan wuz scurryin' along in a 'go as you please' sort ov a way, but wid one idea, to capture Batoche, to set the prisoners free an' avenge the poor boys who had fallin durin' the day. About four hundred yards from the village a man came out wid a flag ov truce, but the Gineril tould him that if Mister Riel wanted fer to chat wid him that he'd have fer to come out himself an' so the fireworks goes on. We cleaned Batoche's house out in short order an' in a few minits afterwards Captain French ov the scouts wuz killed. Now there wuz a fine soldier if I ever seen wan, but he had to go I s'pose. Jack Fox wuz wid him when he wuz hit an' sez he, 'he only said a few words an' thin died.' The next house wuz where the prisoners wuz locked up. Well sor, we soon had thim at liberty an' stampin' about fit to bate the band, an' if ye iver seen a glad lot ov min in yer loife, well it wuz thim.

"'God bless yez, boys. God bless yez, sez they, we wuz goin' to be shot to-night.'

"On we went the rebels scatterin' in all directions. The camp on the bank of the river wuz deserted ex-

ceptin' by wimin and children. We pushed on about a
mile past the village an' halted. The half breeds an'
Injins put for the river like the very mischief an' left
the Gineril in possession, an' that ended the 'Charge on
Batoche,' that is if ye call it a 'charge;' but to tell ye
the truth sor, it wuz nothin' more nor less than a foight
an' a fut race—400 men in skirmishin' order wid their
baynits fixed, runnin', cheerin', yellin', and shootin', all
strugglin' fer first place at the finish—an' if ye call that
a 'charge' then it wuz a 'charge,' an' a good wan at
that. A lot of the poor divils got cowld steel for supper
durin' the 'charge.' Hogan's baynit got jammed in an
Ingin's breast an' Hogan couldn't git it out, sor. So
what does he do but unfix it judgin' the toime loike,
an' come on wid the rest ov us lavin' the baynit stickin'
in the 'good Injin.' The 'charge' wuz a great success
sure enough, but ye know the ould sayin', sor, 'nixt to
defeat the saddest thing is victory.' Poor Liftinint
Fitch, sor, he wuz shot through the heart durin' the
'charge,' an' died without a word. He met his death in
harness loike a soldier an' a man if that's any consolation,
an' he slapes up in Mount Pleasant Cemetery now, sor
enough, enough, poor bye. Captain Brown of the Scouts
was killed too, an' Liftinint Kippin' of Dennises an' a
man named Fraser of the 90th. Our 'Adg.' got a ball in
his foot that put him out of mess for a while, but he
didn't seem to moind it, he jist sez, 'oi wonder if that
wuz mint for me? the divil's got his windage all right,
but his elevation is all wrong, I guess he's shootin with
a 'V.' Major Dawson, he was hit in the ankle an' a
nasty hurt it wuz too, oi'm thinkin', but he would't give

CAPT. J. D. MACKAY.
(Adjutant.)

CAPT. W. T. TASSIE.

in he was knocked out. Captain Caston got a shot through his cap, an' another thro' his tunic, but he didn't seem to moind, he seemed satisfied as long as his shirt wuz 'safe an' sound.' Our Liftinint* got the skin took off the ind of his nose wid a spint ball, an' he turns to Bill Urquhart an' he says, sez he 'By the Lord Harry things seem to be comin' my way at last,' he sez. The Sargint-Major got his shoulder-strap shot off, an' lots of other fellows got hit wan place or another. Hot quarters, ye say, yer roight, sor! It was about five o'clock when we halted, an' shortly afterwards the Gineral forms up an' sez he:

"'Yez have made me the proudest man in Canada this day.'

* * * *

Surgeon G. S. Ryerson published the following letter also, relating the events of Batoche within a few days after they occurred:

"You have long ago seen in the newspapers accounts of the action at Batoche. I can assure you it was very warm, as I was there all the while. I do not think that the accounts, so far as I have seen, do the Grenadiers justice for their charge in the affair. About 1.30 in the afternoon of the 12th, the Grenadiers were ordered to occupy the position they had the day before, which was about 250 yards from the church. When they reached that position, instead of halting, they pushed on, fixed bayonets, they cleared the first bluff—a cluster of poplar trees and underwood, and with a cheer attacked and cap-

---
*NOTE.—The writer, Captain Irving, with characteristic modesty, does not mention that he was the officer referred to.

tured the second line. Then a ravine was occupied and the enemy driven out. The firing here was very heavy. This past, the left swung round and enfiladed the main pits. These were soon emptied, and a rush was made for the houses. It was not till then that the guns and the 90th came up, the former on the hill behind us, the latter on our right. We had 60 of the Midland Regiment with us from the first. They were on the extreme left. The houses were captured after a warm but short fight. We were greatly bothered by marksmen on the opposite side of the river, who fired on us in comparative safety. The 90th were on our right, Boulton's Horse and the Intelligence Corps on their right again. It was a most brilliant affair. The cheering on our side seemed greatly to disturb the enemy's equanimity. The sight of the glittering steel settled the question. They turned and fled, and in doing so, many were shot down. A number were bayoneted; one man's bayonet became jammed in an Indian's breast so that he could not pull it out; he coolly unfixed it from the rifle and left it. * *
* We in the camp were quite taken by surprise when we heard the cheering, we knew something was up. I sent one of my stretchers out with the regiment, but when the men disappeared in the bluff I immediately ordered out the other, and went up with it at the double. My ambulance has pulled out fifteen wounded so far many of them under fire. They have not been backward with the rifle either when the other duties permitted. The officers all expressed satisfaction with their services and with the field hospital.

"As regards the killed, we have had two: Private

Moore was shot in the head by a round ball, which crushed his skull, glanced off through another man's arm and slightly wounded a third. My men brought him out under heavy fire.   *   *   *   The Gatling covered our retreat. The balls were fairly squirted in volleys. He was living but unconscious and died in about four hours. He was a nice boy and greatly liked by his comrades. Poor Fitch was shot right through the heart and died without uttering a word. He is very much missed for he was greatly beloved as a generous, unselfish, good-hearted fellow.

"Captain Mason's wound was much more serious than was at first supposed. An inch further and it would have ended his career. Two slugs went in and came out again. He is doing well and out of danger now. Manley was shot in the sole of the foot and had a narrow shave. Major Dawson's wound was on the outer side of the leg, near the ankle. Caston had one bullet through his hair and another through his coat. Irving had the skin taken off the end of his nose. The Sergeant-Major's shoulder-strap was shot away. Sergeant Curzon attended my ambulance class last winter and learned how to stop bleeding. His knowledge enabled him to save the life of a man who was shot in the main artery of the arm and was fast bleeding to death. He did it 'under fire.'

"We had 21 wounded during the three days work, besides two who hurt themselves badly by falling into the enemy's rifle pits during the charge. We have lost the services of 41 by sickness, wounds, or death since we left, starting with 271 men, we now have 230."

Another account of Batoche is that given by Henty, the war correspondent of the London *Standard*. It was as follows, and was transmitted by cablegram :—

From the *Standard*.
Thursday, May 14th, 1885.
FIGHTING IN CANADA.
BATOCHE, Tuesday.

"This morning General Middleton started on a reconnaissance with the Cavalry, one gun, and a Gatling, towards the hills two miles distance, among which some rebels were encamped.

Shots were exchanged and one of the troops was killed.

A messenger from Riel having come out to say that if any women or children were killed by us the prisoners would be put to death, Lieut. Kippen was sent forward with a flag of truce, to say we did not kill women or children, and that if Riel would put them in a safe place, and inform us of its direction, we would not fire at it.

After the reconnoitering party returned to camp, the troops had their dinner and at one o'clock advanced against the enemy's position, led by the Toronto Grenadiers.

Without a moment's hesitation they dashed into the bush, and with a rush carried the rifle pits from which the enemy had harassed us on Saturday, and then swept the enemy before them down a short valley dotted with bush into the plain, which extends half a mile back from the river bank.

On one side of the plain the enemy had dug a long range of rifle pits, from which they opened fire as we advanced towards the village of Batoche, which stands in the centre of the plain. The ground to be crossed was open, and for the most part under cultivation, though here and there were patches of brushwood.

As the Grenadiers had cleared the valley, the other corps had come up, and the Grenadiers and Boulton's Horse advanced together with the Intelligence corps on their flank.

The scene was a pretty one as the troops advanced, the puffs of smoke darting out from the houses of the village, and fringing the bush covered hills on our flank from the rifle pits at their feet. On our part there was no attempt at advancing in accordance with any military system. The troops moved forward in an irregular body, firing as they went at the village in front.

The enemy were few in number but fought well and steadily, keeping under cover of the houses and seldom showing a head. The troops advanced briskly until near the village, when they hesitated a little and the officers had to expose themselves a good deal to get them forward; the result was that three officers were killed, Captains French and Brown and Lieutenant Fitch, while only two privates fell in the whole day's fighting. This speaks of itself, and shows also the steadiness and accuracy of the aim of the enemy.

We had in all eleven wounded.

After a short pause the troops went at the village with a rush, and the rebels fled instantly from the other side. So quickly was the affair over, that Riel's men had no time to carry off their prisoners with them, and they were all found uninjured.

Several of the enemy were killed as the Grenadiers rushed the rifle pits, and some more were shot as we cleared the valley; but the total number engaged was small, and there can be no doubt that many of those who fought against us on Saturday must have retired before the fighting began.

There is great satisfaction at our having recovered the prisoners uninjured, but although Riel threatened to kill them if we advanced, it is not probable that he intended to do so, as such an act would have placed him and those with him beyond the hope of mercy.

A despatch had been received from the *Northcote*, at whose absence some uneasiness had been felt; she was fired at, but is all right, and is expected here this afternoon.

The two first objective points of the campaign have now been accomplished. Battleford has been relieved and Riel has been driven from Batoche, but the real difficulty of the campaign is only beginning. It was morally certain that with our superior force and artillery we could drive Riel from his position, but a war in the woods is a very different thing. It may be that the Indians will desert Riel, now that he has proved himself unable to hold Batoche, but the engagements of the war, so far, can hardly be discouraging to the half-breeds who could not have hoped to withstand us in the open, but who have proved themselves good fighters in cover."

When the Regiment left Toronto for the Northwest, there were seventeen officers, including two non-combatants, Surgeon Ryerson and Lieutanant Lowe, acting Quarter-Master. The fifteen combatant officers were, Staff:—Lieut.-Col. Grasett, commanding; Major Dawson and Captain Manley, adjutant. Company officers, Capts. Caston, Mason, Spencer, Harston; Lieuts. Howard, Gibson, Irving, Hay, Morrow, Fitch, Michie and Eliot.

During the journey along the North shore, Captain Spencer was completely prostrated by an attack of rheumatism, and Lieut. Morrow was accidently shot in the leg. Both these officers were taken back to Toronto. After the engagement at Fish Creek, while waiting in camp there, Lieuts. Eliot and Gibson, suffering from severe attacks of rheumatism, were placed on board the steamer *Northcote* with other invalid officers, and while on board, aided in the defence of the steamer against the fierce attack made upon her by the rebels when running the gauntlet at Batoche.

During the fighting before Batoche, the Grenadiers had one officer killed, Lieut. Fitch, and three wounded, Major Dawson and Capts. Manley and Mason, so that on the evening of the day on which Batoche was captured there were left efficient only seven combatant officers in the regiment. A special fatality seemed to attach to No. 3 Company; every officer belonging or attached to it being killed or wounded. This goes to show how fully the officers shared with their men the hardships and dangers of the campaign.

The men of the Grenadiers were peculiarly well fitted for this campaign, being hardy, intelligent and strong, able to endure fatigues and privations, and fitted by their various occupations to make themselves peculiarly useful. For instance, on the way along the North shore, in the beginning of the journey, the wheels of the tender jumped the track. This occurred many miles from the nearest station, and what looked like a long delay was speedily put right by some of the men who were regularily employed in the Grand Trunk repair shops, Toronto. Then on the line of march across the prairie the General found it frequently necessary to communicate by wire with different points, the Grenadiers furnished men who were expert at cutting and repairing wires, and so assisted in this matter.

In the matter of courage and pluck they were also conspicuous. Many instances might be related in support of this statement, but one or two will suffice.

When General Middleton made his last halt before advancing on Batoche, camp was formed early in the afternoon, and orders issued that on the following morning every available fighting man must join the attacking column, and all non-combatants and sick or disabled men remain in camp. The details of the plan of attack as ordered by the General, provided that the Grenadiers should have the post of honor, and lead the attack, and it was well known that the resistance would be such that a bloody struggle was anticipated, so the Surgeons of the different corps made an examination of men who were on the sick-list with the view to ascertain whether or not they were fitted for the attack on the following day.

One of the officers of the Grenadiers in passing from one part of the camp to the other heard his name called out, " Captain ———" and looking around he saw the Surgeon, Dr. Ryerson, engaged in a discussion with one of the men of the regiment—Private Martin. This man had his foot frozen in travelling along the north shore of Lake Superior, and so badly, that the great toe was

ON THE WAY TO THE NORTHWEST. 157

almost off, and he had been struggling along for some time with a piece of blanket wrapped around his foot, and wearing a moccasin. Dr. Ryerson told this man he would have to remain in the camp, but Martin insisted upon marching out with his comrades to take part in the fight, and appealed to Captain —— to speak on his behalf. This was done and the man permitted to go. It was rather an unlucky decision for him, as he was very severely wounded, his shoulder being broken, and he has a crippled arm to this day.

An instance to show the spirit of the men. On the last day when they were travelling on sleighs and on foot between the gaps on the North Shore, night found them at the end of the track, and the other end of the track had to be reached by a long march of some hours duration across the ice. This march promised to be the severest struggle of the journey. It was pouring rain, pitch-dark, the snow, nearly three feet on the level, was melting fast and becoming slushy. Many of the men were foot-sore, suffering from frost-bites, colds and rheumatism. All the baggage and supplies had to be transported in sleighs over this gap, and an officer of the Regiment was detailed to superintend that duty. The Commanding Officer suggested to this officer that accommodation might be made for those of the men who were most worn out to ride on the sleighs sitting on the baggage. In order to carry out this suggestion, the officer in charge got the regiment formed up and briefly addressed them, stating that many of them must be suffering severely from exposure and fatigue, that the march before them would test the endurance of the strongest, and said that twenty or thirty could be accommodated with seats in the sleighs, and that those men who felt unable to make this march could fall out on the reverse flank of the column. The result showed the spirit of the men, for not a single man left the ranks, all preferring to share the hardships of their comrades.

In Dr. Ryerson's letter the gallantry and ability of Colour-Sergeant Curzon is referred to, the war correspondent of the Toronto *Mail*, in his account of the action at Batoche, also mentions it thus:

" There was one case of heroism which deserves mention. One of the Grenadiers was seriously wounded at Batoche and would have bled to death had he been left any length of time. Colour-Sergeant Curzon, under a shower of rebel bullets at once knelt down and stopped the hemorrhage and carried his wounded comrade to a place of safety, marching coolly away to the music provided by the guns of the enemy." [It is no disparagement to Sergeant Curzon, indeed it is the reverse to say that the *Mail* correspondent makes a mistake in saying the wounded man was a Grenadier, he was not, but belonged to the Midland regiment.]

It is generally understood that Colour-Sergeant Curzon was recommended for the Victoria Cross for this achievement, why he never received an honor he had so fully earned has never been explained. He died in Toronto.

In another portion of General Middleton's despatches he refers to the rebel losses as well as to some criticisms passed upon himself:

" The Catholic priest reported this morning the following loss of the rebels in the 4 days of fighting:

CAPT. A. J. BOYD.

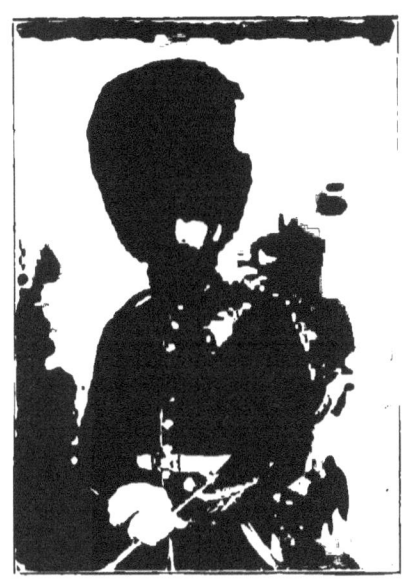

CAPT. A. E. GOODERHAM.

CAPT. H. A. WILLIS.

CAPT. R. O. MONTGOMERY.

"First day, 4 killed and five wounded; second day, 2 wounded; third day, 3 wounded; fourth day, 47 killed, 163 wounded.

"Total, 51 killed, and 173 wounded.

"In one of the English papers I am represented as having been waiting at Fish Creek for reinforcement, of having asked for 1,000 men, and as having been reinforced by the Midland Regiment, and as having fought with 1,000 men, and arms superior to the enemy. The real facts of the case being as follows : I was waiting at Fish Creek, as you know, to get rid of my wounded, and get oats up, and not for reinforcements. Only 100 men of the Midland Regiment reached me then under Lieut.-Col. Williams, and as I had lost, killed and wounded, nearly 60 men, and had to put 35 men on board the *Northcote*, my actual reinforcement was 5 men. As regards the actual number of men engaged out of my total force of 724 officers and men, owing to having to leave 100 men to protect my camp, leaving wounded and sick men, cooks, ammunition carriers, assistants to ambulances, etc., I was only able to bring 495 men into the engagement, and this included the Artillery and Gatling which, owing to the nature of the position, were not able to do so much damage as the infantry. So that with about 400 men we drove with heavy loss of force, (taking the lowest estimation), 600 Half-breeds and Indians, many of them armed with long-range rifles, and who were considered the finest and best prairie fighters in the country, out of a strong position, carefully selected and entrenched by themselves. After this I need say no more concerning the conduct during the engagement, of the whole force. From my second in command, Lieut.-Col. Straubenzie, I received every assistance, and on the 12th, his leading of his brigade was beyond praise.

"The conduct of Lt.-Cols., Montizambert, commanding Artillery; Williams, commanding Midland regiment; Lt.-Col. Grasett, commanding Grenadiers, and Major McKeand, commanding 90th Regiment, was everything I could wish. Lt.-Col. Williams and Lt.-Col. Grasett came prominently to my notice from the gallant way in which they led and cheered their men on the left, rush by rush, until they gained the house on the plain, the former having commenced the rush. The field officers of the different Infantry regiments, Major Smith and Hughes, Midland; Major Dawson, Grenadiers; Major Boswell and Acting Major and Adjt. Buchan, 90th regiment, are equally to be commended for their behaviour on this and other days."

The list of killed and wounded at Batoche is a sad one. A full list of the former and of the wounded belonging to the Grenadiers is here given:

Northwest Field Force under Major-General Middleton, C. B. Return of officers and men killed during the attack on Batoche from 9th to 12th May inclusive.

24th May, 1885.

RANK AND NAMES.	CAUSE OF DEATH.	REMARKS.
" A " Battery :—		
Gr. Wm. Phillips........	Gun shot wound.	9th May.
10th Royal Grenadiers :—		
Lieut. W. Fitch.........	"	12th May.
Pte. T Moore..........	"	9th May.

90th Battalion :—
  Pte. R. R. Hardisty..... Gun shot wound. 10th May.
  Pte. James Fraser.......   "   12th May.

Boulton' Scouts :—
  Capt. E. L. Brown.......   "   12th May.

French's Scouts :—
  Capt. John French......   "   12th May.

Intelligence Corps :—
  Lieut. A. W. Kippen....   "   12th May.

  Recapitulation :—   2   9th May.
                       1   10th   "
                       5   12th   "

           Total   8

WOUNDED OF THE ROYAL GRENADIERS.

10th Royal Grenadiers :
  Pte. Brisbane..........Forehead...........11th May.
   "   Eager.............Jaw................12th "
  Corpl. Foley...........Side...............11th "
  Pte. H. Millsom........Chest..............12th "
   "   A. Martin.........Shoulder...........10th "
   "   Marshall..........Ankle..............12th "
   "   Barber............Head...............12th "
   "   Cantwell..........Hand and thigh...... 9th "
   "   Quigley...........Right arm..........12th "
  Capt. Manley...........Foot...............11th "
  Major Dawson...........Leg................12th "
  Pte. Hughes............Ruptured in action...12th "
  Capt. Mason............Side................ 9th "
  Bugler Gaughan.........Hand...............12th "
  Pte. Cook..............Arm................12th "
   "   Stead.............Arm................ 9th "
   "   Scobel............Arm................10th "
      Total 17
  K

Captain Harston, of the Royal Grenadiers, was appointed after the battle of Batoche, by the Major-General commanding, to the post of Infantry Brigade-Major. Captain Young, of the Winnipeg Field Battery, had held the post up to this date, but he had been detached by the General to take charge of Riel after his surrender, and had gone with him to Regina.

LIEUT. J. G. SMITH.

LIEUT. A. F. R. MARTIN.

LIEUT. H. R. O'REILLY.

LIEUT. D. C. MEYERS

CHAPTER VII.

THE SERGEANT'S DIARY—RETURN TO TORONTO—HOW THE CITY RECEIVED HER SOLDIERS—PROMOTIONS AND APPOINTMENTS—CONCLUSION.

BEFORE concluding the account of the Northwest expedition, so far as the battle of Batoche, a few reminiscences of the Grenadier's journey from Toronto, of their march across country, and of their eventful six weeks from March 30th to May 12th, 1885, may properly be given.

Crossing Lake Superior on the ice, men, footsore and worn with fatigue, refused to take the sleighs belonging to the transport, even when urged by their officers to do so, because they knew so many of their comrades must of necessity march. Again when the Grenadiers were barracked in the schooner, *M. L. Breck*, they actually slept with moisture pouring on to their faces from the thawing ice, with which the sides of the vessel's hold were encrusted, and which the heat of the men's breath melted. It is a comparatively small matter, but it is worth recording that on the railway journey northward, there was at times not even sitting space for the whole of the men, and on one occasion they were sixty-six hours continually in a train. Nor was there for many of them even " the soft side of a board " for a resting place at night. Their only couch was being closely jammed on the seats of the railway cars, without a chance to get any comfortable rest. Yet it was borne brightly and cheerfully, the Grenadiers were "Ready, aye Ready," for anything and for everything.

The regiment had been specially selected by Major-General Middleton to accompany him to Batoche for the following reasons. First, they were commanded by experienced officers, who knew what discipline was and enforced it in this battalion. In the second place, the General knew the Grenadiers were as capable of doing a hard days work at road-making or ditching as they were steady on parade and expert rifle shots.

Nor was this determination of the Grenadiers to do their duty, unnoticed or unappreciated by those who watched them from a distance. Canada was proud of her sons, Toronto gloried in the "Grens.," the "Queen's Own" and the "Body Guards." Were they not from the city, of the city, were they not our neighbors, our brothers or our friends.

The fortunes of the Toronto contingent were followed eagerly by all Toronto; the city gloried in their successes, sympathised with their wounded, and sincerely mourned for their honored dead. Of these last it was written at the time.

> "Not in the quiet churchyard, near those who loved them best,
> But by the wild Saskatchewan they laid them to their rest,
> A simple soldiers' funeral, in that lonely spot was theirs,
> Made consecrate and holy by a nation's tears and prayers."

The poetical account of the Expedition written by S. A. C. (Mrs. Curzon) is so simple and yet so touching that it is given here also:

O, but they sprang at the call !
  The call of the bugle to arms;
Sprang as a man to the fight;
  The fight, not of foreign alarms.

Tramped through the ice and the snow,
  Tramped through the forest and swamp
Lay with the stars for a roof,
  Dried by the dead-branch fire the damp.

Hoar on the hair hung the frost,
  Stiff with the frost the moustache,
Mustachios so silky and soft,
  And curled, to be sharp as a lash !

Rations of hard-tack and tea,
  Rations of nothing for hours ;
But ever the heart of the brave—
  Ever the will that o'erpowers.

Sense of the stress of the time
  Makes of a biscuit a feast,
Strengthens for duty the soul,
  Reckons for comfort the least.

Frozen and cramped of the hands,
  Frozen and cramped of the feet ;
Chill to the marrow, the wind
  Blinding, the rain and the sleet.

Footsore and sleepless and worn,
  Over Superior they go ;
Stumbling mid hummocks of ice,
  Ploutering and plunging through snow,

Onward and onward the march,
  On to broad Saskatchewan ;
Peering to right and to left
  For a sign of the fight that's begun.

Middleton flashes the word ;
  " Grenadiers, here to your post !"
How shall the river that flows
  Like a surge of the sea-tide be crossed ?

" There goes the Gatling again !
  Cross ? We must cross as we may !
Rig this old jerry-scow up;
  Men, there is always a way.

Over the tide they are gone ;
  Taste their first blood at Fish Creek ;
Bury their dead where they fell,
  Follow the foe whom they seek.

O, the wooded ravines of Batoche !
  Frederick lay there with his men,
Firing till scrub there was none,
  Rifle-pits firing again.

Breast on the sod, and the chin
  Resting in hollow it made ;
Beard and the roots of the grass
  Mingling as threads of one blade.

Breast on the sod for three days,
  Sleepless and hungry and black—
O, for a rush on the foe !
  Middleton, wise, held them back.

LIEUT. S. F. SLOANE.

LIEUT. J. T. CRAIG.

LIEUT. J. C. MASON

LIEUT. G. H. C. BROOKE.

Breast on the sod, and the chin
    Resting in hollow it made ;
Lift but an inch from the slope,
    Life is the penalty paid.

Crook but an elbow too high,
    Crack ! and a ball from below ;
O, for the word of command—
    O, for a rush on the foe.

"Charge !" and they sweep like the wind—
    Midlanders, Ninetieth, and Grens.—
Out leap the foe from their holes,
    And scatter like sheep from the pens.

"On to the church, men ; the church !
    There are the women and priests ;
On to the house, men, the house !
    Give the poor prisoners release."

'Tis done. And Batoche is a dream,
    Its terrors, its sufferings, its tears ;
But forever it blazons the flag
    Of your service, O brave Grenadiers.
                                   C.

One more word about the actual fighting at Batoche.

It has often been asked why General Middleton delayed the final attack upon Batoche, many reasons have been assigned, the probable one is this, that he thought he could in time tire out the enemy and that they would capitulate and thus save many lives. It must be borne in mind that the troops in his command were not regulars but militia, that in many, if not in all cases, they were bread-winners, and had others dependent upon them, and, although to many people General Middleton's delay seems inexplicable, the probable reason is the one that has just been stated, the desire to protect as far as possible the lives of his men.

He could certainly have made an advance upon Batoche on May 9th or 10th at the latest, but there is no doubt that had he done so it would have been a hand-to-hand conflict, and that many brave and useful men would have fallen, whose lives, through the tactics General Middleton adopted, were saved to the country, as it was, the loss was very great, not less than eight being killed and 46 wounded on our side, during the four days' attack upon Batoche, from May 9th to the 12th inclusive. Of the killed, one officer and one private were from the Grenadiers also three officers and 15 men more or less seriously wounded.

The following diary was kept by Color-Sergeant F. Francis of the Royal Grenadiers, and may be introduced here most appropriately:

Friday, April 10th.—Left Fort Qu'Appelle at six a.m. in the same waggons; passed through a fine parklike country, a lot of gophers to be seen on the road. The boys had great fun running after them. The country sandy in some parts, went 25 miles, camped on the prairie; started next morning, Saturday 11th, at 7 a.m. A bluffy country with a lot of sloughs; saw a few farms of Half-breeds on the road; reached Touchwood about 5 p.m. Saturday; left a man sick at the Hudson Bay store; two houses besides the store; the hills are rolling but not steep. Had 20 rounds of ball served out to us at Touchwood. Fresh butter served out—a great treat, and fresh bread; more blankets served out here, making three each man. A fine day, but very cold at night; no candles to be had; no salt or sugar.

Sunday April 12th, 7 a.m.—Fine day. Saw a family of Indians picking up the crumbs we left behind—a miserable looking lot of people shivering with the cold —advanced to the big Touchwood hills; no difference in the country only more hilly. Saw a bear in the distance, too far to shoot at; saw a flock of geese and a lot of rabbits; camped on the plain—made about 25 miles; 75 scouts caught up to us here under command of Major Boulton—a hardy looking lot of men mounted on small ponies, all dressed in corduroy breeches and fustian coats with helmets and slouch hats, armed with repeating rifles, revolvers and knives; a very strange saddle with wooden stirrups; they camped with us for the night, and pushed on next day to overtake the General.

Monday morning, April 13th.—Struck camp at 7 a.m. Started for the Salt Plains; had to take enough wood and water for six rations, as there is none to be got on the plains. The water is very salt, not fit to drink. The prairie is very flat and wet, in some places up to the waggon box. Arrived at the middle of the plains at 4 o'clock. Camped on General Middleton's old camping ground. He is a day ahead yet. We have made about eighteen miles; everybody very tired. There is a mail shanty here where the mail changes horses; the ground very damp, but we have had rubber sheets served out, so it does not matter much. Posted some post cards; got a frying pan, a thing that we wanted much. The country a level flat, not a thing to be seen for miles, like being on the lake.

Tuesday morning, April 14th.—Struck tents at 7 a.m. Started on the road; nothing new. I have been with the leading waggon all the way from Qu'Appelle. Encamped on the plains about 5 p.m. Had supper of hard tack and tea.

Wednesday, April 15th.—Struck tents at 7 a.m. Packed our knapsacks into the waggons—the rest of waggons except those with supplies were sent back. We start to march with an advance guard and a rear guard. I was in charge of the leading files of the advance guard. Came to a little bush of wood poplar. A mounted policeman came to meet us; he is posted at Humboldt. Encamped about four miles from Humboldt; in this place one house, where the telegraph man lives. The trail here branches off to Prince Albert. We followed the old trail by the telegraph poles; pitched tents, made about 20 miles; some of us very tired, myself tired but not footsore as a good many of them were.

Thursday, April 16th.—Struck tents at 7 a.m. Had hard-tack and canned meat as usual for rations; started again with advance guard. A fine country but no trees, plenty of small lakes. It was snowing when we started, blowing a hard gale in our faces; made marching very hard; had to ford two or three streams; a hard march; two of my advance files gave out; had to ride on the knapsacks; near played out myself; stopped for dinner at noon, hard-tack, canned meat and water for dinner. Blowing very cold with snow all the time. Saw a fox on the hill; some of the teamsters fired at it, but missed it. Encamped for the night on the prairie. Not much wood to get a little tea with. All very tired indeed, and wet, made 24 miles. The postman arrived soon after we encamped; everyone had a letter but myself; was disappointed. A Toronto *Globe* of April 6th was given to each company; had a good laugh when we were able to read it. We have no candles yet; it is miserable without light, and no one can see in the tents now to cover himself up, or move around with twelve men stretched on the ground. We all miss oatmeal very much; it is wanted bad.

Friday, April 17th.—Started at 7 a.m. A fine country but no wood to be seen; dinner of fresh meat and hardtack; beans for breakfast, plain, boiled in water. It is very cold; had to march with overcoats on ; started again after dinner, encamped on General Middleton's old ground ; made 25 miles this day ; still it first-class health, feet in good order yet; seen no wood for the last two days.

Saturday, April 18th.—General Middleton is still twelve miles ahead, at Clark's Crossing. We started as usual. Made about 11 miles ; had dinner and about one hour's rest, but it is very cold; fixed ourselves up a little and started again for Clark's Crossing. Saw the camp in the distance. Some of the men in camp came out to meet us. General Middleton's camp is on the Saskatchewan River. We marched into camp and pitched tents, etc., and made ourselves comfortable. Had some sugar, hard-tack, one candle, and some pork served out to each company, for a treat. About 4 p.m., the scouts brought in three Indians, they captured them about nine miles from camp ; they are ugly-looking men, one a chief: they are dressed in skins as usual, and armed, one with a rifle and two with shot guns. They were interviewed by Lord Melgund and the General. They were taken, put in a tent under guard; they were well fed and one of them allowed to go and report to their council, of the kindness they had received. There were four Indian scouts seen around our camp on Friday night by some of the men. I suppose they are some of these men.

"A" Battery of 100 men, 100 mounted scouts, 40 of "C" Company, Winnipeg Field Battery, 50 men; 90th Battalion, 280 men; Royal Grenadiers, 264 men. These are all the fighting men in camp, and about 125 two-horse teams to carry our provisions for us. There is no wood here; it has to be drawn three miles for us to use. We all enjoyed a good night's rest. Every day before this we have been up at 4 a.m. This morning (Sunday, April 19th) we were allowed to sleep until 6 a.m.; breakfast of hard-tack, beans and a little piece of pork. Paraded at 10 a.m. for inspection of arms, after which we had divine service. The whole camp attended, Colonel Grasett read the Church of England service. The 90th Band played for the singing: "Onward Christian Soldiers," "Nearer My God to Thee," and "The Old Hundredth." It was very touching. Each man was served out with a New Testament at Touchwood Hills. We are on the Saskatchewan River now; it is a broad stream, about 80 yards wide and very swift, about six miles an hour I think, and very dirty. The ice is piled up very high from the water; the water must be twelve feet lower than it was in the winter. The Temperance Colonization Company own land on each side of the river, fine land; they have a stone house built on the river, about five rooms, but the family cleared out when the trouble began, and went to Moose Jaw. There is another house kept by Mr. Clark; he is doing a good trade now, bread forty cents a loaf, butter seventy-five cents a pound, and so on. Chewing tobacco and matches are very scarce. I bought some fishing tackle in Winnipeg; I set a night line last night but caught no fish. Everybody is busy writing this afternoon; I have been writing this all the afternoon; I kept notes from the time we started till yesterday when I lost my book and had to borrow another party's book for dates, etc. Just had word that Riel and his party are about thirty miles from here on the right bank of the river. I hope he will stay there until we get at him. Just had orders that we march to-morrow, (Monday). We have the post of honor ourselves, and "A" Battery and half of the scouts advance to attack them. The 90th Winnipeg Battery, and "C" Company go on the other side of the river as a blind; we shall soon be through now I suppose; I hope they will take us down home by Swift Current.

Monday, April 20th.—Had orders to cross the river with the Winnipeg Battery, but for some reason the order was countermanded, and we had to stay in camp all day; this morning we had drill; this afternoon was in charge of a party of 25 men fixing an old scow; no trouble; hope to move to-morrow. It will take sometime to take us all over, 50 men at a time. Half of the scouts went over yesterday afternoon.

Tuesday, 21st April.—Reveille at 5 a.m. Orders are to prepare to start after breakfast. We live better now, get full rations of meat and biscuits, but no salt or sugar.

The fresh meat we kill here. The pickets brought in two Indians this morning; they were found prowling around the camp last night. One is armed with a gun, and the other with a bow and arrow—I suppose to take down a sentry without any noise. They are fine built men, but ugly. I don't know what they will do with them. We crossed the river at twelve o'clock, No. 1 Co. first, the supplies after us. We then pitched tents on a level piece of land, a fine place. The Winnipeg Field Battery with two guns is with us.

I set a fish-line in the river this afternoon; they tell me there is fish in the river to be caught sometimes, but it is early in the season to catch them.

Wednesday, 22nd April.—Up at six. Expected to start to-day, but did not do so. Stayed in camp all day; drilled three times in extended order. Had to put *
* in the guard tent; had a false alarm last night; all the boys turned out armed. Am told off to quarter guard this evening; expect to start for Prince Albert to-morrow. They say the wire is cut between here and Hnmboldt; very strange we have had no mail; have had no letters from any one since we left Winnipeg. Every one is looking for a letter. I wish the quartermaster would give us some oatmeal or rice for a change. Have had only one candle since we left Toronto. This is a fine country around here.

Thursday, 23rd April.—Just got breakfast; on guard all night; was away when the visiting and grand rounds came around; made it all right. Nice and warm in the day, but have to make a pillow of our boots at night to keep them from freezing stiff. Passed the night without trouble. We left camp at Clark's Crossing at 7.30 this a.m. Glad to be on the move again; on the way now to Prince Albert; expect to meet Riel at Batoche's Crossing, about forty miles. We left camp in the following order: myself and four men in advance; then the rest of the column; the scouts spread out in front of us for about one-half mile, the guns in rear; passed through a fine country, and encamped for dinner after doing twelve miles; dinner cold; no wood to make tea with. Went on again, and encamped seven miles further on. Posted a very strong guard. General Middleton moved on the other side of the river with us, and encamped opposite us for the night. Riel is reported about ten miles from us now. I walked all the way yesterday; rather tired, as I did not shut my eyes the night before, as I was on guard.

Friday, 24th April.—Struck camp this morning at five o'clock, ready to start at six, when our marching orders were altered, and postponed. They say the eastern mail is with General Middleton; I wish they would deliver it to us here; would like to hear from home. I never was in better health than I am now; can eat more now than I ever did before. It is a healthy country. Each man was served out with ten more rounds of ammunition, making 30 rounds each, Sergeant 50 rounds. I am afraid they will not be wanted as Riel will not stop for us. Everybody is anxious to advance. We have the Prince Albert mail with us to carry through as of course the road is not safe for the mail. We have had no rain since we left Red Rock. They say it never rains here till June. It is rather rough on our men to have to furnish a guard of 54 men every night; the pickets have to lie out all night and march next day. The guard lay in tent except those on duty, but the men do not complain except for a candle at night. Chewing tobacco is very scarce. We had to march through a lot of water yesterday; last night a hard frost. Lord Melgund is on this side with us, dressed like a scout. Every man is expecting to have a brush and closing with the enemy. I hope they may; had orders to start at 10 a.m. No. 1 Company extended twelve paces; No. 2, support, went along for about four miles through a fine country with a little bush. Heavy firing all the time on the other side. Halted and then the old scow was brought up and No. 2 Company crossed over first, then No. 1 Company and No. 4 Company. No. 3 Company and French's Scouts being left behind to guard the supplies. When we arrived we relieved the 90th. Found the enemy down in a hollow about a mile from the river bank. There was a dead Indian about six yards in front of where I lay down on the bluff of a hill. The Indians are just underneath us, but we cannot get at them very well. I have had a few shots; each one of us have had 100 rounds of balls served out to us; there must be a lot of Indians killed; I can count ten dead horses as I lie here; there was an "A" Battery man lying about 20 paces from me, dead; there are about eight of the 90th dead. Captain Wise has just been carried by on a stretcher with a ball in his heel. Some of "A" Battery men have just carried their dead men away. We covered them while they did so. This is all too bad. We shall have to encamp here to-night I suppose; we will have to have a strong guard;

2ND LIEUT. C. S M^cINNES.

2ND LIEUT. C. S. WILKIE.

2ND LIEUT. E. R. STREET.

2ND LIEUT. D. F. CAMPBELL.

have had no dinner to-day; should like to have some. It has just begun to rain. I suppose the rain is brought on by the cannon firing; we do not dare to leave our place but lie still in our tunics and get wet through. The cannon are now firing over our heads at two half-breed houses about 450 yards to our front; they strike every time with shell and ball. It is pretty tough to lie wet through in the cold wind. Just had orders to retire. Everyone else have left the battle field. One 90th man, and one "A" Battery man, lie on the field; they cannot be got at. It is surprising the rumors that fly around. The battlefield is a plain of about 20 acres, surrounded nearly all around with low bush, with a deep ravine running through it. It is in the ravine that the Indians have taken up their stand and cannot be removed to-day. We lay on the top of the bank; the Indians and half-breeds below us. The interpreter has just spoken to them from where they lay; the camp is pitched for the night on the prairie about three-quarters of a mile from the battlefield near the river. We had not got 50 yards from our position when the Indians set up a most unearthly yell. We at once got the order to extend from the centre and cover the rest of the retirement. I expected every moment that they would pour a volley into us but they did not do so. We got orders when about half way to camp to hold some woods to protect the camp; there was nothing for it but to do so; No. 1 Company and No. 4 Company were told off to do it. No. 2 was sent to the river to cover our scow and supplies and prevent reinforcements for the rebels coming in. About eight o'clock it stopped raining and began to snow. We were all wet through with nothing on but our tunics, our overcoats being across the river and no way to get them. Had nothing to eat since six in the morning except a biscuit or two that we had in our haversacks. About 11 o'clock they sent us some canned meat and tea from the camp which did us good. We heard the Indians yelling during the night but did not see them. The 90th relieved us about 2 a.m. We turned into their tents wet and all as we were, and not allowed to remove our boots or anything, and to lay with our arms at our sides. The most miserable night. Our own tents were over on the other side of the river; had to turn out again at seven o'clock to let part of the 90th come in. No. 1 Company had to relieve some of the 90th at 9 a.m. Took up the same ground to guard we had last night. We made up a big fire and dried ourselves; they buried the dead of our own side that they had this morning, eleven I think. There are a lot of wounded men in camp. The other two guns came across the river during the night but No. 3 Company of ours still over there protecting our stores that are not yet removed. We are relieved at 8 p.m.

Sunday, 26th April.—An alarm was sounded at about 2 a.m. A picket fired about a dozen shots at four horsemen. The whole of the camp stood to their arms; the Battery limbered up and all ready to march in three minutes. After standing about ten minutes we were dismissed; turned in again, had to bunk with the 90th; our things are not over yet. Had our breakfast of hardtack and tea. Had divine service at 10 a.m. General Middleton reading the prayers. We were all under arms, strange to go to church with rifles in hand and 100 rounds of ball ammunition. After church a parade party were told off to make roads, another to make litters and other work. I have not got my knapsack yet. They cannot get the cable to work across the river. The scouts captured fourteen horses and about twenty head of cattle.

Monday, 27th April.—Reveille at 6 a.m. The mail came in at eleven o'clock last night, a lot of letters and papers. Two more men buried this afternoon. No. 3 Company crossed over from the other side of the river this morning about two o'clock with all the stores. They had an alarm yesterday, and they all stood to their arms. We have an easy day of it, no duty but to put up tents and sort stores—a long job, but one that was needed. The 90th furnish a picket to-night; the scouts and waggons have been foraging around all day for hay and oats. A man was buried this morning. A scout that was shot through the lungs during the fight on Friday. The 90th and battery have gone on the battlefield this afternoon; we form their support; they have gone to get their dead. I was on the battle ground this afternoon; the Indians left two of their dead on the ground, but there is not a live Indian to be seen. There were from fifty to sixty dead horses on the ground. The houses are a total wreck; all of the wounded are doing well. I do not know when we move from here. All of No. 3 Company are on duty to-night. This place is called Fish Creek; they have brought in twelve more horses to-night.

Tuesday, April 28th.—Nothing occurred to note.

Wednesday, April 29th.—Had drill in the morning

under the General in extended order. In the evening mounted picket; a bad night, rained, and cold; heard a lot of prairie wolves, a nasty howl. Relieved at 7 a m., the 30th.

Thursday, 30th April.—Had drill. Did nothing more. Had fresh meat.

Regimental Orderly Sergeant for the day. Last night the picket caught three Indians. The Indians that were caught at Clarke's Crossing are with us still; they have the run of the camp; they will not leave us. Had a drummer, a defaulter.

Friday, May 1st.—May began with a fine morning. Nothing new to report. The wounded left us this morning on their way to the Hospital at Sakatoon. They had about 20 waggons; the scouts as an escort. Had drill this a.m.; nothing new to report.

Saturday, May 2nd.—Nothing new to report only that I am on picket, and do not like the job to lay out all night; but it cannot be helped.

Sunday, May 3rd.—Got off parade at 11 this a.m. Saw nothing all night only heard the prairie wolves. They made a lot of noise during the night. The mail came in just before we left the camp for picket; was glad to hear from home and to know that they are all well. The mail left this a.m. Saw some swallows yesterday, the first I have seen this year. A lot of men in bathing in the river to-day; had divine service; men with their arms and ammunition.

Monday, May 4th.—Last night had another false alarm, by the picket firing. In some two minutes all turned out. Had no supper last night; our cook undertook to make some dumplings but we could not eat them; they were like lead. The General left camp this a.m. with the scouts for Batoche's Crossing; they returned with about forty head of cattle and horses; were within two miles of Riel's camp but did not go in; we were under arms all day to help the General if he was attacked. It has been a very fine day again; a little cold. Had three days rations served out. I don't know what it may mean but I hope a move on. Mail in to-day; no letters but papers of the 27th.

Tuesday, May 5th.—Two companies of the Midland Battalion came up the river on the *Northcote* this a. m. They left part of the regiment at Clarke's Crossing and Swift Current. They brought a fourteen-day old mail with them; no letter for me. We ought to have sugar and candles. Ought to make it lighter for picket. I was Regimental Orderly Sergeant for the day. The regiment had drill for two hours under the General.

Wednesday, May 6th.—The men took the Gatling gun off the *Northcote*. They had just tried it; it can fire 600 rounds a minute, pretty good work. The *Northcote* is a strange built boat with a paddle wheel behind; they had a great deal of trouble with her coming down the river. I am told off for picket to-night. It is very cold now; I hope it will get warmer before night.

Thursday, May 7th.—Had charge of the pickets last night for the first time, of 15 men; one of my men fired at two men, turned the whole camp out. We moved this a.m. ten miles towards Batoche's Crossing; encamped for the day at about 12 o'clock; as soon as we halted some of the scouts were fired on; the brigade at once threw out a strong picket; we shall certainly have a brush with the enemy to-morrow; I hope we will finish them up then and get home for I am tired of this country although I am in good health. Myself and four men formed the leading files of the advance guard of the whole brigade.

Friday, May 8th.—Left camp at Gabriel's Crossing this a.m. at eight o'clock; expected to meet the rebels every moment, but saw nothing of them; we are as far away from Batoche's as we were last night. We have marched about 18 miles to get around the other side of them. Had a good sleep last night. "C" Company went down the river in a steamboat. They burnt Gabriel Dumont's house before they left this a.m. It was well furnished I believe. The land we passed through to-day is light and sandy.

Saturday, May 9th.—Breakfast this a.m. at 4.30. Started for Batoche at 6 a.m. the scouts in front with the gatling gun. No. 1 Company formed the advance guard, myself in charge of the leading file; all went well till we got near the church when the scouts started some Indians out of a house; we then formed company and extended, No. 1 from the right, No. 2 prolonged to the right, Nos. 3 and 4 in support; came up to a church with a fine two-story house alongside of it, both frame. The Gatling gun fired about 20 rounds through the gable, when a man came to the door and waved a white handkerchief; the General at once advanced. It proved to be a priest and sisters and about a dozen women and children. We passed them by and entered a bush; then the firing began. The enemy retired to their rifle pits in a bluff; they were shelled and the Gatling turned on them but to no purpose;

SURGEON-MAJOR E. E. KING.

REV. A. H. BALDWIN.
(Chaplain.)

2ND LIEUT. A. A. S. WILKINS.

CAPT. D. McD. HOWARD.
(Late Royal Grenadiers.)

they could not be got out of it and this was at 5 p.m. We have been firing at them all day. Captain Mason of No. 2 Company was struck. I have had some bullets near me but so far none of my company are hurt. Just heard that one of the Grenadiers was killed, one scout and one Battery man.

Sunday, May 10th.—Had a hard matter to retire last night. They got all the waggons up from our late camping ground and formed a corral on a piece of ploughed ground with a slough in the centre. Then we threw up some light earthworks about twelve paces on the outside of it. One of our men was shot in the arm and another in the leg (both of No. 2 Coy.) when we were in the corral. These were chance shots for it was too dark to take aim. One of them stood within two feet of me, and was taking a drink out of my water bottle which was still attached to me; another man of the 90th was shot through the head, within four feet of me, when we were retiring, he gave a jump and a yell. We had to lay behind the earthworks all the night in our tunics, no coats or blankets and very cold. This morning we had to move out and surround the camp in extended order before we had any chance to get our breakfast, and here we are now and no chance of getting any, with the rebels firing all around. I have just read the Church service to the men of my section. There are twelve of us in a bluff. We have no one hurt in our company. To-day one of No. 3 Company was hurt and one of the 90th.

It is a job to get a correct account of the number hurt. We had to protect the 90th when they retired to camp. The bullets flew pretty lively then, and after we got in camp, but no one was hurt. Some of the houses were struck. Slept again in the trench that some of the company had thrown up. Had overcoats.

Monday, May 11th.—Had breakfast, and then the regiment was told off in squads to finish the trench which is about five feet high all around the camp, and about two feet below the level of the ground, and six feet wide for the men to sleep in, and then there is another mound thrown up again about twenty paces from the outer one on the inside, so that if we are driven in from the outer one we get behind the inner one; we are quite safe. The rest of the men are out skirmishing; one or two of them have been brought in, and among them, a priest that was wounded, but not by any of our side. Our men have cut down all the bush around the camp for a hundred yards or more. The camp must be half a mile around. The cattle and horses in the centre. The General and the scouts—about sixty of them, that came in last night, went out this morning and caught an Indian. He says they will fight to the last but they have not much powder left. I think the General wants to starve them out. I hope he may, and that soon. The scouts brought in about forty head of cattle and horses. We get all the fresh meat we want. We have not heard the boat whistle to-day. Do not know where she is.

Tuesday, 12th May.—Left camp at 1 p.m. in skirmishing order. No. 1 Company Grenadiers on the right, No. 2, 3 and 4 prolonged to the left; met the rebels about 200 yards from the church. After a stubborn resistance we drove them before us towards the village, and charged them then on the plain, and scattered them in all directions. The fire was very hot; about six killed and thirty wounded on our side. About thirty killed on that of the rebels; released about eight white men that Riel had kept as prisoners of war. Threw up intrenchments on the battlefield and stayed all night. The women and children of the rebels were encamped outside of our encampment. The rebels had been well intrenched in rifle pits. About six of No. 1 Company were wounded. The captain shot through the cap and the back of the coat. General Middleton made us a speech, and then we all turned in, tired out. Found in one of the enemy's tents a basket of eggs and a jar of molasses and took them to the hospital tent for the wounded men.

Wednesday, 13th May.—Every man is allowed to do as he likes this afternoon. I wandered around, saw some dead Indians and half-breeds, and saw our wounded. A great many rebels surrendered themselves under a flag of truce.

Thursday, May 14th.—Left Batoche at 7 a.m., No 1 Company advance guard. We have only one officer present. Had a good night's sleep. One of our men badly hurt by a horse treading on him. We had a good march of about fourteen miles to Guardapuys Crossing, where we encamped for the night.

Several Indians gave themselves up to us on the road; they have all had enough of war. They report 84 killed in the fight. About 115 guns were taken from them; a great deal of ammunition. The guns were all destroyed.

May 15th, Friday.—Camp Guardapuy. Got here last night in the rain, wet through, very uncomfortable. We had no bother to get here at all. About noon the scouts brought in Louis Riel. Myself and 20 men were told off as an escort or guard for him. A little afterwards they brought in Lepine ; he is a man about 50 years old, a little, dark and dull-looking man. The Rev. Mr. Whitcomb, of Toronto, our Chaplain, came in with the mail. The Midland regiment were across the river yesterday. The country all round here is a little light soil with a good deal of scrub. The first pine we have seen since we left Ontario we saw yesterday on the other side of the river.

May 16th, Saturday.—Guardapuy Crossing.—Nothing new to-day only that the 90th and some others crossed the river and encamped on the other side. Several more prisoners brought in and put on the boat.

Sunday, 17th May.—Nothing new to-day. Had divine service ; struck camp at noon, ready to start. No. 3 Company sent four men to Batoche, for Moor's body. Two of the Body Guards came in from Humboldt.

Monday, 18th May.—Crossed the river last night. Left Riel on the boat. Another boat came up from Clarke's Crossing with supplies, Encamped on this side of the river ; this is the prettiest camp we have had yet ; good water ; had a good night's sleep ; we started at ten o'clock for a 15 mile march to Prince Albert; sent Riel back to Regina *via* the River ; pitched camp for the night in charge of Captain Young and a guard of the Grenadiers.

Tuesday, 19th May.—We made fifteen miles yesterday and pitched our tents about half way to Prince Albert. Everything is quiet.

Thursday, 21st May.—Still in camp at Prince Albert. Nothing new, but weather bad, rained all day.

Friday, 22nd May.—Still at Prince Albert. It is a fine morning. Orders to hold ourselves in readiness to start at any moment for Battleford. The Midland Battalion and the scouts started for there this morning on the *Northcote*. Am told off for R.O.S. to-morrow.

Saturday, May 23rd.—All quiet this a.m. Sports all the afternoon, won the foot-race, $6.

Sunday, May 24th.—Up at four a. m. Struck tents and left Prince Albert for Carlton in waggons; the 90th by boat. Camp at fifteen miles.

Monday, May 25th.—Struck tents at 4 a. m. Moved in to Carlton. Reached here at 4 p. m.; a fine place, good land.

Tuesday, May 26th.—Fort Carlton. Got on board the steamer *Marquis*, a fine boat bound for Battleford. Made two hours before night when we had to stop; the boats cannot travel after dark; slept on the hurricane deck.

Wednesday, May 27th.—Got up steam at 3 a.m., and started again. This is a fine river, nothing occurred on the passage. Reached Battleford at 9.30 p.m. All well. Slept on the boat all night.

Thursday, May 28th.—Encamped at Battleford this a.m. It is a fine place, between the Battle river and the Saskatchewan. The camp is badly scattered. Had an invitation to a "Queen's Own" concert at night; it was a good thing; a lot of the Queen's Own and C. Company thought I was killed at Batoche; there was great handshaking when we arrived.

Friday, May 29th.—Nothing new, only drill in the morning. Saw some Indians come in and give themselves up. Had a swim in the river.

Saturday, May 30th.—Nothing new. An order was issued for divine service to-morrow. Soon afterwards orders were issued for *reveille* at four, breakfast at 4.30. Fatigue party all night.

Sunday, May 31st.—Got on the *Marquis* at 8 a.m. for Fort Pitt. The old column, the Queen's Own, feel bad that they are not with us. We are in a pretty rough place; horses and so on all over the deck. During the afternoon we barricaded the boat with planks out of the hold; did not get much sleep all night.

Monday, June 1st.—On boat all day. Nothing new. A fine river; got stuck sometimes. Woodruffe broke his arm; another man was kicked down the hold.

Tuesday, June 2nd.—Landed four miles from Fort Pitt. A fine country, but Big Bear cleared out. He won't show fight. Returned with the men on foot, not able to follow the Indians.

No record was kept from June 2nd to 12th inclusive. It continues:—

13th, 14th, and 15th Nothing new.

16th. General returned.

17th. Nothing new.

18th. General went away again with the mounted men, and Colonel Williams went on the boat to Frog Lake with his men.

19th. Some of Big Bear's prisoners came in.

20th. Nothing.

21st, 22nd, and 23rd. McLean came in, the last of Big Bear's prisoners.

24th. The General returned.

25th, 26th, 27th. General Strange returned with all

the men but one company of the 65th. On the 14th No. 1 Company, including myself, went to Frog Lake; bad place for flies. On the 15th the Toronto stores came in. On the 17th we returned to camp, relieved by a company of the Midlanders.

28th June. Had a review and sports in the evening.

29th. Nothing.

30th. Nothing

July 1st. Had a review and more sports.

July 2nd. Nothing, only the last Company of the 65th came down from Edmonton on the boat.

July 3rd, Friday. The whole of the infantry but the 92nd embarked on board boats for home, the mounted men having already left by rail. The 65th in the *Baroness*, the 90th and Grenadiers, and one company of the 92nd on the *Marquis*. The Midlanders on the *North-West* started for home on Saturday morning, July 4th. One of the 65th died during the night of the 3rd. All went well with us till about nine o'clock when we got stuck on a sand-bar. The *North-West* came alongside and took us on board. Whilst we were on board Colonel Williams died. He had been sick for five days. Got off the bar and went on again. Got strnck three times more; had to tie up for the night. Reached Battleford on Sunday morning early; took Colonel Williams' body ashore with that of the 65th man. We lay there all day, went to the Fort and all over; took on board the G. G. F. G. The *North-West* took on board the Q. O. R. A Battery man was accidentally shot while we lay at Battleford.

Monday, 6th July. Started at daybreak. All three

boats got stuck several times. Tied up for the night.

Tuesday, 7th July. Started at daybreak. Very cold and windy. Stopped at Telegraph coulee there and took on supplies. Found a company of the 7th there; went on again, passed Fort Carlton and tied up for the night.

Wednesday, 8th July. Started at daybreak; still very cold; reached Prince Albert at 9 a.m. Went ashore; saw Big Bear and his son, and his counsellor. They were led out in chains. Left there at noon and made the Forks at about 4 p.m. Stayed there all night with the *Alberta*, which was there with all the sick. Wilson and Eagar were on board here.

Thursday, 9th July. Started at daybreak with the *Alberta*. Saw a few Indians on the banks of the river; tied up for the night. Great fun on board.

Friday, 10th July. Started at daybreak; had great fun with the canoes; went down the river and tied up for the night. The land here a little stony; lots of Indians.

Saturday, 11th July. Started at daybreak. Reached the lake at noon; crossed it and lay to for the night. The lake is about twenty miles across and deep and dangerous, but very pretty with islands.

Sunday, 12th July. Started at daybreak and reached Grand Rapids about 7 o'clock a.m. Unloaded on the tram cars and went to the lake boats about four miles distant. Embarked there on a scow with the Queen's Own; and lay there all night.

Monday, 13th July. Started across Lake Winnipeg in the morning; had it rough that night; a most miserable night; no place to lie down. Nos. 1 and 3 Companies in the hold.

Tuesday, 14th July. Still on the lake, but better weather. A fine lake with islands on it; sometimes out of sight of land. Still on the lake about nine o'clock; entered the Red River, a very poor river, marsh each side. About fifteen miles up we reached Selkirk, landed, and had a lunch that was prepared for us; the Midland got drunk and began to fight about three o'clock. The Midland and 65th left for home; ourselves and the Queen's and G.G.F.G. for Winnipeg, which place we reached at about six o'clock. Landed and had an address from the Mayor, Premier, and others. Had to stand with our packs on for an hour, then march about a mile and pitch camp on the prairie. It began to rain before we had our tents up, and rained all night hard; all of the tents were flooded, and no supper to eat; very miserable indeed.

NOTES.—On June 3rd Major-General Middleton ordered a detachment of 150 men from the column to form a special expeditionary force to go in pursuit of Big Bear and the white prisoners he had with him. Seventy-five men were contributed by the Grenadiers towards this force, under the command of Captain F. A. Caston, with Lieutenant Percy Eliot as subaltern. The detachment succeeded in rescuing the prisoners, but Big Bear eluded capture for a short period longer.

I have not wished to break the continuity of the foregoing diary, so have given it, with but few eliminations, (and those only because they referred to purely personal matters), just as it was written from end to end.

192   HISTORY OF THE ROYAL GRENADIERS.

The following extract from a letter written by Sergeant Francis, dated "Camp Fort Pitt, June 19th, 1885," contains much interesting information, and must be read in connection with the diary:—

"I see by the papers that we get from Toronto that you are all a little mixed up as far as the final charge from Batoche is concerned. Some papers say that the Midland Regiment made the charge, some say the 90th ; neither are right. The way we left the entrenchment was this: The whole of the Grenadiers formed up and marched out of the entrenchment, and then No. 1 Company got the order to extend six paces from the left, by which means we should have taken in the rifle pits on our right. No. 4 Company got the order to prolong the line to the left, which means that they would extend six paces, and then come up on our left. No. 3 Company was told off as our support; No. 2 Company as the support of No. 4 Company. After a time they got the order to extend and join No. 1 Company of the Midland, who were lying in those trenches. They had got the order to extend to the left, which they did, they then formed the left of the line. Two companies then of the 90th got the order to extend to the right and help us, which they did. We were in the centre all the time, for the 90th were away out on our right, and forty men of the Midland on our left on the river bank. They did not charge across the plain at all. The 90th came across the plain, but as they were so much to the right or had so much further to come before they could get to the houses, that we had them all taken before either the 90th or the Midland could possibly reach us. The Battery and the

NORTH-WEST EXPEDITION.

1 Lieut. Michie
2 Capt. Caston
3 Lieut. Eliot
4 Capt. Harston
6 Rev. C. E. Whitcombe
7 Capt. Manley
8 Ass. Surgeon Ryerson
9 Lieut.-Col. Grasett
11 Major Dawson
12 Lieut. Morrow
13 Lieut. Hay
14 Lieut. Gibson
16 Lieut. Lowe
17 Capt. Spencer
18 Lieut. Fitch
19 Capt. Mason

Gatling guns did us good service that day. No. 1 Company must have been in the hottest of the fight, for out of the ten men wounded in our battalion, six of them were out of my own company; anyway I know it was warm enough for me for a time."

Attached to the three columns were numbers of young men who had volunteered for hospital work in any capacity, either as dressers, bearers, or ambulance men. For the most part these were students at the various medical schools in Toronto, who were anxious for work and experience. They performed their duty admirably, working hand in hand with the regular troops, and earning great praise for themselves. The Surgeon-General, in his report after Batoche to the Minister of Militia, thus speaks of them:

* * * * *

"Many of these young men did noble work, regardless of danger. Where the bullets flew thickest, with a heroism that has never been exceeded, they were to be found, removing the wounded and the dying to places of shelter and safety in the rear. Some cases of individual heroism are reported to me, which I feel, call for more than a passing remark, and embolden me to say that among these non-combatant lads and the staff to which they belonged, are to be found some of the greatest heroes of the war. At Batoche I am told that during the fight a flag was thrust from the window of the church, and was observed by a surgeon and a student, who were under shelter from the fire at a couple of hundred yards distance. The student, immediately he perceived it, proposed that a party should at once go to the relief of the one demanding succor. No one appeared willing to second his proposal. To go to the church through the open under such a terrible fire as was being poured from the Half-breed pits seemed to be like proceeding to certain death, but persisting, the surgeon said, 'if you are determined to go, and we can find two volunteers to assist us in carrying a stretcher, I am with you.' Two men from the Grenadiers of Toronto at once stepped forward, and the four started upon their perilous journey, crawling upon their bellies, taking advantage of any little inequality of ground to cover them, and to shield them from the bullets of the Half-breeds. They reached the church, the bullets tearing up the earth all around them, without a scratch, and breathing a short prayer of thankfulness for their deliverance thus far from death and danger, they looked around for him whom they had risked, and were still risking, their lives, to succor and to save. They found him in the person of a venerable priest, who had been wounded in the thigh, and they at once proceeded to remove him, after administering temporary aid. To remain in the church was to court certain death. To return to their corps seemed to be no less perilous, but they chose the latter. When they sortied from the church, so astonished were the Half-breeds at their daring, that they ceased their fire for a moment. This time returning, they had no cover, and were obliged to march erect. Bullets flew thick and fast, but the condition of the wounded man precluded anything like hurry, and they hastened slowly. God watched over them, and protected them, and they reached their comrades in safety, their wounded charge also escaping without further harm. Such conduct deserves recognition, and I beg respectfully to call attention to it in this especial way."

* * * * *

The names of the two Grenadiers referred to in the Surgeon-General's report unfortunately are not known; the other two were Surgeon Gravely, of No. 1 Field Hospital, and Mr. Norris Worthington, from the same hospital.

The journey from Batoche to Winnipeg is very well described in the diary that has been quoted. But there is one thing the author says nothing about, and that is the high state of discipline the Grenadiers had reached. All through this long march and perilous journey, night alarms were of constant occurrence, and these were always promptly responded to, the men ever being on the *qui vive*, alert quick and obedient to orders. When they were halted, drill, not of half an hour or so, but for two hours at a time, was practised, so when the Royal Grenadiers marched into Winnipeg they were a widely different corps to what they were when, as enthusiastic but somewhat untrained men, they left Toronto three months previously.

The sojourn of the Grenadiers at Winnipeg was not a long one, but though the weather was unpropitious, it was most enjoyable.

On July 23rd, the Grenadiers and the Queen's Own Rifles returned to Toronto, and what a welcome they received. The remainder of the Regiment turned out to receive their comrades, wildly cheering them as they appeared. The heading of the account in one of the papers of the time was this:

TORONTO RECEIVES HER HEROES WITH OPEN ARMS.

And then followed a detailed description of the never-to-be-forgotten scene. All down Yonge-street and along King-street marched the soldiers through crowds, such as have never before or since assembled. The men cheered and cheered again as the troops passed, women from every window on the line of route waved their handkerchiefs or small flags; flowers by hundreds of bunches were thrown at the passing heroes. Nothing was left undone by the people of Toronto to show their citizen soldiery how thoroughly their services were appreciated.

The troops marched to the City Hall, where they were received by the Mayor and Corporation, and addresses presented to them. Afterwards at the drill hall they were dismissed to their homes, which they had not seen for four months previously.

The field force remained embodied for several weeks after its return to Toronto, nearly two months elapsing before they rejoined their respective companies in the regiments to which they belonged.

On September 19th, 1885, appeared these Regimental Orders, upon which it is not necessary to make any comment, they were as follows:

" No. 1. The Service Companies of the regiment will be broken up from the 21st inst., and the officers and men composing them will rejoin the companies to which they were posted or attached prior to Regimental Order No. 2, of the 28th March last.

" No. 2. The Lieut.-Colonel commanding desires to take this opportunity of placing on record his high appreciation of the services rendered by all ranks during the recent expedition to the Northwest, and he feels sure that it must be a source of true pride to every officer, non-commissioned officer and man in the regiment to know that their conduct while on active service has met with the approval, not only of Lieut.-Colonel von Straubenzie, who commanded the Infantry Brigade, but also of Major-General Sir Frederick Middleton, C.B., K.C.M.G., who, as Commander-in-Chief of the Forces in the Field, brought the operations to such a successful issue, (vide Field Force Orders, dated Fort Pitt, July 2nd, 1885).

" It therefore only remains to Lieut.-Colonel Grasett to express his grateful thanks to the officers, non-commissioned officers and men, for their ready support and hearty co-operation under all circumstances, which so materially conduced to lighten the responsibility inseparable from the position of Commanding Officer.

OFFICIAL INSPECTION. 197

"Lieut.-Colonel Grasett also desires to sincerely thank those who remained in Toronto for all they did in connection with the regiment, and it will ever be remembered with pleasure, how anxious those in reserve were to join their comrades in arms at the front, when it seemed probable that their services might be required."

On October 28th, 1885, the Regimental Orders contained this announcement:

"It is hereby notified that authority has been received for the Non-commissioned officers of the regiment to wear their chevrons on both arms, as a special case."

The official inspection of the Grenadiers by Major-General Middleton took place on Thursday, November 12th, Lieutenant-Colonel Grasett being in command. The inspection passed off most successfully.

In accordance with District Order, dated November 24th, 1885, the undermentioned officers, non-commissioned officers and men attended the Medical Board, ordered to assemble in the drill shed, on Tuesday, December 1st, 1885, at one o'clock p.m., for the purpose of having their claims for compensation investigated. All concerned were notified to attend by the officers commanding the companies to which they belonged.

Capt. Mason.   Lieut. Morrow.
Priv. Bradford.   Priv. Marshall.
" Billinghurst.   " Martin.
" Cane.   " Milsom.
" Cantwell.   " McIlvean.
" Cook.   " Quigley.
" Eager.   " Scovell.
Corp. Faragher.   " Stead.

Corp. Foley.
Priv. Gaughan.
" Gray.
Priv. Tyler.
" Woodroffe.

Assistant-Surgeon Ryerson will attend the Board.

The story of the Northwest Expedition has hitherto filled up the whole of the regimental history of the Grenadiers for the year 1885, and the promotions and appointments in the commissioned ranks have not been given, they were as follows :—

HEAD QUARTERS,
OTTAWA, 6th February, 1885.
GENERAL ORDERS.
ACTIVE MILITIA.

No. 4. Tenth Battalion Royal Grenadiers.

To be Captains : Lieutenant R. G. Trotter, V.B., vice Harrison, promoted.

Lieutenant F. J. Gosling, V.R., vice J. H. Patterson, resigned.

To be Lieutenants : 2nd Lieutenant Granville Percival Eliot, S.I., vice Trotter, promoted.

2nd Lieutenant Forbes Michie, S.I., vice Gosling promoted.

To be 2nd Lieutenant, provisionally, William S. Lowe, Esquire, vice McDonald, resigned.

HEAD QUARTERS,
OTTAWA, 27th February, 1885.
GENERAL ORDERS.
ACTIVE MILITIA.

No. 4. Tenth Battalion, Royal Grenadiers.

To be Lieutenant : 2nd Lieutenant William Charles Fitch, S.I., vice Paterson, promoted.

The resignation of Captain Peter Brown Ball, is hereby accepted.

HEAD QUARTERS,
OTTAWA, 10th April, 1885.

GENERAL ORDERS.

ACTIVE MILITIA.

No. 4. Tenth Battalion, Royal Grenadiers.

To be Captain, from 27th February, 1885: Lieutenant Charles Greville Harston, formerly Lieutenant in the Royal Marine Light Infantry, *vice* Ball, resigned.

NOTE.—In General Order No. 3 of same date, the Battalion was ordered for actual service in the Northwest Territories, and in accordance with these orders proceeded to the front. The story has already been told.

HEAD QUARTERS,
OTTAWA, 16th October, 1885.

GENERAL ORDERS, (23).

ACTIVE MILITIA.

No. 3. Tenth Battalion, Royal Grenadiers.

To be Lieutenants: 2nd Lieutenant, John Morrow, S.I., *vice* Harston, promoted.

2nd Lieutenant John Dunlop Hay, S.I., *vice* William Charles Fitch, killed in action.

To be 2nd Lieutenant, provisionally, Albert Edward Gooderham, Esq., *vice* Morrow, promoted.

The resignation of Lieutenant G. H. Symons is hereby accepted.

HEAD QUARTERS,
OTTAWA, 30th October, 1885.

GENERAL ORDERS (24.)

ACTIVE MILITIA.

No. 4. Tenth Battalion, Royal Grenadiers.

To be 2nd Lieutenant, provisionally : Charles Edward Burch, Esquire, *vice* Hay, promoted.

The resignation of 2nd Lieutenant (provisionally) Leonard Edward Leigh, is hereby accepted.

Nothing further of any moment occurred in connection with the Royal Grenadiers in 1885. Throughout the winter of 1885-86 there were many social gatherings among the officers N.C.O's. and men of the regiment, but they were more of a private than of a public nature.

The first order for 1886 concerning the regimental parades was this:

HEAD QUARTERS, ROYAL GRENADIERS,
March 1st, 1886.

REGIMENTAL ORDERS.

No. 1. The regiment will commence the annual drill on Thursday, April 1st, when it will parade in drill order with leggings at 8 o'clock p.m., and will also parade on every subsequent Thursday at the same hour unless otherwise ordered. The recruits will assemble on Tuesday, March 9th, at 8 o'clock p.m.

The promotions and appointments to the commissioned ranks of the Grenadiers in 1886 were these :

HEAD QUARTERS,
GENERAL ORDERS. OTTAWA, 29th January, 1886.
ACTIVE MILITIA.

No. 2. Tenth Battalion, Royal Grenadiers.

To be Lieutenant : 2nd Lieutenant Alexander Cecil Gibson, S.I., *vice* Symons, resigned.

HEAD QUARTERS,
GENERAL ORDERS. OTTAWA, 7th May, 1886.
ACTIVE MILITIA.

No. 3. Tenth Battalion, Royal Grenadiers,

To be Quarter Master: Robert Baldwin Ellis, *vice* Bethune.

HEAD QUARTERS,
GENERAL ORDERS. OTTAWA, 21st May, 1886.
ACTIVE MILITIA.

Tenth Battalion, Royal Grenadiers.

To be 2nd Lieutenant, provisionally: Alfred Buell Cameron, Gentleman, *vice* Leigh, resigned.

HEAD QUARTERS,
GENERAL ORDERS. OTTAWA, 4th June, 1886.
ACTIVE MILITIA.

No. 2. Tenth Battalion, Royal Grenadiers.

To be 2nd Lieutenant, provisionally : William Geoffrey Austin Lambe, *vice* Hay, promoted.

To be Surgeon: Assistant Surgeon George Sterling Ryerson, M.D., *vice* J. H. McCollum, resigned.

To be Assistant Surgeon : Edmond Eleazar King, Esq., M.D., *vice* Ryerson, promoted.

HEAD QUARTERS,
OTTAWA, 2nd September, 1886.
CONFIRMATION OF RANK.

2nd Lieutenant Albert Edward Gooderham, S.I., 10th Batt. from 30th June, 1886.

HEAD QUARTERS,
OTTAWA, 17th September, 1886.
GENERAL ORDERS.
ACTIVE MILITIA.

No. 3. Tenth Battalion, Royal Grenadiers.

To be Captain: Lieutenant John I. Davidson, V. B., *vice* John Weir Anderson, retired retaining rank.

To be Lieutenant: 2nd Lieutenant William Standish Lowe, S.I., *vice* Davidson, promoted.

HEAD QUARTERS,
OTTAWA, 22nd October, 1886.
GENERAL ORDERS.
ACTIVE MILITIA.
No. 3. Tenth Battalion, Royal Grenadiers.

The resignation of Captain Francis James Gosling is hereby accepted.

The first Regimental church parade of the year took place to St. Luke's church on Sunday, April 25th. There was a very good muster, nearly the whole of the corps being present.

On May 13th, 1886, the medals awarded to the officers and men of the Grenadiers for their services in the Northwest, were publicly presented to them in the Queen's Park, Toronto, by Lady Middleton. A Toronto paper of May 14th thus describes the scene:

" How many a gallant red coat thought with pleasure, not unmixed with pain, of that day twelve months before, pleasure at the victory of Batoche and the way the Grens. proved themselves—but pain at the cost of it all. No better day than this the 13th of May, 1886, it was indeed all that could be desired, and Toronto you might say was *en fete*. Shortly after 3.30 the " fall in " sounded, and after companies had been proved, Col. Grasett took command and headed by their fine band the Royal Grenadiers, accompanied by immense crowds, it is astonishing what an attraction a scarlet coat is to the civilian, and, well, we won't say, to the dear girls who are there with delight on their faces. Swinging into line on the left of the Queens Own, all awaited the General. At 4.45 p.m. Gen. Sir Fred. Middleton arrived accompanied

THE LATE CAPT. G. PERCY ELIOT.

THE LATE CAPT. A. M. IRVING.

THE NORTH-WEST MEDAL.
(Obverse.)

THE NORTH-WEST MEDAL.
(Reverse.)

by Capt. Wise, A. D. C., and Lt.-Cols. R. B. Denison, D.A.G.; Milsom, B.-Major, and Otter, Commandant C Co. Infantry School, late Commander of the Battleford Column.

"Dismounting, the General took his position on the platform, on which also were Lady Middleton, and other ladies. Some delay was caused by the crowd, who pressed so close that Lady Middleton could not get near the troops, or could they come to the platform. At last space was cleared, but gently, as all Toronto seemed eager to get a medal, for the interest they felt in their boys. About 5 o'clock Gen. Middleton stepped up to the table where Lady Middleton pinned the first medal on his breast, as cheer after cheer went up for the gallant leader. The next was his A.D.C., Capt. Wise, then came Col. Otter and other staff officers. When the turn of the Royal Grenadiers came, Lady Middleton walked over to where they were and pinned the medals on the officer's breasts."

Afterwards the medals for the N.C.O.'s and men were handed to them and on the conclusion of the ceremony the regiment re-formed into column, and after three cheers had been given for the Queen and the General, returned to the drill shed.

The battalion had evidently acquired a taste for northern travel for they decided to make Barrie their destination on the Queen's Birthday, in 1886, and on May 20th, the commanding officer issued the following order:

HEAD QUARTERS, ROYAL GRENADIERS,
May 20th, 1886.

REGIMENTAL ORDERS.

No. 1. Instructions for proposed visit to Barrie for

Queen's Birthday. The regiment will parade in marching order, (with leggings) without haversacks or water-bottles, Saturday, 22nd inst., at 3.15 p.m. and go by special train to destination. Tickets, $1.00 each will be issued to officers commanding companies, to be accounted for on Tuesday, 26th inst., there will be no charge for accommodation or subsistance while in Barrie. The regiment will leave Barrie, Monday evening, so as to reach Toronto about 9 p.m. Knapsacks issued to each man to carry field kit. Each squad to have necessary supply of clothes and blacking-brushes and blacking. All to have forage caps to be carried in place of mess tin.

The regiment duly proceeded to Barrie and the following are the orders as issued there:

HEAD QUARTERS, ROYAL GRENADIERS,
BARRIE, 23rd May, 1886.

REGIMENTAL ORDERS.

Detail. Captain of the day, to-morrow, Capt. Spencer.
        Subt'n   "   "   Lieut. Gibson.
        R.O. Serg't "   "   Sergt. Jack.
        R.O. Corp.   "   "   Cor. Stainsby.

No. 1. The Regiment will parade in drill order at 7.am.

No. 2. The regiment will parade in review order at 9.45 a.m.

No. 3. Blankets folded and packed in bales, and returned into Quarter Master's store before 7 a.m.

The regiment will parade in marching order to return home at 5.45 p.m.

Drill ceased with this visit for the summer months, until the following order was promulgated:

HEAD QUARTERS, ROYAL GRENADIERS,
TORONTO, 23rd Aug., 1886.

REGIMENTAL ORDERS.

No. 1. The regiment will re-assemble for drill on Thursday, Sept. 2nd, when it will parade at the armoury in drill order, with leggings, at 8 o'clock p.m., and also on each subsequent Thursday at same hour and place, until further orders.

A most efficient officer of the Grenadiers was compelled to sever his connection with the regiment towards the end of 1886, this was the Rev. C. E. Whitcombe, and his departure was marked by the following Regimental Order:

Sept. 30th, 1886.

" The Lieutenant-Colonel commanding announces with regret that the Rev. Chas. E. Whitcombe, who was appointed Chaplain to the regiment in the field, and who has acted in that capacity since the return of the regiment from active service, has been obliged to sever his connection with the battalion, owing to intended removal from Toronto. Lieut.-Colonel Grasett is sure that he expresses the feelings of all ranks when he says that the regiment is under many obligations to Mr. Whitcombe for his kindly ministrations while Chaplain of the Royal Grenadiers."

The annual inspection of the regiment by the Major-General commanding the Canadian Militia took place on Saturday, October 30th, 1886, and was satisfactory in its results. Drill then ceased for the year, and was not resumed until Thursday, April 14th, 1887, a somewhat later date than usual.

There were very few alterations among the ranks of the officers in the Grenadiers in 1887, what they were are as follows :—

HEAD QUARTERS,
OTTAWA, 29th April, 1887.

GENERAL ORDERS.
ACTIVE MILITIA.

No. 1. Tenth Battalion, Royal Grenadiers.

To be Captains: Lieutenant Donald Macdonald Howard, *vice* Gosling, resigned.

Lieutenant Granville Percival Eliot, S.I., *vice* Oliph Leigh Leigh-Spencer, retired retaining rank.

To be Lieutenant: 2nd Lieutenant Albert E. Gooderham, S.I., *vice* Andrew Maxwell Irving, resigned.

To be 2nd Lieutenant, provisionally: W. F. Godson, Esquire, *vice* Gooderham, promoted.

HEAD QUARTERS,
OTTAWA, 16th September, 1887.

GENERAL ORDERS.
ACTIVE MILITIA.

No. 4. Tenth Battalion, Royal Grenadiers.

Memo—Adverting to No. 1 of General Orders, 29th April, 1887, in which the resignation is accepted of Lieutenant Andrew Maxwell Irving, *read* "who is hereby permitted to retire retaining rank," *instead of* "whose resignation is hereby accepted."

One of the most noticeable events in the social life of the Royal Grenadiers, took place on February 17th, 1887, it being the ball given by Lieutenant Colonel Grasett and the officers of the regiment to the citizens of Toronto, in recognition of the kindness shown, and aid given to the corps from the city while the Grenadiers were on active service. It was one of the most unique, as well as one of the most brilliant and successful events held in Toronto for many years. All of the arrangements were made on a scale of magnificence seldom attempted, and were carried out to perfection. The success was worthy of the circumstances the ball was designed to celebrate, the patriotic feeling called forth by the Northwest troubles.

In the fall of 1885, when the regiment returned from the Northwest from active service, the officers were desirous of giving a public entertainment to the ladies of Toronto, to show their appreciation of the kind manner in which the ladies looked after the wives and families of the men, and after the men's own comfort in sending them clothing and supplies. That winter the idea was abandoned, owing to a bereavement in Colonel Grasett's family, but taken up again in 1886-87, and a ball decided on as the most fitting mode. The work of decoration, undertaken by Mr. Clark, of Jno. Kay & Co., justified the choice of the decorator, and the work presented a scene of rare beauty.

A guard of honor of 60 men was formed in the centre of the hall, facing inwards, five paces apart. As the guests arrived they passed between the ranks and were received at the front by Lieut.-Col. Grasett and Mrs. Dawson.

Shortly before 10 o'clock, an avenue was forced through the company to the dais, for the Lieut.-Governor, who was received by a general salute, the band playing "God save the Queen."

His Honor's party included Mrs. Beverley Robinson,

Captain and Mrs. Forsyth Grant, Captain Geddes and Miss Robinson. When Major General Sir Fred. Middleton and party arrived, the guard again presented arms, the band playing the general salute. Accompanying General Middleton were Lady Middleton, Col. and Mrs. Otter, Captain Wise, A.D.C., Miss Crookes, Lieut. Sears, and Miss Otter. The first set in the opening quadrille was composed of the following :—Gen. Middleton and Mrs. Ryerson, The Lieut.-Governor and Mrs. Dawson, Col. Grasett and Miss Robinson, Col. Otter and Mrs. Goldwin Smith, Lt.-Col. Fred. Denison and Mrs. Mason, Major Dawson and Lady Middleton, Major Harrison and Mrs. D'Alton McCarthy, Major Smith (7th Battalion) and Mrs. Harston.

Supper was served in a large annexe off the north aisle specially erected for the occasion.

The officers of the Grenadiers wore mourning badges in memory of Lieutenant Fitch who was killed at Batoche.

It was estimated that between 500 and 600 couples were present.

The invited guests came from far and near, and never before had there been such a gathering of representatives of fair Canada socially. Cabinet Ministers from Ottawa, ministers of all denominations and cities, society people from Ottawa, Manitoba, Regina, N.W.T., Quebec, Montreal, Kingston, London, St. Catharines, Halifax, N.S., Brantford, Barrie, Buffalo and Elmira, N.Y., Victoria, B.C.

Of the ladies dresses, it must content us to say that as each one came in view each appeared the better and all were wonderfully lovely creations.

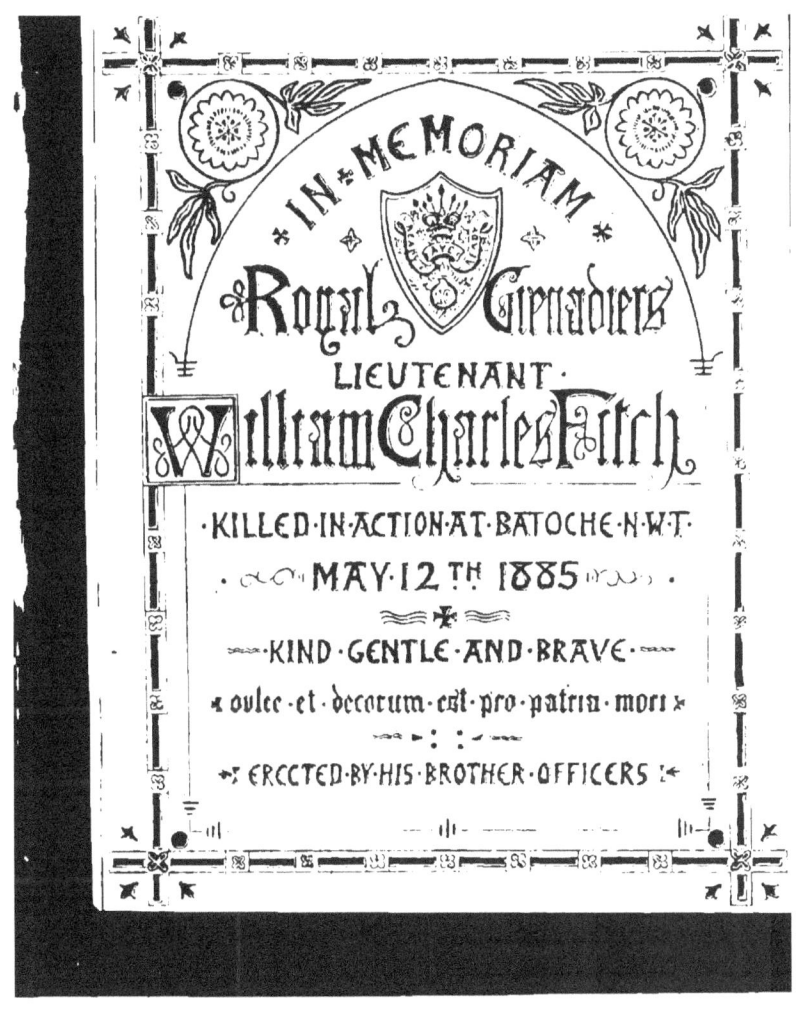

THE TABLET IN ST. JAMES' CATHEDRAL, TORONTO, IN HONOR OF LIEUT.

One great want experienced by the officers of the Grenadiers to this date was the insufficient mess room accommodation they were able to obtain, this was in some measure rectified early in 1887, when this intimation appeared in Regimental Orders :

HEAD QUARTERS, ROYAL GRENADIERS,
TORONTO, March 30th, 1887.

Memo—The officers are informed that the new regimental and mess rooms, 42 King St. East, will be opened on Saturday, April 2nd, on which occasion the Mess Committee hope that every officer will make it his business to be present.

Memories of the Northwest campaign and of its results are brought back by the following extract from the Order Book of the regiment:

HEAD QUARTERS, ROYAL GRENADIERS,
TORONTO, May 10th, 1887.

REGIMENTAL ORDERS.

No. 1. The regiment will parade in review order (without side arms) on Sunday, May 15th inst., at 3 o'clock p.m., in the Queen's Park (north), and attend divine service at Mount Pleasant Cemetery, where the memorial to Privates Moore and Hughes will also be unveiled.

At this parade there was a very large attendance, every member of the corps feeling it to be specially his duty to be present.

On May 24th, the Grenadiers proceeded to the Queen's Park, and there " trooped " the Queen's color before His Excellency, the Governor-General, and amidst an enormous concourse of spectators. The scene was a most impressive one, and called forth from the facile pen of Mrs. J. W. F. Harrison, the following stirring lines, supposed to be the utterances of an old guardsman, a Waterloo veteran:—

> Come! What are ye waitin' there for?
>   Don't ye 'ear what the people say?
> Don't ye want to join the procession?
>   Don't you know its the Queen's birthday?
> If I was the one as faltered,
>   And grumbled and looked kind o' black,
> It might be forgiven me surely,
>   With ninety years at my back.
> But, there! I'm as willin' as ever,
>   Although I can't 'ear 'em play,
> To join with the band in singin'
>   "God Save 'Er," on 'er birthday!
>
> She's sixty-eight and I'm ninety;
>   We're both gettin' on, I know,
> She's the Duke o' Kent's little daughter,
>   I mind 'er openin' show.
> 'Twas in the black old Abbey—
>   How the London crowd did pour
> 'Long the Strand from dock and city,
>   And cheered 'er at the door!
> And I was there, and your father,
>   And we both elbowed our way
> To the side o' the Royal Carriage
>   On the Coronation Day!
>
> She give us a smile, I remember
>   And we came away satisfied,
> I see 'er next at 'er weddin',
>   With Prince Albert at 'er side.
> I didn't sulk and grumble
>   As some o' you young uns do.
> I'd been used to crowds afore—why, boy!
>   I was at Waterloo;

And in crowds, mind, do as I do,
　　Just push and fight your way ;
Or ye'll find—'ere, boy ! your arm, lad
　　Pretty work on a Queen's Birthday !

They had almost ridden me down, like,
　　'Tis a pity old folks can't 'ear,
But my sight is as good as ever,
　　And there goes a Grenadier !
A splendid fellow he is, too—
　　A chip off the fine old block,
And 'ere is the Governor-General,
　　Sharp to his 'leven o'clock !
Ay, ay, but it takes me back, lad,
　　And England seems far away,
And I wish I could cheer as I'd like to
　　For 'er Sixty-Eighth Birthday.

But you—why, I'm 'alf ashamed o' ye !
　　Ye don't give as lusty a cheer
As me, with my bent old shoulders,
　　As me with my ninety year !
Ye've got hold o' new ideas ;
　　"Beant English "—well, that may be ;
Yes " wan't born in England,"—
　　But your father was—and me,
And ye live in the Queen's Dominions,
　　And ye owe her every way,
And it's nothin' more than duty,
　　To cheer on the Queen's Birthday.

For what if your mother was Irish,
　　And what if ye don't just like
The ways of some around ye,
　　And feel sort o' set on strike !
Take me—I come out in—'40
　　To this 'ere Canadian land,
And there's many things as I know
　　I don't yet 'alf understand—
Why the Quality's twice as 'aughty,

> Why the Parks must be sold away,
> And why we must drink in water
>   'Er 'ealth on the Queen's Birthday.
>
> But though I'm a loyal Briton,
>   I love the new land, too ;
>   *   *   *   *
>
> 'Tis a fair young land, in truth, lad,
>   Look around, and ye'll see how fair,
> With the glory o' springtime grasses,
>   With the chestnut smell in the air,
> Why, a prettier spot than this, lad,
>   And people in finer array,
> Could 'ardly be found in old England,
>   A-keepin' the Queen's Birthday !
>
> And we look to all you youngsters
>   To keep your land fair and young,
> To take no man for a leader,
>   As hasn't an honest tongue.
> There, watch the eddykongs gallop !
>   And 'ark to the British cheer !
>   *   *   *   *
>
> And I wish that the Queen 'erself was
>   Able to see the display,
> And the loyal crowds as is keepin'
>   'Er Sixty-Eighth Birthday !

Twice in June of 1887 did the Grenadiers make what may be termed "official" appearances. It is a somewhat unusual thing for any summer parades to be held after that which takes place on the Queen's Birthday, which had been held as has been told.

The two following Regimental Orders will explain the reason for these additional parades :

THE LATE MAJOR A. B. GARRISON.

HEAD QUARTERS ROYAL GRENADIERS,
TORONTO, June 10th, 1887.

REGIMENTAL ORDERS.

No. 1. The Regiment will parade in review order, with leggings, in the Queen's Park, at 2.15 p.m., on Sunday the 15th instant and march to St. James' Cathedral for Divine Service in celebration of *Her Majesty's Jubilee.*

HEAD QUARTERS, ROYAL GRENADIERS,
TORONTO, June 27th, 1887.

REGIMENTAL ORDERS.

No. 1. The Regiment will parade in review order with cross-belts and leggings, at the drill shed, on Friday the 1st prox, at 10.15 a.m., for the purpose of participating in the procession on the occasion of the celebration of *Her Majesty's Jubilee.*

The Annual Inspection of the corps was held on Saturday, November 5th, by the Major-General commanding the district, and like all its predecessors was satisfactory both to the General and for the Grenadiers.

The spring drills for the year 1888 began in the latter end of March, being held on Thursday evenings, as heretofore.

The year was an eventful one in many respects for the Grenadiers, there being some very important changes in the commissioned ranks of the regiment; what these were will be found in the following list.

HEAD QUARTERS,
OTTAWA, 8th May, 1888.

GENERAL ORDERS.

ACTIVE MILITIA.

No. 6. Tenth Battalion, Royal Grenadiers.

To be Captain: Lieutenant Forbes Michie, S. I., *vice* Bruce, appointed paymaster.

To be 2nd Lieutenant: Alfred Buell Cameron, R. S. I., *vice* Albert Edward Gooderham, resigned.

To be 2nd Lieutenant: James Drummond Mackay, M. Q., *vice* Cameron, promoted.

Frederick W. G. Fitzgerald, provisionally, *vice* W. F. Godson, left limits.

To be Paymaster, with honorary rank of Captain: John Bruce, V. B., (formerly Captain,) *vice* Nicol Kingsmill, who, having relative rank of Captain is hereby permitted to retire with honorary rank of Captain.

HEAD QUARTERS,
OTTAWA, 1st June, 1888.

GENERAL ORDERS.

ACTIVE MILITIA.

No. 6. Tenth Battalion, Royal Grenadiers.

Authority has been given this Battalion to wear upon their colors the word "Batoche," in recognition of the corps having been in that engagement during the Northwest Campaign of 1885.

To be Lieut.-Colonel: Major George Dudley Dawson (late Lieut. 47th Ft.), *vice* Henry J. Grasett, retired retaining rank.

To be Lieutenant: Captain John Bayne McLean, G. S. I., from the Adjutancy 31st Battalion, *vice* Michie, promoted.

HEAD QUARTERS,
OTTAWA, 7th September, 1888.

GENERAL ORDERS.

ACTIVE MILITIA.

No. 4. Tenth Battalion, Royal Grenadiers.

To be Major: Captain James Mason, R.S.I., *vice* Dawson, promoted.

To be Captain: Lieutenant John Morrow, S.I., *vice* Mason, promoted.

To be Lieutenant: 2nd Lieutenant James D. McKay, M.Q., *vice* Morrow, promoted.

HEAD QUARTERS,
OTTAWA, 16th November, 1888.

GENERAL ORDERS.

ACTIVE MILITIA.

No. 2. Tenth Battalion, Royal Grenadiers.

To be 2nd Lieutenant, provisionally, from 9th Nov., 1888: John Donald Maclennan, Esquire, *vice* Mackay, promoted.

HEAD QUARTERS,
OTTAWA, 23rd November, 1888.

GENERAL ORDERS.

ACTIVE MILITIA.

No. 2. Tenth Battalion, Royal Grenadiers.

2nd Lieutenant, provisionally, Charles Edward Burch having "failed to qualify," his name is hereby removed from the list of Officers of the Active Militia.

Early in 1888 it became known that Lieut.-Colonel Grasett, would in consequence of his having received an important municipal appointment, have to resign the command of the Grenadiers, and early in April the following R. O. appeared.

HEAD QUARTERS, ROYAL GRENADIERS,
TORONTO, 11th April, 1888.

REGIMENTAL ORDERS.

"No. 1. In accordance with Para. 78 Militia Orders, 1887.

"The transfer of all stores, etc., in charge of the Regiment will be made to Major Dawson at the Armoury on Tuesday next, the 17th inst.

"Officers commanding companies will attend at their respective Armouries on the above date, and will take care to have all Rifles, Bayonets, Pouches, and other equipment (in their possession) ready for inspection. The Quarter Master will also attend with his books."

The Governor-General, Lord Lansdowne, paid his farewell official visit to Toronto prior to his return to England, on May 7th and 8th, 1888. Consequent upon this visit the officer commanding the Grenadiers published the following order :

"HEAD QUARTERS, ROYAL GRENADIERS,
"TORONTO, May 5th, 1888.
" REGIMENTAL MEMO.

" Adverting to District Memo of 3rd inst. The reception of officers of the Garrison, will be held by His Excellency the Governor-General, on Tuesday next, the 8th inst., at Government House, at 5.15 p.m. The commanding officer considers it incumbent on every officer to be present at this the farewell reception of Lord Lansdowne."

It is only necessary to mention in connection with the foregoing order that it was issued, as it " goes without saying " that the officers of the Grenadiers would not fail in paying every respect to the representative of their sovereign.

The church parade of the regiment was held at St. Stephen's church, on Sunday, May 13th, and on May 24th the battalion spent the day in Guelph, where a review was held and the officers and men of the corps entertained afterwards by the inhabitants of the " Royal City."

On June 1st, 1888, Lieutenant-Colonel Henry James Grasett retired from the command of the regiment consequent on his appointment as Chief of Police for Toronto City. A few days later he issued the following dignified valedictory order :

HEAD QUARTERS, ROYAL GRENADIERS,
June 9th, 1888.

No. 3. Lieut.-Colonel Grasett in resigning the command and taking leave of the regiment, desires to place on record his grateful appreciation of the services rendered by all the corps since he was appointed its Lieutenant-Colonel. The success attending the re-organization of the battalion was largely due to the united exertions of the officers and non-commissioned officers combined with the co-operation of the rank and file, without which the attempt would have been a failure. The credit and prestige which the regiment has since gained both in quarters and in the field is the result of discipline, engendering that *esprit de corps* which is so essential to the well-being of every military organization. Lieut.-Colonel Grasett feels sure that by following the same lines the battalion will sustain and increase the high reputation it now enjoys. He congratulates the regiment upon the permission accorded to bear on its colors the honors they gained with such distinction in the face of the enemy, and though tardy was this recognition of its services to the country, it will serve as an incentive for those who come after to do their duty as loyally and as faithfully when occasion demands. Lieut.-Colonel Grasett desires to bespeak for his successor the same measure of confidence and support from all ranks that had been extended to him, and begs to say farewell to the Royal Grenadiers with every expression of gratitude for the past, and a full assurance that they will ever be for Canada "Ready, aye Ready."

By order,

FRED. F. MANLEY,

Capt. and Adjt.

Drill for the autumn of 1888 was resumed on Thursday, September 6th, and was continued until November 15th, when the annual inspection took place, a review being held at the same time in High Park.

Immediately preceding the annual inspection a most pleasing event took place in connection once again with the ladies of Toronto and the Royal Grenadiers.

The Colors of the Regiment had for some time, owing to their time-worn condition been exercising the minds of the Ladies of Toronto. For just twenty-five years these standards had been carried, first by the 10th Royals, and afterwards by the Royal Grenadiers, and they had become very much dilapidated. But other things had also happened since their presentation, the Grenadiers had earned the right to have an "honour" emblazoned on those colors, and so the ladies decided to give themselves what they considered the pleasurable privilege of, so far as possible, repairing the old flags and embroidering on their folds the word "Batoche." This work was accomplished, and on November 13th, 1888, at a grand parade held in the Pavilion of the Horticultural Gardens, the colors were re-presented to the Corps.

The Regiment under the command of Lieut.-Col. Dawson, formed up one-half on each side of the building which was beautifully draped with flags, &c.

To grace the occasion were Gen'l. Sir F. Middleton, Lt.-Col. Otter, Commanding C. Co., Lt.-Col. Grasett, ex-Commanding officer Grenadiers, Lt.-Col. G. T. Denison, G.G.B.G., Lt.-Col. Allen, Q.O.R., Major Delemere, Q.O.R., the Hons. G. W. Allan, G. W. Ross, and the Mayor, Mr. E. F. Clarke.

The Ladies Committee was as follows: Mrs. Cumberland, Mrs. Worthington, Mrs. Warring Kennedy, Mrs. McLean Howard, Mrs. Geo. Gooderham, Mrs. Goldwin Smith, Mrs. Fletcher, Mrs. Dawson, Mrs. Ryerson, Mrs. Mason, Mrs. Davidson, Mrs. Grasett.

His Worship the Mayor, Mr. E. F. Clarke, addressing the commanding officer said: "Col. Dawson, Officers and men of the Royal Grenadiers, I have to congratulate you on behalf of your fellow citizens for the noble name the Regiment has earned. These colours were given you in July, 1863, and the same lady who then presented the Colors to the Regiment will do so now."

Mrs. F. W. Cumberland then came forward, and in clear tones said: "A quarter of a century ago on 7th July, 1863, I had the honor on behalf of the Ladies of Toronto, of presenting these Colors to the Regiment. We have watched with pride and joy the course of the Regiment, and having embroidered the word "Batoche" on their folds, now return them to you with renewed confidence that the Royal Grenadiers will be ever loyal and true, "Ready, aye Ready.'"

Col. Dawson in a few well chosen words warmly thanked Mrs. Cumberland and the Ladies of Toronto, not alone for their addition to the Colors, but for the warm sympathy and good wishes which incited them all to do their best.

Hon. G. W. Allan addressing Lieut.-Col. Dawson and the officers of the Royal Grenadiers, said it gave him great pleasure to be with them on the occasion. He referred to a similar occurrence nearly three-quarters of a century previously, when the ladies of Toronto gave Colors to the "Third Regiment of York Militia," his father being in command of the regiment, whose motto was "Deeds Speak!"

Hon. G. W. Ross then spoke at length on the deeds of the regiment and the pride Canada takes in her militia.

General Middleton was then loudly called upon, and on coming forward said: "I have to apologise for not being in my 'war paint,' that is my military clothes, but had I stopped to change would have been too late for this occasion, which I would not on any account miss." He spoke in flattering terms of the Royal Grenadiers, and said Her Majesty had no more faithful soldiers than they.

With hearty expressions of admiration and good will on every side, the meeting then broke up, and the Royal Grenadiers then returned to their quarters.

There were fewer changes among the officers of the Grenadiers in the next year, 1889, than had been the case in any year since the first formation of the corps in 1860, and with the single exception of that of Captain Tassie to the important post of Quarter Master, they were all junior officers who were gazetted to the battalion. The appointments were these:

HEAD QUARTERS,
OTTAWA, 29th March, 1889.
GENERAL ORDERS.
ACTIVE MILITIA.

No. 7. Tenth Battalion, Royal Grenadiers.

To be 2nd Lieutenants, provisionally, from 19th March, 1889 : Stephen Augustus Heward, Esquire, *vice* Gibson, promoted.

Archibald Hayes McDonell, Esquire, *vice* Lowe promoted.

HEAD QUARTERS,
OTTAWA, 14th June, 1889.
GENERAL ORDERS.
ACTIVE MILITIA.

No. 4. Tenth Battalion, Royal Grenadiers.

To be 2nd Lieutenant, provisionally : Thomas Fraser Homer Dixon, *vice* Burch.

HEAD QUARTERS,
OTTAWA, 27th September, 1889.
GENERAL ORDERS.
ACTIVE MILITIA.

No. 1. Tenth Battalion, Royal Grenadiers.

To be Quarter Master, with honorary rank of Captain : William Tassie Tassie, Esquire, *vice* Robert Baldwin Ellis, resigned.

On Friday, January 4th, 1889, the newly appointed Governor-General of Canada, Lord Stanley of Preston, visited Toronto in order to be present at the annual dinner of the Board of Trade. On this occasion the Guard of Honor was furnished by the Royal Grenadiers. In reference to this incident the following extract from the Regimental records is given:

HEAD QUARTERS, ROYAL GRENADIERS,
TORONTO, 10th January, 1889.
REGIMENTAL ORDERS.

No. 1. The Commanding Officer has great pleasure in publishing the following letter received from Captain Colville, Military Secretary to His Excellency the Governor-General:—

GOVERNMENT HOUSE,
OTTAWA, 7th January, 1889.

SIR,—I am directed by His Excellency the Governor-General to ask you to be good enough to convey to those officers, non-commissioned officers and men of the Regiment under your command, who formed the Guard of Honor on Friday last, January 4th, at the Toronto Board of Trade dinner, his best thanks for volunteering their services on that occasion.

I have the honor to be, Sir,
Your obedient servant,
CHAS. COLVILLE, Captain,
Military Secretary.

The spring drill of the battalion began on April 3rd, and was continued as usual until the Queen's Birthday, when the Regiment went to Berlin for the day. Later the Regiment took part in the festivities held in Toronto on Dominion Day, July 1st.

Sergeants Mitchell and Curzon of the Grenadiers were members of the Wimbledon Rifle team in 1889, and proceeded to England accordingly.

The autumnal drill of the Grenadiers commenced about September 20th, and continued until November 7th, the following being the orders issued for the last parade of the year:

HEAD QUARTERS, ROYAL GRENADIERS,
5th November, 1889.
REGIMENTAL ORDERS.

No. 2. The regiment will parade in drill order, with leggings, at the Armoury on Thursday the 7th inst., at 8.30 p.m., and will proceed by train to grounds west of High Park, where a Field Day will take place, followed by the Annual Inspection by the Major-General commanding the Militia. Fifteen rounds of ammunition will be issued to each man.

An important appointment among the non-commissioned ranks of the Regiment was notified early in the next year, 1890, it was this:

HEAD QUARTERS, ROYAL GRENADIERS,
TORONTO, 4th January, 1890.
REGIMENTAL ORDERS.

No. 2. The Commanding Officer has been pleased to confirm the appointment of James Cox as Sergt.-Major and Warrant Officer (retired).

The year 1890 presented a marked contrast in one respect with that of its predecessor, as there were numerous and important changes among the officers of the regiment, which are here set forth as they occurred:—

HEAD QUARTERS,
OTTAWA, 31st January, 1890.
GENERAL ORDERS.
ACTIVE MILITIA.

No. 2. Tenth Battalion, Royal Grenadiers.

To be Captain: Lieutenant J. D. Hay, S.I., *vice* J. I. Davidson, retired retaining rank.

To be Lieutenants: 2nd Lieutenant F. W. G. Fitzgerald, R.S.I., *vice* Hay, promoted.

2nd Lieutenant Stephen Augustus Heward, R.S.I.

2nd Lieutenant Archibald Hayes Macdonell, R.S.I.

HEAD QUARTERS,
OTTAWA, 18th April, 1890.
GENERAL ORDERS.
ACTIVE MILITIA.

No. 5. Tenth Battalion, Royal Grenadiers.

Captain Charles Greville-Harston, has been permitted to accept the appointment of Honorary Aide-de-Camp to His Honor, the Lieutenant-Governor of the Province of Ontario, to date from 8th March, 1890.

HEAD QUARTERS,
OTTAWA, 5th September, 1890.
GENERAL ORDERS.
ACTIVE MILITIA.

No. 3. Tenth Battalion, Royal Grenadiers, Toronto.

To be 2nd Lieutenant, provisionally: D'Arcy Hugh Kirkland MacMahon, Esq., *vice* F. W. G. Fitzgerald, promoted.

The resignation of 2nd Lieutenant W. Geoffrey Austin Lambe is hereby accepted.

HEAD QUARTERS,
GENERAL ORDERS. OTTAWA, 31st October, 1890.
ACTIVE MILITIA.

No. 2. Tenth Battalion, Royal Grenadiers, Toronto.

To be Lieutenant: 2nd Lieutenant John D. Maclennan, R.S.I., vice F. W. G. Fitzgerald, resigned.

To be 2nd Lieutenant, provisionally: Alexander Claude Forster Bolton, Esq., vice J. D. Maclennan, promoted.

HEAD QUARTERS,
OTTAWA, 31st December, 1890.
GENERAL ORDERS.
ACTIVE MILITIA.

No. 1. Tenth Battalion, Royal Grenadiers, Toronto.

To be Captains: Captain F. F. Manley, V.B., from the Adjutancy vice Donald Macdonald Howard, retired retaining rank.

Lieutenant Alexander Cecil Gibson, S.I., vice J. Morrow, retired retaining rank.

To be Lieutenant: Andrew Maxwell Irving, V.B., from the Retired List of Lieutenants, vice A. C. Gibson, promoted.

To be Adjutant: Lieutenant and Captain John Bayne McLean, G.S.I., vice F. F. Manley, who vacates that appointment.

Captain Howard retired from the regiment to join the Northwest Mounted Police in which he had been appointed Inspector. He had served with the Grenadiers in the Northwest and was a most enthusiastic soldier.

The Regiment paraded on Friday May 30th, 1890, and marched to Front street, forming up in front of the Queen's Hotel, where they were inspected by H.R.H. the

Duke of Connaught, who was passing through Toronto on his way home to England from his Indian Command, having come *via* the C.P.R. from Vancouver. H.R.H. expressed himself afterwards as being highly pleased with the appearance of the regiment, and the approval was duly notified in General Orders.

On June 26th took place in Toronto what was described as "The Carnival." It was a pleasing entertainment, and the Grenadiers took part in the military portion of the pageant.

Staff-Sergeant Frederick Curzon who had served so gallantly in the Northwest campaign of 1885, died on August 13th, 1890, after an illness of three weeks. He was interred with military honours on August 15th, in Mount Pleasant Cemetery. The *Globe* of August 16th remarked in reference to Sergeant Curzon's death:—" It is not often that a military funeral takes place in Toronto, but there are few men deserving such an honour more than the late Staff-Sergeant Curzon, who, while comparatively a young man, had given a decade of his life to the service of his country."

Autumn drill began on September 25th, and concluded on November 6th, when a Field day was held in High Park which proved highly successful.

The following order speaks for itself, and requires no comment. It marks though one more forward step in the regimental history.

HEAD QUARTERS, ROYAL GRENADIERS,
TORONTO, 2nd October, 1890.
REGIMENTAL ORDERS.

No. 5. A Sergeants' Mess being formed in connection

with the Regiment, the Commanding Officer directs that all Staff-Sergeants and Sergeants must be members.

Progress, steady progress, still marked the course of the Royal Grenadiers, for in January, 1891, the battalion was increased in strength from eight to ten companies, and there was not the slighest difficulty in obtaining recruits, in fact, if the regiment had been increased to twelve companies the men would have been forthcoming.

Consequent upon this augmentation, and also from other causes, there were many changes among the officers of the Grenadiers in 1891. Almost every month throughout the year did these occur, they constitute a somewhat long list, which is now given:

HEAD QUARTERS,
OTTAWA, 30th January, 1891.
GENERAL ORDERS.
ACTIVE MILITIA.

No. 3. Tenth Battalion, Royal Grenadiers, Toronto, Ont.

To be 2nd Lieutenant, provisionally: George A. Stimson, Esq., *vice* S. A. Heward, promoted.

HEAD QUARTERS,
OTTAWA, 20th March, 1891.
GENERAL ORDERS.
ACTIVE MILITIA.

No. 1. Tenth Battalion, Royal Grenadiers, Toronto, Ont.

To be Captains: Lieutenant W. Standish Lowe, S.I., on augmentation.

Francis James Gosling, Esquire, S.I., on augmentation.

To be 2nd Lieutenant, provisionally : Alexander James Boyd, Esquire, *vice* A. H. Macdonell, promoted.

HEAD QUARTERS,
OTTAWA, 24th April, 1891.

GENERAL ORDERS.

ACTIVE MILITIA.

No. 4. Tenth Battalion, Royal Grenadiers.

To be 2nd Lieutenant, provisionally : Arthur Robert Sweatman, Esquire, *vice* W. G. A. Lambe, resigned.

Major James Mason is permitted to retire, retaining rank.

HEAD QUARTERS,
OTTAWA, 22nd May, 1891.

GENERAL ORDERS.

ACTIVE MILITIA.

No. 1. Tenth Battalion, Royal Grenadiers.

To be Captain : Lieutenant A. B. Cameron, R.S.I., *vice* Forbes Michie, deceased.

Lieutenant and Captain J. B. McLean, Adjutant, with seniority immediately next to and below Captain A. B. Cameron.

To be Lieutenant : 2nd Lieutenant D'Arcy Hugh Kirkland MacMahon, R.S.I., *vice* W. S. Lowe, promoted.

To be 2nd Lieutenant, provisionally : Wm. Lehmann, Esq., *vice* D'A. H. K. MacMahon, promoted.

HEAD QUARTERS,
OTTAWA, 26th June, 1891.

GENERAL ORDERS.

ACTIVE MILITIA.

No. 1. Tenth Battalion, Royal Grenadiers.

To be 2nd Lieutenant, provisionally: Wm. R. Pringle, Esq, *vice* T. F. Homer Dixon, transferred to 7th Battalion.

HEAD QUARTERS,
GENERAL ORDERS.   OTTAWA, 16th July, 1891.
ACTIVE MILITIA.

No. 2. Tenth Battalion, Royal Grenadiers.

To be Lieutenant: 2nd Lieutenant A. R. Sweatman, R.S.I., *vice* A. B. Cameron, promoted.

2nd Lieutenant William Lehmann, R.S.I.

Lieutenant Wm. Craven Vaux Chadwick, from the Adjutancy, 36th Battalion.

HEAD QUARTERS,
OTTAWA, 28th August, 1891.
GENERAL ORDERS.
ACTIVE MILITIA.

No. 3. Tenth Battalion, Royal Grenadiers.

To be Captain: Lieutenant J. D. Mackay, M.Q., *vice* William Standish Lowe, retired with rank of Lieutenant.

HEAD QUARTERS,
GENERAL ORDERS.   OTTAWA, 18th Sept., 1891.
ACTIVE MILITIA.

No. 2. Tenth Battalion, Royal Grenadiers.

To be Lieutenants: 2nd Lieutenant A. C. F. Boulton, R.S.I, *vice* J. D. Mackay, promoted.

2nd Lieutenant G. A. Stimson, R.S.I., to complete establishment.

HEAD QUARTERS,
OTTAWA, 20th Nov., 1891.
GENERAL ORDERS.
ACTIVE MILITIA.

No. 5. Tenth Battalion, Royal Grenadiers.

To be 2nd Lieutenants: 2nd Lieutenant Cesare J. Marani, R.S I., from No. 7 Company, 34th Battalion, *vice* A. R. Sweatman, promoted.

James Wm. Bain, Esq., provisionally, *vice* Lehmann, promoted.

HEAD QUARTERS,
OTTAWA, 24th December, 1891.

GENERAL ORDERS.

ACTIVE MILITIA.

No. 2. Tenth Battalion, Royal Grenadiers, Toronto, Ont.

To be Captain: Lieutenant Stephen A. Heward, R. S. I., *vice* G. P. Eliot, retired retaining rank.

To be Lieutenant: 2nd Lieutenant Alexander J. Boyd, R.S.I., *vice* Heward, promoted.

To be 2nd Lieutenants, provisionally: J. W. S. Corley, *vice* Boyd, promoted.

John T. Thompson, to complete establishment.

The spring drill commenced as usual, early in March for recruits and on the 17th for the entire battalion, being continued without intermission until May 24th.

Divine service parade took place on May 10th, and was attended by almost the entire regiment.

Much sorrow was felt by all ranks in the regiment at the death, on May 5th 1891, of Captain Forbes Michie. He had served throughout the whole of the Northwest campaign and had been connected with the Grenadiers for nearly ten years.

The regiment's excursion to Woodstock in 1891, was a somewhat notable one, as it extended over three days.

HEAD QUARTERS
TORONTO, 28th May, 1891.

The following extract from a letter from His Excellency the Governor-General is published for the information of all concerned:—

" His Excellency the Governor-General desires to express the pleasure which it gave him to see the regiment Saturday evening, May 23rd. He had heard much of their reputation and although the circumstances under which they marched past were such as make it difficult for any corps to show what it could do in the way of drill, His Excellency was fully satisfied from the steadiness, physique and general appearance of the men that they and their officers maintain the best traditions of the service and that they would do ample credit to themselves at all times."

The battalion paraded in review order with helmets and leggings at the Armoury at 3 p.m., on Tuesday the 2nd of June, and took part in the 25th anniversary celebration of the Battle of Ridgeway.

The autumnal drills began in September and were brought to a close by the annual inspection, which took place on November 12th, upon the common, north side of Kingston Road, east of Norway and south of York Station, G.T.R.

The inspection was preceded by a church parade to Oak street Presbyterian church on Sunday, November 8th, which was fully attended by all ranks.

The following promotions and appointments took place in the regiment during 1892, they were published officially thus:

HEAD QUARTERS,
OTTAWA, 24th March, 1892.
GENERAL ORDERS.
ACTIVE MILITIA.

No. 6. Tenth Battalion, Royal Grenadiers, Toronto, Ont.

To be Lieutenant: 2nd Lieutenant William Robert Pringle, R.S.I., vice J. D. Maclennan, promoted into the 6th Battalion.

HEAD QUARTERS,
OTTAWA, 12th May, 1892.
GENERAL ORDERS.
ACTIVE MILITIA.

No. 4. Tenth Battalion, Royal Grenadiers, Toronto, Ont.

To be Lieutenant: 2nd Lieutenant Cesare, J. Marani, R.S.I., vice, A. H. Macdonell, appointed to the Infantry School Corps.

To be 2nd Lieutenant, provisionally : A. W. Croil, Esq., vice A. C. F. Boulton, promoted.

Lieutenant A. C. F. Boulton resigns his commission.

2nd Lieutenant J. W. S. Corley retires from the service.

HEAD QUARTERS,
OTTAWA, 3rd June, 1892.
GENERAL ORDERS.
ACTIVE MILITIA.

No. 1. Tenth Battalion, Royal Grenadiers, Toronto, Ont.

The retirement of Major James Mason, notified in General Orders, 24th April, 1891, is hereby cancelled.

Major Arthur Bagshaw Harrison is permitted to retire, retaining rank.

HEAD QUARTERS,
OTTAWA, 30th September, 1892.

GENERAL ORDERS.

ACTIVE SERVICE.

Tenth Battalion, Royal Grenadiers, Toronto, Ont.

To be Lieutenants: 2nd Lieutenant J. W. Bain, R.S.I., *vice* A. C. F. Boulton, resigned.

Lieutenant W. H. McClive, R S.I., from No. 2 Company, 19th Battalion, *vice* D'A. H. K. MacMahon, appointed to Canadian Regiment of Infantry.

2nd Lieutenant Arthur Wellesley Croil retires from the service.

HEAD QUARTERS,
OTTAWA, 28th October, 1892.

GENERAL ORDERS.

ACTIVE MILITIA.

Tenth Battalion, Royal Grenadiers, Toronto, Ont.

To be 2nd Lieutenants, provisionally: James Grayson Smith, Esquire, *vice* G. A. Stimson, promoted.

Cyrus Stiles, Esquire, *vice* W. R Pringle, promoted.

HEAD QUARTERS,
OTTAWA, 16th December, 1892.

GENERAL ORDERS.

ACTIVE MILITIA.

Tenth Battalion, Royal Grenadiers, Toronto, Ont.

To be Major: Captain John Dunlop Hay, R.S.I., *vice* A. B. Harrison retired.

The annual drill for 1892 began as usual in March, the church parade took place to St. George's on April 10th, being well attended, and on May 24th, spring drill concluded by an excursion to Windsor, which though most successful and highly enjoyed by both officers and men, does not call for any special comment beyond recording the hearty reception given the battalion in Windsor.

The autumnal drills began on September 22nd and continued until November 10th when the inspection was ordered to take place in High Park, but owing to the bad weather which prevailed, the parade was at the last moment cancelled. Divine service for the battalion was held at the Northern Congregational Church, on October 2nd.

There were several notable changes among the officers of the Grenadiers, in 1893, Lieutenant-Colonel Dawson retiring at the close of the year, being succeeded by Major Mason, all these changes will be found duly recorded in the following General Orders:

HEAD QUARTERS,
OTTAWA, 20th January, 1893.
GENERAL ORDERS.
ACTIVE MILITIA.

Tenth Battalion, Royal Grenadiers, Toronto, Ont.

To be Captain : Lieutenant Andrew Maxwell Irving, R.S.I., *vice* J. D. Hay, promoted.

HEAD QUARTERS,
OTTAWA, 3rd February, 1893.
GENERAL ORDERS.
ACTIVE MILITIA.

Tenth Battalion, Royal Grenadiers, Toronto, Ont.

To be Lieutenant: 2nd Lieutenant Harvey A. Willis, R.S.I., from No. 6 Company, 36th Battalion, *vice* A. M. Irving promoted.

HEAD QUARTERS,
OTTAWA, 24th February, 1893.

GENERAL ORDERS.

ACTIVE MILITIA.

Tenth Battalion, Royal Grenadiers, Toronto, Ont.

Lieutenant William Robert Pringle resigns his commission.

HEAD QUARTERS,
OTTAWA, 5th May, 1893.

GENERAL ORDERS.

ACTIVE MILITIA.

Tenth Battalion, Royal Grenadiers, Toronto, Ont.

Lieutenant Cesare J. Marani resigns his commission.

2nd Lieutenant Cyrus Stiles retires from the service.

Paymaster and Honorary Captain John Bruce is granted the honorary rank of Major, to date from 25th September, 1892.

HEAD QUARTERS,
OTTAWA, 15th September, 1893.

GENERAL ORDER.

ACTIVE MILITIA.

Tenth Battalion, Royal Grenadiers, Toronto, Ont.

To be Lieutenant: 2nd Lieutenant James Grayson Smith, R.S.I., *vice* W. R. Pringle, resigned.

2nd Lieutenant John T. Thompson, retires from the service.

HEAD QUARTERS,
OTTAWA, 2nd November, 1893.
GENERAL ORDER.
ACTIVE MILITIA.

Tenth Battalion, Royal Grenadiers, Toronto, Ont.

Captain and Brevet Major Frederick F. Manley is permitted to retire retaining rank.

HEAD QUARTERS,
OTTAWA, 1st December, 1893.
GENERAL ORDER.
ACTIVE MILITIA.

Tenth Battalion, Royal Grenadiers, Toronto, Ont.

To be Lieutenant-Colonel: Major James Mason, R.S I., *vice* George Dudley Dawson, who is permitted to retire retaining rank.

Drill for the battalion commenced in 1893 as in previous years in March. There was the usual regimental church parade in April, and the battalion of course took part in the first Garrison church parade, which was held at the Pavilion in the Horticultural Gardens, on the second Sunday in May.

There was a departure from precedent in 1893, as the battalion remained in Toronto for the Queen's Birthday, and "trooped" the Queen's color on the old Cricket Ground in Queen's Park.

Colonel Sir Casimir Gzowski, K.C.M.G., was the reviewing officer. The day was fine, and there was an immense number of spectators. Among those present were Major-General Sandham, Lieut.-Colonel Grasett, Lieut.-Colonel G. T. Denison, G.G.B.G.; Lieut.-Colonel

G. A. Shaw, R.L.; and hundreds of ladies. The Queen's Own Rifles on the same day were brigaded with the Governor-General's Foot Guards from Ottawa, and fired a *feu de joie* at the Lacrosse Grounds in Rosedale.

After the various parades were ended, the officers of the three regiments proceeded to the Woodbine race course, and saw the Queen's Plate run for.

Drill was resumed in the latter end of September, 1893, though the autumn, so far as the Grenadiers were concerned, was unmarked by any special incident. The Garrison church parade was held at the Pavilion, Horticultural Gardens on November 12th, when the Grenadiers wore their new "bearskins" for the first time. Major-General Herbert was present, and marched at the head of the column, accompanied by his A.D.C. and the D.A.G. of the district. Drill concluded for the year with a field day in High Park on Thanksgiving day, and most laborious work it was for all concerned, the troops being under arms from 7 a.m. until 6 p.m.

The corps who took part in the proceedings were—A. troop R.C.D., a half troop of the Governor-General's Body Guard, C. Company R.R.C.I., the Queen's Own Rifles, the Royal Grenadiers, 13th Battalion from Hamilton, and the 48th Highlanders of Toronto. They were commanded respectively by Captain Lessard, R.C.D.; Captain Fleming, G.G.B.G.; Lieutenant Laurie, R.R.C.I.; Lieutenant-Colonels Hamilton, Q.O.R.; Dawson, R.G.; Hon. J. M. Gibson, 13th; Davidson, 48th.

The Queen's Own Rifles, aided by the G.G.B.G., who acted as scouts, were the defending brigade, and held Toronto against the attacking force, who were advancing on the city by High Park and the Lake Shore road. The battle terminated about 3 o'clock, Major-General Herbert being well satisfied with the men's work.

After the battle was over, the troops marched to the Exhibition Grounds, and marched past before the Major-General, who, on its conclusion, spoke of the entire parade as "being the best he had seen since he came to Canada."

The day's proceedings concluded with a dinner of the whole of the officers at Webb's.

At this parade the Grenadiers turned out 450 strong.

Lieutenant-Colonel Dawson's valedictory address to the Regiment on his retirement, read thus:

"Lieutenant-Colonel Dawson, in taking leave of the Royal Grenadiers, in which he has served for thirteen years, and has had the honor to command for the past six, desires to tender his thanks to the officers, non-commissioned officers and men of the regiment for their support and co-operation during his period of command. He takes pride in the fact that during his command:

"Two companies were added to the strength of the regiment. The colors were re-decorated by the ladies of Toronto, when the name 'Batoche'* was emblazoned on their folds, and that the enthusiasm and *esprit de corps* of all ranks were never greater than at the present time. Lieutenant-Colonel Dawson now says farewell to the Grenadiers, with the assurance that the corps will

---

*"The Honour" of "Batoche" on the colours of the R. G. was actually granted during Lieut.-Col. Grasett's command, and as Lieut.-Col., Dawson says, carried into effect in his.

always keep and maintain in the future the distinguished position and prestige it has earned in the past, both on the field and in their native city, and that they will hold fast to their motto, 'Ready, Aye Ready.'"

There were not many changes among the officers of the Grenadiers in 1894, though no less than six of the vacant 2nd Lieutenancies were filled up. The General Orders relating to promotions and appointments were these:

HEAD QUARTERS,
OTTAWA, 31st January, 1894.

GENERAL ORDERS.

ACTIVE MILITIA.

Tenth Battalion, Royal Grenadiers, Toronto, Ont.

To be Lieutenant: William Robert Pringle, Esq., *vice* C. J. Marani, resigned.

Lieutenant Walter Hugh McClive resigns his commission.

HEAD QUARTERS,
OTTAWA, 20th April, 1894.

GENERAL ORDERS.

ACTIVE MILITIA.

Tenth Battalion, Royal Grenadiers, Toronto, Ont.

Paymaster and Honorary Major John Bruce, to be Major and to perform the duties of Paymaster in accordance with General Order 33, of the 19th August, 1892.

To be Adjutant: Captain A. M. Irving, R.S.I., *vice* Maclean, who resigns the Adjutancy.

To be Captain: Honorary Captain and Quartermaster Wm. T. Tassie, R.S.I., *vice* Gosling, retired, retaining rank.

To be Quartermaster: Captain (Retired List) G. P. Eliot, *vice* Tassie.

To be 2nd Lieutenants (provisionally): Alexis Francis Ramsay Martin, Henry Rowsell O'Reilly, James Tolmie Craig, Samuel Foote Sloane, and Donald Campbell Meyers.

HEAD QUARTERS,
OTTAWA, 10th May, 1894.

GENERAL ORDER.

ACTIVE MILITIA.

Tenth Battalion, Royal Grenadiers, Toronto, Ont.

Captain C. Greville Harston is permitted to retire, retaining his rank.

To be Captains: Lieutenant A. R. Sweatman, *vice* Manley.

Lieutenant William Lehmann, *vice* Greville Harston, retired.

HEAD QUARTERS,
OTTAWA, Sept. 8th, 1894.

GENERAL ORDERS

ACTIVE MILITIA.

Tenth Battalion, Royal Grenadiers, Toronto, Ont.

To be 2nd Lieutenant provisionally: James Cooper Mason, Gentleman, to complete establishment.

Drill began for 1894 in March, and was continued until May 24th, when the battalion went to Galt for the day, being brigaded with the 13th Battalion. Though the people of that pleasant town did their utmost to welcome the Grenadiers, the Regiments pleasure was marred by the torrents of rain which fell during the greater part of the day.

PROMOTIONS AND APPOINTMENTS. 241

A useful N.C.O. of the regiment, one who had gone through the Northwest campaign, Hospital Sergeant Dent, died on May 27th, 1894. He was interred with military honors two days later. Sergeant Dent had been a pleasing writer on military matters for some years previously.

Drill was resumed in the autumn on August 30th, and concluded with a field day on November 13th, on the ground to the immediate west of the continuation of Spadina road, north of Davenport road. The troops engaged were one troop of the Royal Canadian Dragoons and one company of the R.R.C.I., the three Toronto regiments and the 13th Battalion from Hamilton. The final march past was by half companies in column, and took place on St. George street before Lieutenant-Colonel Otter, D.A.G.

The changes among the officers of the Grenadiers in 1895 were as follows:

HEAD QUARTERS,
OTTAWA, 26th January, 1895.
GENERAL ORDERS.
ACTIVE MILITIA.

Tenth Battalion, Royal Grenadiers, Toronto, Ont.

Lieutenant William Craven Vaux Chadwick is permitted to resign his commission.

HEAD QUARTERS,
OTTAWA, 9th February, 1895.
GENERAL ORDERS.
ACTIVE MILITIA.

Tenth Royal Grenadiers, Toronto, Ont.

Captain Stephen A. Heward is permitted to resign his commission, and to retain the rank of Captain on retirement.

To be Captain: Lieutenant George Alexander Stimson, vice Heward, resigned.

To be Lieutenant: Charles S. McInnes, Gentleman, to complete establishment.

HEAD QUARTERS,
OTTAWA, 13th April, 1895.
GENERAL ORDERS.
ACTIVE MILITIA.

Tenth Royal Grenadiers, Toronto, Ont.

Captain Alexander Cecil Gibson is permitted to resign his commission, and to retain the rank of Captain on retirement.

To be Captain: Lieutenant Alexander James Foyd, vice Gibson retired.

To be 2nd Lieutenants provisionally: Coote Nisbitt Shanly, Gentleman; George Allen Case, Gentleman.

HEAD QUARTERS,
OTTAWA, 21st Sept., 1895.
GENERAL ORDERS.
ACTIVE MILITIA.

Tenth Royal Grenadiers, Toronto, Ont.

To be Lieutenants: 2nd Lieutenants A. F. R. Martin; H. R. O'Reilly; D. C. Meyers; S. F. Sloane; J. T. Craig; J. C. Mason, and G. H. C. Brooke, from the retired list of Captains, to complete establishment.

That part of General Orders, 11th May, 1895, permitting Lieutenant W. R. Pringle to resign his Commission is amended by the following, ' and to retain the rank of Lieutenant on retirement."

HEAD QUARTERS,
OTTAWA, 12th October, 1895.

GENERAL ORDERS.

ACTIVE MILITIA.

Tenth Royal Grenadiers, Toronto, Ont.

To be 2nd Lieutenant provisionally: Albert Amos Stuart Wilkins, Gentleman.

HEAD QUARTERS,
OTTAWA, 9th November, 1895.

GENERAL ORDERS.

ACTIVE MILITIA.

Tenth Royal Grenadiers, Toronto, Ont.

To be 2nd Lieutenant provisionally: Robert Oliver Montgomery, Gentleman.

On the 4th April, 1895, for the last time, the Royal Grenadiers paraded in the Old Armoury, at the foot of Jarvis and West Market-streets.

About five minutes past eight the buglers on duty for the evening sounded the " Fall in," and well did the Royal Grenadiers respond to the summons. Rarely, if ever, has such a muster been seen. Sometime elapsed owing to the crowded drill shed before it was possible for the Adjutant to order the Sergeant-Major to sound " orderly sergeants " so as to collect the company "states," but it was accomplished just before nine. Markers were then thrown out and the companies marched upon them forming a ten company battalion at quarter distance, right in front, colours in the centre.

The adjutant rode up to Lieutenant-Colonel Mason, reporting all correct, then the latter took command. The scene which followed was thus described by one of the newspapers of the day:

"ROYAL GRENADIERS, 'TENTION," called the Colonel, and as one man the regiment sprang to attention. The Colonel then told the battalion that an enterprising and artistic photographer being present a picture of the Royal Grenadiers was going to be taken, and they must stand like rocks. The commanding officer proceeded to form the regiment into column of companies at three paces distance with the pioneers, band, and drums in front; ordered the men to fix bayonets, slope arms, and wait. They had not long to do the latter, a tremendous flash, a cloud of smoke, and a cry of "Oh!" from a number of young ladies who were in the galleries announced that the picture had been taken. "Order arms." "Unfix bayonets," were the next commands, followed by "Stand at ease, stand easy," then the gallant soldiers waited again, no one seemed to understand exactly what for. Presently it was learned that another photograph was to be taken and that the aforesaid 'artistic and enterprising" photographer had to prepare his lights. It was a long wait, and while it lasted the drummers whistled, and did it very well, too, the popular air of "Tommy Atkins."

"At last the artist informed Colonel Mason that 'all was ready,' and again the R. G.'s were called to attention and ordered to 'slope' their arms, but not to fix bayonets. A second flash, another cloud of smoke, and yet another exclamation of dismay from the ladies, and the second picture was duly taken.

"Then came the order from the Colonel to open the great gates facing West Market street, and as the band played 'Auld Lang Syne,' the Royal Grenadiers marched out of the building, headed by Lieutenant-Colonel Mason.

"Assembled in the Armory to see the 'Grens' depart were many officers and ex-officers of the city corps. Numbers of men belonging to the R.R.C.I., the R.C.D., the G.G.B.G., the 'Queen's Own,' and the 'Kilties' also turned up to see the Grenadiers take their departure. There were four men on parade who were in the corps when it was the 10th Royals, and one officer, Captain Caston, who has on no less than four occasions refused promotion to higher rank.

Of survivors of the Northwest campaign still in the ranks, though some two or three were unavoidably absent from parade, there are six officers and thirty non-commissioned officers and men, distributed as follows:

B Company		3
C	"	3
D	"	5
E	"	2
F	"	3
G	"	4
H	"	6
K	"	3
Drummers		1
	Total	30

Before leaving the drill shed Colonel Mason faced the men to the left, and thus addressed them:

"Men of the Royal Grenadiers:

"Before leaving the hall I wish to address a few words to you, and they shall be very few. It is fourteen years since this regiment was re-organized, and in that time it has grown from six to eight, and from eight to ten companies. The growth of the regiment was under discouraging circumstances, but owing to the zeal and good judgment of your first commanding officer, Lieutenant-Colonel Grasett, every difficulty was overcome, and when Lieutenant-Colonel Dawson assumed the command, he kept the battalion up to a high state of efficiency. It is for the present members of the regiment to prove themselves worthy successors of those who have preceded them, and by our exertions, by our zeal, and by the pride we take in our corps, to maintain our good name, and also to maintain the character of the regiment. For although we may not be in some unimportant points quite up to other corps, I think I may safely say, that, as a fighting machine, for that is what we are, we are not second to any regiment in the active militia of Canada. I trust every member will at all times show that he is proud of being one of the Royal Grenadiers."

The battalion, after leaving the shed, proceeded *via* King, Yonge and Queen streets to University avenue until the new Armoury was reached. As they marched up the avenue the band played "Men of the Northern Zone," and as they entered the new quarters, "A Soldier and a Man." Inside the building, the regiment, formed into column were halted, closed to quarter distance, and then the Colonel, in a very few words, addressed the regiment, saying, he hoped they would all make the Company Armouries as much of a club as possible, and that he was highly gratified at the splendid turn out of the evening. The colours were then marched off to the tune of the "British Grenadiers," and the parade was at an end.

There were 26 officers and 526 non-commissioned officers and men on parade, including band, drums, ambulance, signal men, and pioneers. The Queen's colour was borne by Lieutenant Martin, the Regimental by Lieutenant Mason. All ranks vied with each other in making the day a memorable one in the history of the Royal Grenadiers.

In 1895 the year's drill began in the new Armuories on University street, on April 4th, a somewhat later date than usual, and continued until May 24th, when it closed with an excursion by the regiment to Collingwood. When they arrived there they were welcomed by the Mayor, and later in the day a review took place on the Fair grounds. At night a grand entertainment by the band and drums of the battalion took place in the town hall, and on its conclusion the band went on a moonlight excursion on the Georgian Bay to Meaford. Next day was Saturday, and the regiment marched through the town with unfurled colours and band playing to a suburban park, where a short rest was taken. They then returned to the Fair ground, reaching there about 1 p.m. The remainder of the afternoon was given up to amusement, and at 7 o'clock the regiment took train for Toronto. The scene at the station was lively in the extreme ; all Collingwood was there to see the "Grens" depart, and when the train moved out of the station it was amidst what a country paper described next day as "a tempest of cheers."

The Batoche dinner of the officers of the Grenadiers took place in the new Armouries on May 12th. It was an all but purely private affair, yet there was one guest not belonging to or in anyway connected with the regiment who was present, namely, Senator and Lieut.-Colonel Boulton, formerly of the 100th P. W. R. C. Regiment, who during the Northwest campaign was in command of Boulton's Scouts serving "shoulder to shoulder" with the Grenadiers.

The anunal drill season commenced in 1895 early in September; the Regimental church parade was held at All Saints church on October 13th, and the Garrison church parade when the Grenadiers turned out 600 strong, beating their record, on November 3rd, Major-General Gascoigne being present.

A few days later the following communication from the Major-General was published in Regimental Orders.

HEAD QUARTERS,
TORONTO, November 7th, 1895.

GARRISON ORDERS.

Major-General Gascoigne has been pleased to express his satisfaction with the Garrison Parade on the 3rd inst. in the following letter received by Lt.-Col. Buchan, acting D. A. G.

TORONTO, 3rd November., 1895.

THE OFFICER COMMANDING No. 2 DISTRICT,—

Please express to all ranks of the Toronto Garrison, both Permanent Force, as well as Active Militia, my extreme satisfaction at the remarkably good turn out. I witnessed the divine service parade this afternoon, not only in numbers did it exceed my expectation, but the general smartness and magnificent appearance of the troops, as well as the steadiness and evident knowledge of drill and training, gave me the highest gratification. I am proud to have the honor of commanding such troops. Your own arrangements also were exceedingly good and well carried out.

      W. J. GASCOIGNE,
       Major-General Commanding.

 Another officer of the Grenadiers who had served throughout the Northwest campaign, Captain and Quarter Master G. P. Eliot, died on November 15th, 1895, and was interred with military honors on November 17th. Many officers of other corps were present at the funeral, in addition to those of the Grenadiers.

 Two months had barely elapsed when on January 11th, 1896, Captain and Adjutant Andrew Maxwell Irving, was, after a very brief illness, removed by death. He was lamented by all ranks and mourned for most sincerely. Every Toronto newspaper gave a lengthy notice of his life and career, and all spoke in the highest terms of the man and of the soldier. "It was his thorough unselfishness, his desire to let others shine rather than himself that made the character of Andrew Irving such a thoroughly lovable one," wrote one paper, and all who read it knew the words to be true.

 The Regimental Orders of January 16th thus referred to the sad event.

 "By the death of Captain Irving, the regiment has lost the services of a most capable and efficient officer, one who during his long connection with it faithfully and thoroughly performed every duty assigned to him and always made the interests and advancement of the regiment his first consideration, and who by the thoughtful and kindly but firm manner in which he discharged his various duties, endeared himself to his brother officers and won the enduring respect and esteem of all ranks."

At the express wish of Captain Irving's family, the funeral on January 13th, was private, but the pall-bearers were representative men, namely: Lieut.-Colonel's Grasett, Dawson, Davidson, Mason, Messrs. John R. Robinson and H. Brophy,

From January to June, 1896, when this history closes, the only changes among the officers of the Grenadiers were as is thus told in General Orders.

HEAD QUARTERS,
OTTAWA, 25th January, 1896.

GENERAL ORDERS.

ACTIVE MILITIA.

Tenth Royal Grenadiers, Toronto, Ont.

To be 2nd Lieutenant, provisionally: Charles Stuart Wilkie, Gentleman.

HEAD QUARTERS,
OTTAWA, 7th March, 1896.

GENERAL ORDERS.

ACTIVE MILITIA.

Tenth Royal Grenadiers, Toronto, Ont.

To be 2nd Lieutenant, from 25th Feb., 1896: Edmund Rochfort Street, Gentleman.

IN LOVING MEMORY
OF
CAPTAIN
Andrew Maxwell Irving
ADJUTANT ROYAL GRENADIERS

 BORN AUGUST 31ST 1860.
DIED JANUARY 11TH 1896.

ERECTED BY HIS BROTHER OFFICERS

IRVING MEMORIAL TABLET, ST. JAMES' CATHEDRAL.

HEAD QUARTERS,
OTTAWA, June 12th, 1896.

GENERAL ORDERS.

ACTIVE MILITIA.

Tenth Battalion, Royal Grenadiers, Toronto, Ont.

To be Quartermaster, with honorary rank of Captain: Provisional 2nd Lieutenant, Robert O. Montgomery, *vice* Eliot, deceased.

To be 2nd Lieutenant, provisionally: Duncan F. Campbell.

Mr. Campbell is the grandson of the late Lieut.-Col. Cumberland, and nephew of Capt. F. Barlow Cumberland, the only instance in a Canadian Infantry corps where three generations of one family have held commissions in the same Regiment. In the G. G. B. G. four generations of one family have served, but that corps has a history of 60 years

The condition of the Royal Grenadiers at the close of the drill season for the spring season of 1896 is such as to cause every member of the regiment to feel a pardonable pride in belonging to such a corps. The authorized strength is 420 men of all ranks, excluding commissioned officers; but the actual strength exceeds 600. The men over and above the authorized establishment have to be clothed and equipped at the expense of the regiment, thereby entailing from year to year a heavy drain upon the financial resources of both officers and companies. The amount disbursed each year more than doubling the total amount received from the government for all purposes.

Not only is the battalion numerically strong, but it is in an excellent state of drill, also of discipline, not excelled by any other corps in the Dominion.

The band, under Mr. Waldron's able directorate, is in the highest state of efficiency, and its services are in constant demand for various entertainments from January until December. The drummers and buglers are also well trained by Sergeant-drummer Farmer, and they display that zeal and devotion to their duties which is happily a characteristic of the entire regiment.

Before bringing the history to a close it will not be out of place to refer briefly to the part the Grenadiers of all ranks have taken in the social life of the city. The famous ball given by the officers after the regiment's return from the Northwest has been fully described in former pages. Notable as this event was, it was only one of many occasions when the Grenadiers were "ready, aye ready" to afford enjoyment to their fellow citizens in the exercise of the most profuse and graceful hospitality. The assemblies held for many years by the Grenadier officers are looked back to with pleasure by all those who had the privilege of attending them. Toronto's fairest matrons and maids graced these assemblages by their presence, and in doing so felt that they were as much honored by, as conferring honor upon, their hosts.

The dramatic performances given under the auspices of the Grenadiers have also been a great source of pleasure to a large number of Toronto residents.

The non-commissioned ranks of the regiment have also proved themselves to be kindly hosts and genial

RGT.-MAJOR JAMES T. COX, W.O. BANDMASTER J. WALDRON, W.O.
COLOR-SERGT. G. SCULLY.
ARTERMASTER-SERGT. H. W. JOHNSTON. PAYMASTER-SERGT. W. J. BEWLEY.

entertainers. The annual dinner of the Sergeants and of the Band and Drummers being events eagerly participated in by all those who have the honor to be invited.

The Sergeants' Mess of the regiment is yet a young institution; but under its effective and practical management it can not fail to be one of the most popular adjuncts of the corps, besides one of the sources of its strength.

One of the most pleasing matters in connection with the church parades of the Royal Grenadiers is the appearance, attached to them, of the Upper Canada College company of Cadets. These youths, in their neat uniform of blue and silver, their smart drill and good discipline always receive a great deal of well merited attention.

There is little now to relate respecting the Royal Grenadiers as the present year is not yet expired. Drill began on March 26th, 1896, and ended for the summer with the regiment's return to Toronto, after a most enjoyable trip to Berlin, extending from May 23d to early morning on May 26th. This was the largest holiday parade on record, 502 of all ranks being present. It would be impossible to speak too highly of the enthusiasm shown by the people of Berlin in the welcome they extended to and the hospitality they bestowed upon all ranks of the regiment.

* * * * * * * * *

My work is finished, I have tried to tell the story of the regiment for the thirty-five years of its existence, fairly and accurately and I can only ask those who read the book to overlook any small errors and to believe that I have tried to do justice to the regiment particularly, and to all others generally.

June 15th, 1896.

APPENDIX.

10TH BATTALION ROYAL GRENADIERS.

"BATOCHE."

Uniform, Scarlet; Facings, Blue; Lace, Gold; Head-dress, Bearskins with Red and White Plume.

MOTTO—"READY, AYE READY."

Badge, in centre on Shield, figure 10 with crosses on top, behind both and showing above Crown and 10, a sheaf of spears, on dexter side Thistle and Shamrock, on sinister's de Roses, and on base Maple Leaves. The Shield surrounded with Garter bearing the motto "*Ready, aye Ready,*" which is surrounded by a wreath of laurel leaves, behind which and extending outside wreath, a Military star. The whole surmounted by a Royal Crown.

LIEUTENANT COLONEL—James Mason,[1] Captain, Sept. 29, 1882; Major, Sept. 7, 1888; Lieut.-Col. Dec. 1, 1893.

MAJORS.	2nd Lieutenant	Lieutenant.	Captain.	Major.
John Dunlop Hay[2]	Jan. 25, 1884	Oct. 16, 1885	Jan. 31, 1890	Dec. 16, 1892
John Bruce	....	Jan. 13, 1881	Sept. 15, 1882	Apr. 20, 1894
CAPTAINS.				
Frederic Albert Caston[3]	....	....	Jan. 28, 1881	
Robert Goodall Trotter	Nov. 11, 1881	Nov. 24, 1882	Feb. 6, 1885	
Alfred Buell Cameron	May 21, 1886	May 12, 1888	May 22, 1891	
John Bayne McLean	....	June 7, 1886	May 27, 1891	
James Drummond Mackay (*Acting Adjutant*)	May 12, 1888	Sept. 7, 1888	Aug. 28, 1891	
William Tassie Tassie*	....	....	Apr. 20, 1891	
George Alexander Stimson	May 22, 1891	July 16, 1891	Feb. 18, 1894	
Alexander James Boyd[4]	Jan. 30, 1891	Sept. 18, 1891	Feb. 9, 1895	
	Mar. 20, 1891	Dec. 24, 1891	Apr. 13, 1895	

WAR SERVICES OF OFFICERS.

1. Lieutenant-Colonel Mason served throughout the Northwest campaign of 1885. Was present at the engagement at Fish Creek and the capture of Batoche (severely wounded.) Medal and clasp.
2. Major Hay served in the Northwest campaign of 1885. Was present at Fish Creek and Batoche. Medal and clasp.
3. Captain Caston served in the Northwest campaign of 1885. Was present at Fish Creek and Batoche. Medal and clasp.
4. Captain Boyd served in the Battleford Column during the Northwest campaign, with the Queen's Own Rifles. Present at the engagement at Cut Knife Hill. Medal and clasp.

* Captain Tassie joined the Royal Grenadiers as Quartermaster (Honorary Capta'n) September 27th, 1889.

APPENDIX.—Continued.

	2nd Lieutenant	Lieutenant.	Captain.	Major.
LIEUTENANTS.				
James William Bain	Nov. 20, 1891	Oct. 1, 1892		
Harvey Archelaus Willis		Feb. 4, 1892		
James Grayson Smith	Oct. 28, 1892	Sept. 15, 1893		
Alexis Francis Ramsay Martin	Apr. 20, 1894	Sept. 21, 1895		
Henry Rowsell O'Reilly	do.	do.		
Donald Campbell Meyers	do.	do.		
Samuel Foote Sloane	do.	do.		
James Tolmie Craig	do.	do.		
James Cooper Mason	Sept. 8, 1894	do.		
George Hiram Capron Brooke[5] (Captain in Militia)				
2nd LIEUTENANTS.				
Charles Stephen McInnes	Feb. 9, 1895			
Coote Nisbett Shanly	Apr. 13, 1895			
George Allen Case	do.			
Albert Amos Stuart Wilkins	Oct. 12, 1895			
Charles Stuart Wilkie	Jan. 25, 1896			
Edmund Rochfort Street	Mar. 7, 1896			
Duncan Frederic Campbell	June 12, 1896			
ASSISTANT SURGEON.				
Edmond Eleazar King[6]	Assistant Surgeon,		June 4th, 1886.	
QUARTERMASTER.				
Robert Oliver Montgomery	Nov. 9, 1895		Quartermaster, June 12th, 1896. (Honorary Captain.)	

WAR SERVICES OF OFFICERS.—(Continued).

5. Captain and Lieutenant Brooke served in the Humboldt Column during the Northwest campaign with the York and Simcoe Battalion. Medal.
6. Assistant Surgeon King served in the Northwest on the Medical staff during the campaign of 1885. Medal.

ROYAL GRENADIERS.

LIST OF OFFICERS.

Conclusion of Drill Season 1895.

LIEUTENANT-COLONEL.—James Mason.

MAJORS.—John Dunlop Hay, John Bruce.

CAPTAINS.—Frederick Albert Caston, Robert Goodall Trotter, Alfred Buell Cameron, John Bayne McLean, James Drummond Mackay, Andrew Maxwell Irving, Adjt., William Tassie Tassie, William Lehmann, George Alexander Stimson, Alexander James Boyd.

LIEUTENANTS.—James William Bain, Harvey Archelaus Willis, James Grayson Smith, Alexis Francis Ramsay Martin, Henry Rowsell O'Reilly, Donald Campbell Meyers, Samuel Foote Sloane, James Tolmie Craig, James Cooper Mason, George Hiram Capron Brooke, (Capt. in Militia).

2ND LIEUTENANTS.—Charles Stephen McInnes, Coote Nisbett Shanly, Geo. Allen Case, Albert Amos Stuart Wilkins, Robert Oliver Montgomery.

ADJUTANT.—Captain Andrew Maxwell Irving.

SURGEON.—George Sterling Ryerson.

ASSISTANT SURGEON.—Edmund Eleazar King.

QUARTERMASTER.—Captain Granville Percival Eliot.

REGIMENTAL ROLL.

STAFF SERGEANTS.—Sergeant-Major, J. T. Cox ; Band Master, J. Waldron ; Quartermaster-Sergeant, H. W. Johnston ; Paymaster Sergeant, W. J. Bewley ; Orderly-room Sergeant, W. J. Weatherly ; Sergeant Instructor of Musketry, A. Bell ; Armourer Sergeant, G. Brooks ; Assistant Sergeant-Major, F. Francis ; Assistant Quartermaster-Sergeant, J. Ewart ; Assistant Sergeant Instructor of Musketry, R. McVittie.

ASSISTANT DRILL INSTRUCTORS.—Color-Sergeant, P. Foley ; Sergeant, O Freemantle.

BAND.

SERGEANT.—Tressam, T.

CORPORAL.—Barnard, T. H.

PRIVATES.—Alderson, J., Bagnall, J., Blight, M., Brickenden, A. J., Brickenden, T. E., Carrier, C. J., Chisholm, D., Clegg, T., Cull, H. J., Grogan, C., Harris, J., Henderson, W., Herbert, J., (Howard, J. T.), Jackman, W., Jacobs, R., Johnstone, H. W., Johnston, W. C., King, J. H., Lovatt, W., Lucas, J., McBride, J., McClure, J., Martin, C., Mills, W.

Q

A., Moore, W. J., Murley, J., Palmer, T., Pratt, J., Pye, C. A., Pye,
H., Pye, H. A., Savage, C., Smith, C., Stoneberg, F., Stump, J., Van
Valkenberg, M., Williams, T., Wilson, R., Winlow, F.

DRUMMERS.

SERGEANT-DRUMMER.—Farmer, J. T.
SERGEANT.—Havard, T.
LANCE-SERGEANT.—Kilford, E. J.
CORPORAL.—Stewart, J.
DRUMMERS.—Bond, W., Bonsteel, A., L.C. Bourne, A., Bourne Arthur,
Brown, J., Burnett, R. W., Carter, W., Cheeseworth, F., Clink, W.,
Coleman, G., Cully, C., L.C. Dennet, A., French, W., Gee, W. H., Gillespie, A., Gurnett, W., Hay, F., Hay, J., Hughes, A. H., Jewell, W.
J., Jordan, R., Kerr, G., Kerr, K., Kerrison, E., Latimer, J., Matthews,
E., L. C. Mathews, T., Oster, J., Palmer, S., Parker, G., Pippy, W.,
Skipper, C., Stanley, E., Wild, J., Witheridge, F., Wray, W., Wray,
W. H.

PIONEERS.

SERGEANT.—R. Lea.
CORPORAL.—C. Collett.
PRIVATES.—R. Burton, G. Douglass, H. Hele, A. Lusty, G. McCleary,
W. McIntosh, W. Switzer, W. Wallwork, W. E. Watson.

AMBULANCE AND SIGNAL MEN.

HOSPITAL-SERGEANT.—A. Taylor.
SIGNAL-SERGEANT.—W. Cane.
SERGEANT.—S. W. Knight.
CORPORALS.—J. Isbister, J. Law, L. E. Martin, G. Moat, W. E. Till, J.
Young.
PRIVATES.—V. G. Bell, E. Boyd, F. C. Chandler, C. Creed, J. C. Farquharson, J. Gimblet, S. Gowans, A. W. Green, A. Johnston, F. B. Johnston,
F. G. King, W. Martin, T. J. Mitchell, H. E. Reid, H. Ritchie, R. S.
Ritchie, W. Rooke, T. Tate, P. R. Wakeman, G. White, W. H. Wilson,
F. Workman.

"A" COMPANY.

COLOR-SERGEANT.—F. Smith.
SERGEANTS.—A. Davies, G. Stemman.
LANCE-SERGEANT.—L. A. Kirkland.
CORPORALS.—C. H. Leggott, W. White.
PRIVATES.—J. Aikens, A. A. Allen, J. Andrew, J. Bowman, T. Byrne,
E. Clink, T. H. Conder, W. Cuthbert, W. Davis, L. Elliott, W. Farley
F. Forgie, (L.C.), C. J. Fox, C. Fox, J. H. Fox, A. Gordon, (L.C.)

APPENDIX. 259

W. Griffiths, Chas. Hindle, Geo. Hindle, W. J. Hird, G. Hopkins, J. Hopkins, T. Hopkins, H. Hunt, H. Jones, J. Kavanagh, J. Kembly, J. Kilby, G. Long, J. McCuaig, (L.C.), R. R. McCuaig, S. A. Marchment, H. Marsh, (L.C.), G. Nesbitt, W. J. Nesbitt, A. Orr, C. Perrin, J. Pickering, L. Rees, W. E. Reid, R. L. Riggs, A. Saunders, T. R. Seeley, D. A. Serviss, W. Stanley, F. Swain, W. Thomas, E. Wills.

"B" COMPANY.

COLOR-SERGEANT.—McClinton, D.
SERGEANTS.—Craig, D., Phillips, J.
LANCE-SERGEANT.—Magone, R.
CORPORALS.—McBrien, T., Sink, E., Sweet, O.
PRIVATES.—Bates, D., Bates, G. E., Bell, H., Bloxam, C., Campbell, A., Cassidy, N., Clarke, F. A., Cordingley, E., Cumming, W., Daniels, W., Eames, G., Eckhardt, E. H., Forster, J. (L.C.), Forster, Wm., Glenn, W., Gonder, A., Graham, W., Harris, A. (L.C.), Henderson, W., Hewitt, E., Ingram, G., Levell, W., Long, H., Micks, G., Mitchell, W. J., Murphy, J. D., Morris, J. S., Osler, A., Phibbs, R., Phillips, C. E., Phillips, E., Phillips, R. S., Reid, G., Robinson, G., Roulston, J. R., Sewrey, J., Simmons, C., Stitzel, W., Surphlis, R., Taylor, W. (L.C.), Tomlin, A., Webb, H., Wilson, G.

"C" COMPANY.

COLOR-SERGEANT.—Leith, Wm.
SERGEANTS.—Botsford, W., Eaton, Ryerson, Lance-Sergeant, Norris, H. G.
CORPORAL.—Leith, D.
PRIVATES.—Banks, W., Beatty, S. (L.C.), Beynon, J., Brown, R., Carpenter, J., Carroll, R., Carter, A., Chesher, A., Cooper, A., Cowan, W., Conhan, A., Cruickshank, Wm. (L.C.), Duff, D. (L.C.), Fell, Wm., Hill, G., Hornshaw, S., Hussey, Jas., Ibbotson, Joe, Kent, E., Legier, T., Leonard M., Ludlow, Wm., McKnight, R., Milloy, N., Newton, A., Osborne, T., Owston, P., Rabjohn, A., Rabjohn, F. (L.C.), Robertson, R., Russell, James, Scott, Wm., Stacy, Jas. A., Tassie, H., Walker, S. (L,C.), Williams, R., Wray, W., Yeomans, R.

"D" COMPANY.

COLOR-SERGEANT.—Scully, Geo.
SERGEANTS.—Richardson, Geo., Smith, W., Lce.-Sergeant, Wadsworth, A.
CORPORALS.—Braun, R., Britton, F., Edwards, W.
PRIVATES.—Auchincloss, G., Breckenreid, W., Brooks, G., Bull, C., Calhoun, A., Calhoun, W., Campbell, W., Chinn, J., Coghill, J., Connell, J. J., Culligan, S., Dale, T., Dean, T., Dyson, W.A., Friend, W., Garland, R., Gee, P., Gillam, A., Gladwin, Jas., Hagen, T., Hockridge, A., Hum-

phrey, E., Humphrey, J., Jones, C. M., Lane, P., Lewis, C., MacNally, M., Marsh, A., Metcalf, F., Milne, T., Moore, R., Mortimer, G., Newman, E., Nelson, G., Parsons, W. S., Richardson, J. R., Scott, H., Stephen, J. T., Tansley, C., Todd, J. H., Voss, J., Walker, T., Watts, C., Watts, W. A., Weldon, G., White, A., Wilson, J.

"E" COMPANY.

COLOR-SERGEANT.—Bennett, W. K.
SERGEANTS.—Hall, T., Robinson, T.,
LANCE-SERGEANT.—McHugh, D.
CORPORALS.—Bennett, J. H., Edmondson, W.
PRIVATES.—Bach, W., Barker, A. J., Barker, W., Barnes, W., Bennett, T., Bourne, R., Brown, J., Brown, I. H., (L.C.), Browne, C. F. W., Bryson, H., Caldwell, R., Calvert, F. M., Campbell, J., Chalmers, G. A., Charters, T., Cloutman, A., Colcock, W., Croot, J. T., Crowly, W. Cook, B. W., Davis, H., Dear, H., Donald, R., Forsyth, C., Frauce, L., Gallagher, J. G., Gallagher, P., Gould, D., Hall, I., Hall, W., Hampton, R., Harrington, A. N., Harrison, R. S., (L. C.), Harrison, W., Head, W. A., Hogan, P. J., Hurrell, J., King, W. J., Lowry, A., Lynn, D. A., McHugh, E., Magennis, J., Murley, J., Poulton, H. M., Powis, W., Rodway, F., Roome, R., Seale, C., Seale, F., Smith, J., Starr, N., Van Iderstein F., Williams, E., Wright, G., Wyley, W.

"F" COMPANY.

COLOR-SERGEANT.—Nolan, J.
SERGEANTS.—Doherty, R., Weston, J.
LANCE-SERGANT.—Comber, B. T.
CORPORALS.—Noble, J., Smith, A. J.
PRIVATES.—Abraham, G., Ball, E. H-, (L. C.), Bedford, E., Bennett, A. Bishop, W., Brown, G. R., Brown, R., Butcher, W., Carwardine, A., Coe, Chas., Colyer, L., (L. C.), Constable, Thos., Elsworth, R., Ferguson, John, (L. C.), Fleming, Wm., Green, H., Hamilton, Geo., Hanna, J., Hunt, D., Jackson, Chas., Joyce, H., Kenmare, J., (L. C.), Love, Thos., McDonald, Jas., Mack, M., Mayne, S., Moffitt, Jas., Moore, H., Mullen, A., Scott, J., Snider, F., Stephens, W., Stearn, A. E., Weir, J. Thompson, S., Whitley, R., Whitley, W., Wilson W.

"G" COMPANY.

COLOR-SERGEANT.—Dempster, R.
SERGEANTS.—Cartwright, G., Hill, H.
LANCE-SERGEANT.—Dicks, G.
CORPORAL.—Beales, S.
PRIVATES.—Atkinson, E. G., Atkinson, J., Baylis, J. (L.C.), Beasley, J.,

APPENDIX. 261

Brambles, T., Brimley, N. (L.C.), Broesnan, T., Campbell, W., Claridge, C., Cook, A. J., Colls, W., Cruickshank, H. (L.C.), Davis, W., Forscyth, A. J., Gilmour, W., Glenholm, H., Grey, G., Griffiths, J., Hammond, H., Hill, A., Hind, J., Hull, J. A., Hyde, A. P., Kemp, J. G., Kenny, T., Knott, A., Leng, J., Leslie, W., Libby, H., McKay, J. E., McKee, W., Menzies, J. (L.C.), Mumby, J. H., Nicholl, S., Pickens, C., Raynor, J., Reaston, V. W., Slingsby, T. E , Stewart, G., Sullens, C., Warren, S. Waters, T., Watt, J.

"H" COMPANY.

COLOR-SERGEANT.—Middleton, H.
SERGEANTS.—Ferris, J. E., McLim, F. F.
LANCE-SERGEANT.—Jones, W. B.
CORPORALS.—Young, N. S., Hunt, W.
PRIVATES.—Armstrong, C. (L.C.), Bailey, T. C., Bayles, T. S., Bourne, G. R., Chapman, W. H., Cusack, H. M. (L.C.), Davidson, W. J., Dunham, C., Earl, C., Fowler, W. G., Gimblet, John, Gordon, W. J., Graham, R., Graham, T., Hawkins, G., Heller, H. B., Hickey, J.C. (L.C.), Houlden, H., Howard, C., Jones, J. H., Kingsnorth, J., Kirk, R., Langdon, E., Lennox, D. J., Lloyd, T., Louma, J., Lowrey, W., Mack, T., McLearn, A. J., McMurray, F. G., Maiden, A. W., Martin, A., Martin, W. E., Meyers, C., Middleton, J. R., Norris, J., Page, G., Pollard, J., Reid, S., Ross, C., Scholes, J. L., Seymour, C., Sherwood, W., Simpson, J. H., Sprinks, W., Stewart, H. R., Taggart, W. J., Taylor, J. S., Tyers, H., Wilbur, A. M., Windatt, C. A. (L.C.).

"I" COMPANY.

COLOR-SERGEANT.—Mole, A.
SERGEANTS.—Ironside. G.. Williams, R.
LANCE-SERGEANT.—McDonald, G. A.
CORPORALS.—Addy, R., Buchanan, A. E.
PRIVATES.—Aitcheson, H., Allen, C., Barlow, W., Barnard, A., Barron, F., Bryant, F., Carpenter, W., Cradock, J., Daughton, T., Drummond T. A., Fairhall, J. W,, Ferguson, J. R., Flanagan, D., Franks, A., Fyfe, J., Gardiner, F., Giles, J., Hudson, G. T., Jefferies, W., Jefferies, W. H. E., Linn, F., McCartney, J., McClyment, A. (L.C.), McMillian, H., Mackie, J., Mason, T: W., Meen, W., Middleton, A., Moat, J., Moore, E., Oldbury, J., Parker, A. E., Parsons, A., Philip, F. F., Playter, C., Playter, F. (L.C.), Rogers, H., Spafford, W. C., Thompson, A., Townsend, W., Wall, O., Walsh, W.

"K" COMPANY.

COLOR-SERGEANT.— J. McDonald.
SERGEANTS.—J. Elmer, C. J. Saunders, Lance-Sergeant, P. Armstrong.

CORPORALS.—G. Hammond, L. Keele.
PRIVATES.—A. Adams. F. Appleton, G. Black, H. Black, J. Bush, J. Callon, H. Cast, A. Caswell, J. Clarke, A. Coggins, W. Cook, H. Cousins, J. A. Davidson, M. Dodsen, H. Dryland, D. Deckinson, E. A. Flaxman, F. Francis, S. Francis, J. T. French, G. Gibbons, J. Hackett (L.C.), E. Hodgson, R. Hyde, T. Lane, S. Latimer, W. J. Laverty, J. Long, R. McCleary, N. McEachren, M. Mercer, A. Mitchell, H. Nixon, J. Orrett, G. Penny, G. Pellow, A. Pillow, A. Robinson (L.C.), M. H. Sheppard, W. Spence, L. Sherrif, J. Silvester, C. Standish, E. Taylor, W. D. Titus, W. J. Titus, W. W. Townsend, J. Van Wyck, J. E. Warring, A. Weston, J. A. Williams, J. A. Wilson, W. Withers, R. Worden.

STRENGTH OF REGIMENT.

RECAPITULATION.

Officers	30	D Co	54
Staff-Sergeants	12	E "	62
Band	42	F "	44
Drummers	41	G "	48
Pioneers	11	H "	57
Ambulance and Signal Men	31	I "	48
A Co	54	K "	60
B "	49		
C "	43		686

THE NORTH-WEST CAMPAIGN.

LIST OF OFFICERS, NON-COMMISSIONED OFFICERS AND MEN.

STAFF.—Lieut.-Col., H. J. Grasett; Major, G. D. Dawson; Adj.-Capt., F. F. Manley; Asst.-Surgeon, Dr. G. S. Ryerson; Act.-Quartermaster, Lieut. W. S. Lowe.
STAFF-SERGEANTS.—Alf. Curran, Q.M.S.; James Hutchison, O.R.C.; Acting Sergt.-Maj., J. S. Monroe; Drum-Maj., W. Bewley; Hosp.-Sergt., R. Hazelton; Pion.-Sergt., C. W. Harding.

NO. 1 COMPANY.

CAPTAIN.—F. A. Caston.
LIEUTENANT.—D. M. Howard.
2ND LIEUTENANT.—A. C. Gibson.
COLOR-SERGEANT.—F. Francis.
SERGEANTS.—J. G. Goodman, G. P. Magner, R. Davis.
CORPORALS.—A. E. Moore, I. G. Craig, J. Foley, W. Rogers, C. M. Thrush, J. W., Bolton, V. E. Ashdown, W. W. Small.
PRIVATES.—T. J. Allan, A. E. Barnes, J. Blevins, J. W. Beattie, C. Bloxam,

H. Boothe, J. Boyd, W. J. Carter, G. Cook, J. Richardson, B. W. Smith, G. Smith, R. Wiggins, G. Wood, G. White, Private Moberly, J. Gray, G. Congalton, A. B. Curran, S. H. Dye, J. M. Edgar, W. Fraser, G. A. Geasley, H. Green, D. M. Haines, H. J. Hare, R. G. Henry, J. Ibbotson, J. J. Kilby, J. McDonald, E. Major, J. R. Martin, H. Milson, H. V. Mitchell, J. H. Mitchell, J. H. McDonald, J. A. McKenzie, J. A. McQuillan, J. O'Malley, G. Peters, A. Price, J. Quigley,

BUGLER—Michael Gaughan.
DRUMMERS.—J. King, J. Miles ; Assistants—J. Hunter, A. Taylor.
PIONEER.—G. Bradford.

NO. 2. COMPANY.

CAPTAIN.—Jas. Mason.
LIEUTENANT.—A. M. Irving.
2ND LIEUTENANT.—John D. Hay.
COLOR-SERGEANTS.—H. W. Johnston, and Theo. Lane.
SERGEANTS.—Wm. Medcalfe, Wm. Jack, Geo. Nelson.
CORPORALS.—Geo. C. Moody, James Wishart, Dr. Farragher, John Sinclair, W. H. Coxon, David Anderson.
PRIVATES.—Richard Cooke, James Richardson, Thos. A. Williams, Robt. Reynolds, John Smith, John Moss, Louis Stead, W. J. Cantwell, Charles W. Rogers, Frank Rogers, Arthur Ward, Robt. A. Stanley, George Croucher, Phillip Beaugil, John Griffin, Fred Petty, Christ. Steirn, Thos. Blake, Benj. Pearson, Albert Bruce, Thomas Dean, William Gibson, Oscar Freemantle, Samuel Downey, Thomas Milner, Wm. Blythe, D. Snell, John Mitchell, George Sculley, John Billinghurst, Andrew Murdison, Robert Thorpe, Robert Newman, Wallace Dossitt, Patrick Cronin, Wm. Richardson, James Baxter, Arthur Aikins, Eli Jeffries, Ernest Worsdell, Thomas Stanley, Albert Roberts, John Reid, James Marshall, John Streeton, Ernest Newman, W. D. Whiting.

AMBULANCE CORPS.—Swan Fearn, Jos. Bell.
PIONEER.—D. Shepherd.
BUGLERS.—Thomas Cuthbert, Geo. Baker.
DRUMMER.—Wm. Cuthbert.
FIFER.—Hugh. Burke.

NO. 3 COMPANY.

CAPTAIN.—O. L. Spencer.
LIEUTENANT.—W. C. Fitch.
2ND LIEUTENANT.—John Morrow.
STAFF-SERGEANT.—J. Hutchinson.
COLOR SERGEANT.—Wm. Dale.
SERGEANTS.—G. Knight, W. Mowat, John Nolan, John Jameson.
CORPORALS.—Robert Moore, Robert Whiteacre, Thomas Johnston, W. G.

Fowler, W. Taylor, W. Marsh, Robt. Blevins, George Dickson, Wm. Butcher.

LANCE CORPORAL.—John Coulter.

PRIVATES.—R. G. Beeman, George Brennan, Alfred Burridge, James Campbell, Albert Coburn, Robert Cook, Richard Culley, William Drake, Henry Fletcher, Alfred Hambleton, Arthur Hatch, Thomas Hicks, Thomas Hunter, Robert March, Alfred Meade, George Meade, Thomas Medcalfe, John Menary, William Mitchell, Thomas Moor, John Pollard, Walter Randall, Henry Riddle, Henry Roberts, Alfred Scovell, C. Spice, John Stayne, Robert Studham, Thomas Taylor, Adam Trotter, Richard Tyler, James Wylie, John Welby, A. Woodruffe, James Woodward.

PIONEER.—Lawrence Belz.

AMBULANCE CORP.—C. Haultain, Percy Scharsmidt.

DRUMMERS.—John McDonald, Wm. Holden.

BUGLERS.—Frank Nixon, Walter Impey.

NO. 4 COMPANY.

CAPTAIN.—C. G. Harston.

LIEUTENANT.—G. P. Elliot.

2ND LIEUTENANT.—F. J. Michie.

COLOR-SERGEANTS.—F. W. Curzon, N. Cusick.

SERGEANTS.—I. Dent, T. W. Mitchell, F. Kitchener.

CORPORALS.—F. Godfrey, F. W. Dent, E. C. Currie, T. McMullen, I. Stainsby, W. Jefferies.

LANCE CORPORAL.—L. Judge.

PRIVATES.—H. Watson, A. G. Ross, H. Brisbane, R. Tipton, W. J. Urquhart, G. Phillips, G. Tansley, R. F. Simmons, W. J. Delahunty, J. Davis, A. Gordon, W. Roberts, H. E. Peagram, W. R. Hawkins, J. Hughes, J. Hughes, M. Ross, B. Burtchell, J. Bennett, F. G. McMurray, J. Urquhart, R. F. Joseph, E. C. T. Doole, F. Hughes, S. Calderwood, R. Ross, W. Egles, J. Egles, R. Dempster, J. H. Fox, W. Donnelly, G. F. Lenoir, F. Hancy, A. S. Martin, C. C. Hammond, D. Hambly, W. Colls, S. Bennett, C. McGreevy, R. C. Campbell, D. Smith, F. J. Smythe, J. M. McIlvean, F. Smith, Felix Haney, J. Cain, P. Riggan.

AMBULANCE CORP.—W. E. Mitchell, C. Holman.

PIONEER.—C. Golback.

BUGLERS.—T. Johnson, J. Hume, J. Brickenden, J. W. Marshall.

RIFLE MATCHES.

Apart from the regimental shooting competitions, certain "challenge cups" are offered each year, upon certain conditions, for competition by the

Ontario Rifle Association. They are the Ladies' Cup, the Tait Cup, the Gzowski Cup, the Brassey Cup and the Elkington Cup.

In addition to these there have been the Aldwell and the Merchants' Cup.

In the Ladies' Cup, which is valued at one hundred and fifty dollars, the competition is restricted to teams of five members from each regiment or rifle association, and has to be shot for annually. It was founded in 1871 and in that year was won by the 10th Royals Rifle Association. Sixteen years elapsed before victory rested again with the Grenadiers, as it did in 1887, and again six years later in 1893.

The Tait Cup, which was presented by Sir Peter Tait, of London, England, in 1872, is of the value of two hundred and fifty dollars, is open to battalion teams of the Dominion and has to be competed for annually. In 1872 by the 10th Royals, in 1882 by the Royal Grenadiers, and again in 1888 by the same regiment.

The conditions attaching to the Gzowski Cup were changed some years after its first institution. The cup was presented in 1874 by Colonel Sir Cassimir Gzowski, A.D.C. to the Queen, to be competed for annually by twelve members of each military district in Ontario. In 1882 the conditions were changed and the prize was opened to the Dominion, for highest aggregate of battalion teams of five in skirmishing and volley firing.

For three years in succession, namely, 1886, 1887 and 1888, the Royal Grenadiers carried off this prize. Again in 1890 and 1891 were they successful, and yet again in 1894.

The Brassey Cup, which was presented in 1870 by the late Mr. Thomas Brassey, of Hastings, England, is valued at one hundred and twenty-five dollars, and has to be competed for by company teams, and won three times consecutively before becoming absolute property. In 1872 it was won by No. 2 Company of the 10th Royals, but victory did not again rest with the regiment until 1885, when "G" Company of the Royal Grenadiers secured the prize, as they did again for the second time in 1888.

One of the most famous prizes offered for rifle shooting in Great Britain is the Elkington Challenge Shield, open to volunteers from all parts of the United Kingdom. The Elkington Cup, competed for annually by the Canadian Militia, was presented by the same firm of eminent silversmiths who instituted the Challenge Shield. The conditions are for the highest aggregate in the second, third, fourth, fifth, sixth and seventh matches of the O.R.A. In 1872, Private A. Bell, of the 10th Royals obtained this distinction, and it was again his in 1879. In 1881, Sergeant Mitchell, of the Royal Grenadiers, was the prizeman. Since then it has not fallen to any officer, non-commissioned officer or private of the Grenadiers.

The Aldwell and the Merchants' Cups were presented by Messrs. Aldwell & Co., brewers, and the merchants of Toronto, respectively. They were valued at two hundred and two hundred and fifty dollars. The first of these two cups was open to battalion teams of ten, and when it had been won for two years consecutively by the same regiment, it became the absolute property of the winners. It was founded in 1869, and in that year was won by the Queen's Own Rifles, but in 1870 and the year following the 10th Royals were the winners, and consequently the competition ceased to exist.

The Merchants' Cup was open to battalion teams from the Province of Ontario and had to be won three times in succession before becoming the absolute property of any battalion. In this competition, founded in 1872, and existing till 1880, when the Thirteenth of Hamilton were the victors, neither the 10th Royals or the Grenadiers were successful.

The winners in the Royal Grenadiers for shooting medals have been as follows: The National Rifle Association Silver Medal was won by Staff-Sergeant T. Mitchell in 1889. The Governor-General's Silver Medal fell in 1891 to Color-Sergeant Fowler, and in 1894, Lieutenant W. R. Pringle was the winner of the Govermer-General's Bronze Medal. There are many others belonging to the regiment who have won shooting medals or decorations from the Dominion or Ontario Rifle Associations in the Regimental contests, but these decorations which have just been referred to are national instead of local importance.

In the Dominion Rifle Association Matches, very few years have elapsed without some member of the regiment winning a place on the Wimbledon, or as it is now called, the Bisley Team.

In 1875, the Battalion Match 1st prize of $200 was won by the 10th Battalion, the 2nd individual prize of $40 being won by Captain Anderson. In 1878, the 1st Battalion Team prize of $150 and the second prize in the Affiliated Association Match was captured by a team from the regiment. In 1879, the 3rd prize in the Affiliated Association Match was won by a team from the R. G., as in 1880, the 3rd prize in the Battalion Team Match was also won.

In 1882, the R. G. Team stood first in volley firing, second in skirmishing. It also carried of the 1st Battalion Team prize in the Dominion of Canada Match. In 1883, was won the Gzowski Cup, given for skirmishing and volley firing, and in 1888, 1st Battalion Prize in the Dominion of Canada Match.

In 1891, the R. G. Team won the 1st prize in the Dominion of Canada Match, and the 4th prize in the Lansdown Aggregate Match, and in 1894 they won the 3rd prize in the Skirmishing Match, 4th prize in the British Challenge Shield.

APPENDIX. 267

Since the inception of the Ontario Rifle Association and the Dominion Rifle Association Matches, individual members and also the teams, representing the 10th Royals, afterwards the Royal Grenadiers, have taken a prominent part in these matches, and have won many valuable prizes.

In 1872, the Tait Cup, being the 1st Battalion Match prize, was won by the 10th Royals, No. 2 Company being the successful contestants.

In 1873, the second prize in the Battalion Match was captured by the 10th Royals, and in 1875 the 4th prize in the Battalion Match, and the 3rd prize in the Tait Cup Match was also won.

In 1877, the 2nd prize in the Affiliated Associations Match. In 1878, the 3rd prize in the Affiliated Associations Match, and the 3rd prize in the Battalion Team Match. In 1879, 3rd prize in the Battalion Team Match, and in 1880 the 3rd prize in the Skirmishing Match were won by this Regiment.

In 1882, the 1st prize in the Battalion Match, the Tait-Brassey Cup, was won by the Royal Grenadiers, E Company winning the 2nd prize in the Company Match. In the same year they won the 4th prize in the Skirmishing and 3rd prize in the Volley Firing Matches, while in 1883, the 5th prize in the Tait-Brassey Match and the 4th prize in the Skirmishing were also won.

In 1884, they held the same position in these matches, winning also the 2nd prize in the Skirmishing and 2nd in the Volley Firing Matches. In 1885, the team from this regiment stood fifth in the Walker Match, third in the Tait-Brassey, second in the Skirmishing, and second in the Volley Firing Matches, G Company winning the Brassey Cup. In 1886, 5th prize in the Tait-Brassey, 3rd prize in the Skirmishing, 1st prize in the Volley Firing, and the Gzowski Cup were won by teams from this regiment. In 1887, the team from this regiment captured the Ladies' Cup in the Walker Match, being the 1st prize. They won also the Gzowski Cup, standing first in the Skirmishing and third in the Volley Firing. They also stood third in the Tait-Brassey Match, G Company winning the 2nd Company Prize. In 1888, the Tait-Brassey Cup, being the 1st Battalion Prize, was again captured by a team from the R. G., G Company winning the Brassey Cup. The regimental team also won 2nd prize in the Skirmishing, and 1st in the Volley Firing, winning the Gzowski Cup. In 1889, the team carried off 5th prize in the Tait-Brassey Match, 2nd in the Skirmishing Match, and the 5th in the Volley Firing Match, and in 1890 carried off the 1st prize in the team competitions in the Canada Company Match, 1st prize in the Skirmishing Match, 2nd prize in the Volley Match, winning the Gzowski Cup for the aggregate points in those two matches.

In 1891, the regiment won the 3rd prize in the Walker Match, 2nd in the Tait-Brassey, 3rd in the Skirmishing, 2nd in the Volley Firing, winning also the Gzowski Cup, and in 1892, won the Carslake Cup at the Quebec Rifle Association Matches, standing also second in the Militia Battalion Match, 1st in the Volley Firing, 2nd in the Skirmishing and winning the Houghton Cup for the aggregate points in these two latter matches. The R. G. team also stood second in the Association Match and carried off the 1st prize in the Aggregate Team Match, winning the silver cup. In 1893, at the Province of Quebec Rifle Matches, the team carried off the 4th prize in the Skirmishing Match, the Active Militia Match and the Carslake Match.

At the O.R.A. Matches the R. G's. carried off the Ladies' Challenge Cup, being the 1st prize in the Walker Match ; the 3rd prize in the Skirmishing Match, 4th in the Volley Match, and the 3rd prize in the Tait-Brassey Match. In 1894, was won the 2nd prize in the Tait-Brassey Match, also the Gzowski Cup for Skirmishing and Volley Firing.

In 1895, the regiment was represented at the Quebec Rifle Association Match, carrying off the following team prizes:—
Active Militia Match, 2nd prize ; Carslake Match, 3rd prize ; Skirmishing Match, 3rd prize ; Houghton Cup Match, 2nd prize.

At the O.R.A. Matches the regimental team again carried off the Ladies' Challenge Cup, being the 1st prize in the Walker Match. In the Gzowski Match they also stood second.

Major John Bruce, R. G., proceeded to England in June, 1896, as Adjutant of the Dominion Rifle team sent to Bisley.

THE CUMBERLAND CUP.

The Cumberland Drill Competition was instituted by Capt. F. Barlow Cumberland in 1882, as a memorial of his father, the first Lieut.-Colonel, and founder of the Regiment, and has been of much advantage in creating a healthy competition in perfecting their drill by the various companies. The competition has taken place annually each year since 1884. The prize is a handsome solid silver cup, which is held by the winning company for the year. The ebony base of the cup is surrounded by silver shields upon which are engraved the names of the officers of the winning companies.

A money prize of $50 is added yearly, part by the donor and part by the regiment. Capt. Cumberland also gives each year a large metal shield, to be placed in the armoury of the winning company ; on it are displayed the names of the officers and the color-sergeant, and which remains in possession of the company as a permanent record of its success.

The terms of the competition include not only excellence in performing before competent judges a series of movements in company drill and manual exercise, but points are also included for average attendance at each of the regular drills in proportion to the enrolled strength of each company. The competition is therefore not confined only to excellence in drill, but is also a factor in cultivating regular attendance at the weekly drills during the regular season, the success of the company being thus brought home to each individual man in the ranks.

The competition throughout has been keen, and the winning of the "Cumberland Cup" is looked on as being a red letter year in the history of each company.

The records in the several years have been as follows:

Year.	Company.	Officer Commanding.
1884	G Co	Captain Bruce.
1885	* *	No competition. Regiment being on active service.
1886	G Co	Captain Bruce.
1887	F Co	" Eliot.
1888	F Co	" Eliot.
1889	A Co	" Davidson.
1890	F Co	" Eliot.
1891	F Co	" Eliot.
1892	B Co	" Cameron.
1893	A Co	" Irving.
1894	B Co	" Cameron.

N.B.—Captain Eliot's Company enjoys the distinction of having been successful on no less than four occasions. It is also to be noted, though, that the same officer was a subaltern in G Co. when they were winners in 1884 and 1886.

[The portraits and other pictures contained in this History are by the Photo. Engraving process from photographs by Messrs. Dixon, Yonge Street, J. F. Bryce, King Street West, Simpson, of College Street, and others, and are the work of Messrs. Moore & Alexander, of Adelaide Street, and the "Grip" Publishing Company, both of Toronto. The "Colors" and Memorial Tablets are from half-tone drawings by Miss Esther Knightley Westmacott and Miss Hetty Hancock, also of Toronto.]

NOTES.

(OFFICERS.)

Lieutenant-Colonel Frederic William Cumberland, who was chiefly instrumental in raising the 10th Royals, was an Englishman by birth, and came to Canada in 1847. His first commission in the Canadian Militia was given him in the 3rd Battalion (Sedentary) Militia of the 5th Military District of Upper Canada, in which he held a captain's commission, when he was appointed, on March 14th, 1862, Major in the 10th Royals, and on March 28th, just a fortnight later, its Lieutenant-Colonel and first commanding officer. During Lieutenant-Colonel Cumberland's command, the regiment was increased from seven to eight companies, had their colours presented to them by the ladies of Toronto, and gave the first strictly military ball that had taken place in Toronto for a great number of years. Two companies of the 10th were also called out for frontier duty in the summer of 1864, and formed a portion of the administrative battalion doing duty at Laprairie. (P. 44.) Lieutenant-Colonel Cumberland retired from the 10th Royals July 21st, 1865. (P. 45, 46.) He died in Toronto August 5th, 1881.

The second officer who commanded the 10th Royals was Lieutenant-Colonel Alfred Brunel, who was appointed on the same date as his predecessor resigned. The principal event connected with Lieutenant-Colonel Brunel's command was the regiment's being embodied for active service in April, May and June, 1866, in consequence of the anticipated and actual Fenian Raids. (P. 53-57.) Lieutenant-Colonel Brunel retired from the command, retaining rank, February 24th, 1870. He afterwards removed to Ottawa, where he died.

Succeeding Lieutenant-Colonel Brunel came Lieutenant-Colonel John Boxall, whose command extended from February 24th, 1870, until November 21st, 1873. On the latter date Lieutenant-Colonel Boxall retired from the service. (P. 73.)

The next Lieutenant Colonel was William Stollery, whose commission in that rank was dated November 5th, 1875, the 10th having been for two years without a Lieutenant-Colonel, though Major and Brevet-Lieutenant-Colonel Stollery had been fulfilling the duties. The only event of any note connected with Lieutenant-Colonel Stollery's regime was the adoption of the Regimental badge since worn by the corps. (P. 82.) He retired from the service retaining his rank, December 5th, 1879.

The fifth Lieutenant-Colonel, appointed to the command of the 10th Royals April 9th, 1880, was George Alexander Shaw. (P. 85.) He only retained command for six months, being retired on November 5th, 1880, "retaining his rank as a special case." (P. 83.) Following Lieutenant-Colonel Shaw's resignation came the reorganization of the battalion, with an all but complete change of officers.

Henry James Grasett, formerly Lieutenant in H. M. 100th Regiment, was the first Lieutenant-Colonel commanding the reorganized battalion being gazetted to that rank on November 5th, 1880. The principal events of Lieut.-Colonel Grasett's command were :—The Regiment's title was changed August 5th, 1881, from that of 10th Royals, to 10th Royal Grenadiers, the strength was increased from a six (as it had been since reorganization) to an eight company battalion, the North-West Expedition (p. 113-197), and the train of events consequent thereupon. Lieutenant-Colonel Grasett retired from the Regiment, retaining his rank, June 1st, 1888. (P. 217.)

Lieutenant Colonel Dawson followed Lieutenant-Colonel Grasett in command of the Grenadiers, his appointment being gazetted on the same date as was the former's resignation. He continued in command until December 1st, 1893, and during his term had the satisfaction of seeing the Regiment reviewed by the Duke of Connaught. The battalion was also increased during his command from eight to ten companies. (P. 238.)

Lieutenant-Colonel James Mason's connection with the Canadian Militia dates from 1863 when he joined the Q.O.R., serving therein until 1866. He also held a commission as Lieutenant in the 5th Battalion York Militia. He was gazetted to the Grenadiers as captain in September, 1882, when the battalion was augmented from six to eight companies. There are only three officers in the Grenadiers who have been connected with the Regiment longer than he has, namely, Major Bruce (Lieut., January 13th, 1881), Captain Caston (Captain, January 28th, 1881), the only officer in the Grenadiers who also served in the 10th Royals, and Captain Trotter (2nd Lieut., November 11, 1881). Major Bruce has filled the post of Paymaster, and still discharges the duties of that office, in addition to his other duties. Captain McLean was Regimental Adjutant from December, 1890, until April, 1894. Lieutenant Willis held a commission in the 36th Battalion and was gazetted to the Grenadiers from that regiment. Lieut. and Captain Brooke formerly served in the 12th York Rangers.

(N.C.O'S AND MEN.)

In the ranks of the Grenadiers are several men who have been serving their country either in the regular army or in the Grenadiers for an exceptionally long period. Among these are the Bandmaster, Mr. J. Waldron, who joined H. M. 88th Regiment (Connaught Rangers) so far back as 1856. Mr. Waldron served with the 88th in India and elsewhere for many years, and was subsequently transferred to the 8th Kings Regiment as Bandmaster. On March 9th, 1838, Mr. Waldron joined the Grenadiers in the same capacity, it is only doing him simple justice to say that he has while filling that post discharged his duties in such a manner as to reflect credit alike upon the battalion and upon himself.

Sergeant-Major Cox is almost as old a soldier as the bandmaster, he joined the 16th Foot (Bedfordshire Regiment) in October, 1857, was promoted corporal, January 1st, 1862, and attained the rank of Sergeant-Major January, 14th, 1874, (Warrant Officer, July 1st, 1881). Medal for "long service and good conduct." After leaving the 16th Regiment on a retiring pension he served with the Royal Jersey Militia from March, 1881, until September 1st, 1888. Joined the Royal Grenadiers, September 12th, 1888.

Quarter Master Sergeant H. W. Johnston has served in the 10th Royals and in the Grenadiers for more than twenty years. He went through the Northwest campaign of 1885, and was within a few feet of Lieutenant Fitch when the latter fell mortally wounded.

Colour-Sergeant John Nolan joined the 100th P. W. R. C. Regiment as a boy in 1862. He served therein for many years subsequently entering the Royal Grenadiers in 1883, and serving in the Northwest campaign.

Lance-Sergeant H. G. Norris formerly served in the 6th Carabineers until his discharge on pension in 1880, after seventeen years service. He joined the Royal Grenadiers in 1894. He saw much service in his old corps and possesses medals for Afghanistan, for the Soudan, where he served in the corps of Canadian Voyageurs and also for long service.

Private H. Libby was formerly in the 6th Royal Warwickshire Regiment. Discharged on pension after twenty-six years service, in July, 1888. Had the rank of Colour Sergeant. Possesses medals for Hazara campaign, 1868, and for Afghanistan 78, 79, 80, and for " long service and good conduct."

Sergeant-Drummer Farmer served in the Grenadier Guards and in other regiments and has seen much service in various parts of the world.

PROMOTIONS AND APPOINTMENTS.

(Received after going to press.)

HEAD QUARTERS,

OTTAWA, 27th July, 1896.

10TH BATTALION ROYAL GRENADIERS.

Lieutenant James Grayson Smith is permitted to resign his commission 22nd June, 1896.

Surgeon-Captain Edmund Eleazer King is granted the honorary rank of Surgeon-Major, under the provisions of paragraph 94, Regulations and Orders of the Militia, 1887.

To be Lieutenant : Albert Edward Gooderham, gentleman ; vice Smith retired 22nd June, 1896.

HEAD QUARTERS,

OTTAWA, Aug. 29th, 1896.

10TH BATALLION, ROYAL GRENADIERS.

To be Honorary Chaplain as a special case, Rev. Arthur Henry Baldwin.

Lieut. James William Bain is permitted to resign his commission, Aug. 26th, 1896.

To be Captains: Lieut. Albert Edward Gooderham, *vice* Sweatman, transferred; and Lieut. Harvey A. Willis, *vice* MacLean, transferred Aug. 26th, 1896.

To be Second Lieutenant: George Osborn Hayne, to complete establishment, August 26th, 1896.

To be Adjutant: Capt. James Drummond Mackay, *vice* Irving, deceased, Aug. 26th, 1896.

TABLE OF CONTENTS.

CHAPTER I.

The first Militia Act. The Act of 1822. The Training Days. Interesting Details. - - - - - - - - pp. 7–11.

CHAPTER II.

The Canadian Militia in 1837. The Royal Canadian Rifles. "A Dull Time." The Crimean War. The Militia Act of 1855. pp. 12–18.

CHAPTER III.

The 100th Regiment. The Trent Affair of 1861. The Military Enthusiasm of the Period. The 10th Gazetted. - - pp. 19–34.

CHAPTER IV.

Presentation of Colours to the Regiment by Mrs. Cumberland. Lieutenant-Colonel Cumberland Retires. The Fenian Raid. pp. 35–85.

CHAPTER V.

The Reorganization of the Regiment under Lt.-Col. Grasett. Five Eventful Years. - - - - - - - - pp. 86–120.

CHAPTER VI.

On the Way to the Northwest. Incidents of the Journey. The Battles at Fish Creek and Batoche. The Killed and Wounded. The Return to Toronto. Conclusion. - - - - pp. 121–256

APPENDIX.

Roll of officers. Roll of the Regiment. Names of the officers and men who formed the North-West expedition. Rifle Matches. Cumberland Cup. Notes. Index, etc. - - - pp. 255 to end.

INDEX.

A.

Allan, G. W., 90, 97, 219.
Adamson, W., 62, 66, 69.
Anderson, A., 66, 68, 69, 78, 80, 83.
Anderson, J. Weir, 99, 102.
Allen, Lieut.-Col., 219.
Appelbe, R. S., 97, 102, 103.
Andrews, W. G., 76.
Albiston, John, 23, 25, 30.
Allison, John B., 66, 69.
Arthur, Prince, 65.

B.

Bailey, Jno., 69, 70, 75, 83.
Bradley, A., 70, 72.
Baker, D., 134.
Blake, Ed., 122.
Blake, Ed., Mrs., 122.
Brant, E. E., 66.
Ball, Grenadiers', 208.
Bain, J. W., 230, 233.
Batoche Killed and Wounded, 160, 161.
Ball, P. B., 99, 104, 199.
Barrett, W., 51, 59, 62, 66.
Bell, A., 76.
Bethune, G. E. C., 89, 108.
Bescoby, H. F., 25, 29, 30, 33, 44.
Benson, James, 41.
Bell, W. A., 77, 84.
Bigelow, N. G., 66, 70, 88, 91.
Boyd, Alex., 228, 230, 242.
Boulton, Claude A., 126, 197, 225, 229, 232.
Boswell, F. E., 59, 64.
Boomer, Geo. A., 61, 62, 64, 90.
Brown, Geo., 73, 102, 103, 104.
Brooke, G. H. C., 242.
Brown, Gilbert, 70.
Brooke, G., Captain, 18.
Brown, H. F., 44, 51, 60, 64.
Brophy, H., 250.
Brock, Isaac, General, 10.
Boxall, John, 23, 25, 30, 32, 33, 52, 54, 67, 73.
Boulton, Lieut.-Col., 248.
Boxall, Mrs., 33.
Boswell, Major, 160.
Boulton's Scouts, 126-197.
Brunel, A. J., 22, 23, 24, 25, 47, 49, 54, 55, 59, 61, 67.
Brunel, A. J., Mrs., 33.
Buchanan, Dr., 23.
Burch, E. E., 200, 215.
Brunel, Geo., 68.
Bruce, J., 90, 99, 102, 214, 235, 239.
Buchan, L., 160, 248.
Buchanan, Mrs., 33.
Brunel, Troilus, 33, 53.
Buchanan, W., 132.
Bryant, Ebenezer, 63, 67.

C.

Chapman, A., 72, 77, 79, 80.
Cameron, A. B., 201, 214, 228.
Camp Desolation, 124.
Campbell, Duncan F., 251.
Clarke, E. F., 219.
Cardwell, E., 54.
Caston, F. A., 72, 74, 81, 88, 96, 102, 155.
Carroll, Geo., 22, 25, 30.
Capreol, James L., 61, 66.
Craig, J. T., 240, 242.
Carlisle, Mr., 57.
Carleton Place, 121.
Cantwell, Private, 140.
Chadwick, W. C. Vaux, 229, 241.
Canavan, W. B., 70, 71, 72, 79.
Cleghorn, John, 79, 80, 81, 88, 89, 90.
Chisholm, Colonel, 13.
Crint, W., 76.
Coleman, Arthur, 50, 59, 72, 73, 83.
Croil, A. W., 232, 233.
Coleman, Ben, 66.
Connon, C. H., 44, 51, 52 62.
Colville, Captain, 222.
Connaught, Duke of, 226.
Coatsworth, E., 23, 24, 30, 33.
Cox, James, 223.
Corley, J. W. S., 230, 232.
Crozier, Major, 111.

Cooper, W. H., 70, 72.
Cooper, W. N., 78, 81, 88, 91.
Colwell, W. W., 23.
Curzon, Color-Sergt., 158, 223, 226.
Curtiss, E. G., 63, 64, 65.
Cumberland, F. B., 59, 61, 62, 69, 107, 219.
Cumberland, F. W., 18, 22, 23, 25, 30, 36, 37, 43, 50.
Cumberland, Mrs., 33, 37, 38.

D.

Dawson, G. D., 56, 89, 151, 214, 234, 236, 237, 238, 246, 250.
Darling, F., 90.
Davidson, J. I. Mrs., 219.
Davidson, J. I., 104, 107, 201, 237.
De Grassi, A., 22, 24, 29, 30, 44, 45.
De Rottenburg, Col., 17, 19.
De La Hooke, E. D. A., 72, 76, 79, 88.
Denison, G. T., Lieut.-Col. G.G.-B.G., 236.
Denison, G. T. Lieut.-Col., 12, 17, 37.
Delamere, J. T., 219.
Drew, Maxwell, 137-197.
Denison, R. B., 57, 112.
Dennis, R., 23, 25, 31, 32.
Dent, Sergeant, 241.
Dixon, Homer D. F., 221.
Dickey, J. J., 23, 25, 30, 32, 51.
Dumont, Gabriel, 110, 130, 197.
Drummond, Gordon, Sir., 10.
Durie, Lieut-Col., 34, 36.
Ducklake Massacre, 110, 111, 112.
Dudley, W. H., 63, 64, 70.

E.

Edwards, John, 34.
Erie, Fort, 55.
Eliot, G. P., 105, 136, 155, 198, 206, 239, 240.
Ellis, R. B., 201.

F.

Francis, F., 168.
Fleming, Andrew, 63, 64, 80.
Fleming, Captain, 237.
French, Captain, 143.
Feehan, D. K., 18.
Fleming, D., 23, 25.
Fitz-Gerald, F. W. G., 214, 224.
Fletcher, Mrs., 219.
Fleming, Sandford, 22, 24, 29, 30, 44.
Fitz-Gerald, W. D., 214.
Fitz Gibbon, Jas., Col., 13.
Fitch, W. C., 108, 155, 198.
Fitch, W. C., (Death of), 143.
Fort Carleton, 111.
Foster, W. F., 58.
Furnival, G., 77, 81, 88, 91.
Flynn, T., 78, 79, 88.

G.

Grasett, Henry James, 20, 88, 105, 112, 197, 206, 214, 217, 236, 246, 250.
Graham, J. E., 70, 79.
Grasett, Mrs., 219.
Gascoigne, Major-Gen., 248.
Grenadiers arrive in Winnipeg, 126.
Grenadier's Ball, 208.
Greer, E. F., 70.
Gritz, J., 23.
German, W. M., 81.
George III.
Gibson, A. C., 108, 136, 155, 200, 225, 242.
Gibson, J. M., 109, 237.
Griffith, F. D., 76, 83.
Gilmore, Major, 57.
Gooderham, A. E., 199, 201, 206.
Gzowski, Casimir, Sir., 236.
Gosling, F. J., 99, 105, 198, 202, 227.
Gordon, G. B., 76, 77.
Gooderham, Geo., Mrs., 219.
Godson, W. F., 206.
Gundry, 22, 24, 29.

H.

Harrison, A. B., 90, 102, 104, 233.
Hague, Capt., 130, 133, 197.
Harston, C. G., 105, 155, 199, 224, 240.
Hamilton, Geo., R., 23, 25, 29, 33, 54, 62, 237.
Harwood, Henry, 32.
Hay, J. D., 107, 155, 199, 224, 233.
Harrison, J. W. F., Mrs., 211.
Head, Edmund, Walker, Sir., 16, 19.
Head, Francis, Bond, Sir., 12, 13.
Henty, G. A., 152.
Hetherington, J. W., 51, 52, 53, 54, 59, 60, 67, 73.
Herbert, Major-Gen., 237, 238.

Heward, S. A., 221, 224, 230, 242.
Helm. Sergt.-Major, 37.
Hirschfelder, A. E., 72, 73, 74.
Hill, H. J., 71, 72, 79, 82, 83.
Hirschfelder, R. G., 69, 73.
Howard, Captain, U. S. A., 138.
Howard, D. MacD., 99, 155, 206, 225.
Howard, McLean, Mrs., 219.

I.

Irving, A. M., 100, 105, 155, 206, 225, 233, 239, 249, 250.
Irvine, Colonel, 110.

J.

Jarvis, Major, 131.
Jarvis, Sheriff, 13.
Jones, J. T., 71, 73.
Joseph, R. F., 68, 74.

K.

Kennedy, Mrs., 219.
King, G. G., 201.
Kippen, Lieut., 152.
Kingsmill, N., 98, 214.
Killaly, R. L., 59, 61.
Killed and Wounded at Batoche, 160, 161.

L.

Latham, Capt., 31.
Lawrence, J. W., 33, 51, 52, 54, 59, 70.
Laurie, Lieut., R. R. C. I., 237.
Lansdowne, Marquis, 105.
Lawrence, Samuel, 70, 76.
Lambe, W. G. A., 201, 224.
Leith, A. A., 76.
Lessard, Captain, 237.
Leigh, L. E., 100, 200.
Lehmann, W., 228, 229, 240.
Lowry, Colonel, 96.
Lovekin, L. A., 76, 82.
Lowe, S., 198, 201, 227.
Luard, Major-Gen., 102, 106.

M.

MacNab, Alan N. Sir, 13.
Manning, A., 22.
Martin, A. F. R., 240, 242, 247.
Marani, C. J., 230, 232, 235.
MacMahon, D'Arcy, 224, 228.

Mason, J. C., 240, 247.
Macdonald, H. J., 136.
Marshall, J., 62, 66.
Mackay, J. D., 214, 215, 229.
Maclennan, J. D., 215, 225.
Mason, Jas. Mrs., 219.
Mason, Jas., 98, 102, 106, 133, 196, 215, 232, 234, 236, 244, 246, 250.
Manley, F. F., 89, 98, 155, 218, 225, 236.
Martin, Private, 155.
" Powell, 66, 67, 71, 74.
" R. T., 70.
" R. S., 70, 73.
Mason and Slidell, 18.
Mackenzie, W. Lyon, 12.
Macfarlane, W. T., 91, 98.
Meyers, D. C., 240, 242.
Mead, J. H., 75, 76.
Metcalfe, John, 70, 84.
Melgund, Lord, 128.
Medals, Presentation of, 202, 203.
Michie, Forbes, 108, 155, 190, 211, 230.
Millard, E. A., 69, 72.
Michel, John Sir, 50.
Mills, J. R., 76, 80, 82, 88, 91.
Miller, Lieut.-Col., 112.
Middleton, Maj.-Gen., 109, 128-197.

Mc.

McCaul, Rev. Dr., 37, 38.
McEachren, N., 79, 88, 91.
McGrath, J. G., 22, 25, 29, 44.
McSpadden, W. M., 81, 88, 91.
McGee, John, 22, 24.
McLean, A. Lieut.-Col., 12.
McLean, J. B., 214, 225, 228.
McLean, Mrs. Justice, 17.
McLellan, D., 61.
McClive, W. H., 233, 239.
McInnes, Chas. S., 242.
McIntyre, I. A. D., 99, 100.
McCollum, J. H., 79, 85, 88, 89, 201.
McDonald, C. E., 107, 108.
McDowell, A. H., 221, 224.
McCulloch, H., 77, 79.
McMurrich, Geo., 31, 44, 50, 51, 52, 54, 66.

N.

Napier, Maj.-Gen., 37.
Newcombe, Jas. Dr., 51, 70.

Nickinson, J. Captain, 18.
Noverre, F. H., 59, 62, 69, 73, 77.
Northwest Medals, 202, 203.
" Wounded, 197, 198.

O.

O'Hara, Lt.-Col., 17.
O'Dea, Dr., 23.
O'Reilly, H. R., 240, 242.
Otter, W. D., 115, 122, 241.
Orton, Dr., 135.

P.

Passmore, F. F., 23, 25, 29, 32.
Patterson, John, 59, 62, 67, 69, 88.
Paterson, J. H., 92, 103.
Platt, Samuel, 72, 76.
Peters, Captain, 131.
Peacocke, Colonel, 93.
Peel, E., 23, 25.
Percival, L. V., 90; 98, 104.
Peile, 29.
Price, Chas., 66, 69.
" Jas., 23.
Prince, John Colonel, 17.
Phipps, W. A., 69, 70, 78, 88.
Pringle, W. R., 229, 232, 235, 239, 242.
Pyne, R. A., 85, 87, 88.

Q.

Queen's Jubilee, 213.

R.

Ramsey, David, 23.
Ramsay, Jas., 72.
Ramsey, J., 70.
Ramsey, W. J., 62, 66, 75.
Reid, Chas., 74, 79, 88, 90, 99.
Richardson, Fred., 52, 59, 62.
Richey, J. H., 33, 52, 53.
Richardson, J. H. Dr., 51, 84.
Ridout, J. Gibbs, 19, 44, 45, 47, 48, 50.
Ridout, Mrs., 33.
Riel, Louis, 110.
Robertson, Alex. J., 53, 62, 67.
Robertson, Colonel, 37, 41, 45.
Rottenburg De, Col., 17, 19.
Royal Grenadiers (Created) 96, 97.
Ross, G. W., 219.

Roberts, Henry, 23, 25, 29, 31, 33.
Rolph, J. W., 33, 63.
Robinson, J. R., 250.
Robertson, L. H., 51, 90, 104.
Robinson, Mrs. J. B., 207.
Robinson, J. B. Sir, 17.
Rogers, W. D., 60, 61, 67.
Ruttan, Captain, 131.
Ruttan, Henry Lieut.-Col., 17.
Ryerson, G. S., 90, 98, 103, 149, 156, 157, 158, 201.
Ryerson, Mrs., 219.

S.

Shaw, Aeneas, 85.
S. A. C., 164-167.
Shanly, Coote Nesbitt, 242.
Shaw, Geo. A., 42, 53, 59, 60, 61, 72, 75, 84, 236.
Saskatoon Hospital, 133.
Sandham, Maj.-Gen., 236.
Stanley of Preston, Lord, 221.
Sweatman, A., 228, 229, 240.
Sergeants' Diary, 168-193.
Stewart, Ed., 42.
Street, E. R., 250.
Sears, J. W., 117.
Sherwood, Levius P., 34, 42, 51.
Steamer *Northcote*, 133.
Spencer, O. L. L., 97, 100, 104, 125, 155.
Stead, Private, 104.
Sherwood, Samuel, 34.
Sergeants' Story, 144-197.
Steward, W., 23, 24, 29, 30, 31, 52.
Smith, A. M., 18.
Stiles, Cyrus, 233, 235.
Smith, C. H., 81, 82.
Smith, E. A., 82, 88, 91, 97.
Simcoe, Gen., 7.
Smith, G. B., 23.
Smith, Goldwin Mrs., 219.
Stimson, Geo. A., 227, 229, 242.
Smith, J. Greyson, 233, 235.
Skinner, Rufus, 59, 69.
Scott, Allan, S., 72, 74, 76.
Schooner, *M. L. Breck*, 163.
Sloane, S. F., 240, 242.
Stollery, W. A., 23, 25, 29, 30, 32, 50, 54, 64, 73, 75, 82.
Storm, W, G., 22.
Stuart, John, 22.
Seymour, C. H., 100, 105, 199.
Spry, Daniel, 66, 68.

T.

Tassie, W. T., 221, 239.
Thomson, E. W., Lieut.-Col., 12, 17.
Thompson, J. T., 69, 72, 78, 88, 230, 235.
Thompson, Thos., 62, 79.
Trotter, R. G., 98, 100, 198.

U.

Unitt, F. W., 72, 73, 76, 79, 84, 88.

V.

Vankoughnet, Phil., 61, 62, 67.
Vanstraubenzie, Lieut.-Col. 136.

W.

Waldron, John, 252.
Webb, Harry, 238.
Weatherstone, N., 90, 97.
Wells, R. M., 89, 98.
Weston, W. Henry, 69, 70, 74, 82, 84, 88.
Winstanley, C. J. H., 51, 52, 62.
Wise, Captain, 130.
Willis, Harvey, 235.
Wiley, Jas., 62, 66.
Williams, Lieut.-Col., 140, 197.
Whitcombe, Rev. C. E., 205.
Wilkie, Stuart, A., 243, 250.
Worthington, Jas., 22, 29, 30, 50, 52, 64.
Worthington, Jas., Mrs., 33.
Worthington, John, 22, 23, 24, 25, 29, 30.
Wounded and Killed at Batoche, 160, 161.
Worthington, Mrs., 219.
Worthington, Mrs., 33.
Worthington, Norris, 194.

ERRATA.

Page 40—*For* Fenian Rail *read* Fenian Raid.
" 60— " Glneral Orders *read* General Orders.
" 61— " James L. Capreole *read* James L. Capreol.
" 137— " Humbolt *read* Humboldt.
" 140— " Middieton *read* Middleton.
" 167— " Poetical account C. *read* S.A C.
" 180— " Sakatoon *read* Saskatoon.
" 186— " Rev. Mr. Whitcomb *read* Rev. C. E. Whitcombe.
" 191— " Lt. Percy Eliot *read* Lt. G. Percival Eliot.
" 207— " Mrs. Beverley Robinson *read* Mrs. John Beverley Robinson
" 208— " Lt.-Col. Fred. Denison *read* Lt.-Col. Fred. C. Denison.
" 256— " Harvey Archelaus Willis, Feby. 4th, 1892, *read* Feby. 4th, 1893.

Omitted on page 232:

HEAD QUARTERS,
OTTAWA, 28th January, 1892.
GENERAL ORDERS.

10TH BATTALION, ROYAL GRENADIERS.

Lieutenant John Donald Maclennan is transferred to the 6th Fusiliers with the rank of Captain.

Brevet: To be Major: Captain Frederick Fitzpayne Manley, V.B., from 28th October, 1891.

www.ingramcontent.com/pod-product-compliance
Lightning Source LLC
Chambersburg PA
CBHW022042230426
43672CB00008B/1049